Countdown to Catastrophe

Why It Happened
What Was Overlooked
Who's To Blame
Where Else Was Affected
What To Do About It
What Happens Next

With an *Exclusive* **Interview with Mr. Adam Smith**

by

STEPHEN R. HILL

Duck Editions

An Imprint of
DUCKWORTH
Literary Entertainments Limited

First Published in Great Britain on 31st December 2009

Published by
Duck Editions

An Imprint Of
Duckworth
Literary Entertainments Limited

ISBN 978-0-9564346-2-3

Typeset, Printed and bound by
L.P.P.S., Wellingborough, Northants

Contents

PART III: WHO'S TO BLAME   PAGE 41

Part IV: Where Else Was Affected   PAGE 147

Part V: What To Do About It   PAGE 193

Part VI: What Happens Next   PAGE 241

PART I:

Why It Happened

"If it's so big, why didn't anyone see it coming?"

THIS was the obvious question about Global Crunch, the
question that just demanded to be asked on a suitable occasion, in this case by a youthful but elderly and wise Lady,
complete with hand-bag and hat-pin. Her Majesty Queen Elizabeth
II of Great Britain was the one to pop this inevitable question when
she visited the LSE, the London School of Economics, on 5th
November 2008, a day immortalised in British tradition as the
'Gunpowder Plot', the day Guy Fawkes attempted to blow up
Parliament in 1605. Her Majesty QE II was there that day to open a
new £75.0 million facility, but her hat-pin of a question pricked the
pride of the professors of this globally-renowned institution and
when she swung her hand-bag it just about blew up modern economics as they did, or didn't, know it. None of them had foreseen the

1

world's biggest credit crisis, you see, before it hit them, and that was before that royal handbag really walloped them.

Two stunned so-called economists at the LSE belatedly wrote an extraordinary letter to Her Majesty Queen Elizabeth II to give their answer to her question: "It was a failure of the collective imagination of many bright people. Everyone was to blame, meaning no one was to blame". I doubt whether that one was framed for the royal privy, but was probably flushed down it instead. The global failure of economists generally to see the crisis coming led to the formulation of a new collective noun, as in a Ruination of Macro-economists, until some wag suggested transposing the first two letters.

"It's impossible to foresee a crisis," asserted the former Chairman of the US Federal Reserve Alan Greenspan in a Bloomberg TV interview, unconvincingly, on Friday 12 September 2008, the last working day before the crisis exploded in the world's face. Yes, this is the same beknighted Sir Alan Greenspan, I promise you, who was invited to London by Prime Minister Tony Blair in 2002 to open Her Majesty's new Treasury building and receive an honorary knighthood, by kneeling in time-honoured tradition before Her Majesty Queen Elizabeth II herself at Buckingham Palace, as she raised her sword of state and lightly touched him on each shoulder, thereby ennobling him ... wait for the drum roll ... for "his services to global economic stability"! Her Majesty must have wondered, on that Bonfire Day just six years later, if all these expensive new buildings were of any use at all in fostering stability in the real economy.

Sir Alan Greenspan was the long-serving Chairman, for 18 years until 2006, of the US Federal Reserve who gave that warning in late-1996 that the stock markets were exhibiting "irrational exuberance", but then he did nothing about it except leave interest rates at catastrophically low levels, down to just 1.0% in 2003/4 after the 9/11 attacks on New York and Washington, until mid-2004 for 18 months, and below 2.5% from November 2001 to February 2005, for 38 months, thereby enabling Vodka and Whiskey to be poured into the punch-bowl and now make the markets drunk with Russian exuberance. This was the making of the crisis, as on the back of this very low interest rate, subprime mortgage origination in the US increased by 300.0% between 2002 and 2005, and the level of securitisation of these mortgages into CMOs/CDOs, or the bundling of mortgages or other debts up into parcels called 'Collateralised Mortgage Obligations' or 'Collateralised Debt Obligations' for onward sale to investors, had risen to 80.0% of all subprime mortgages by the last quarter of 2005. Subprime origination between 2004 and 2006 totalled $1.7 trillion, of which $1.3 trillion, or three-quarters, was securitised.

These mortgages now included 'No Deposits', 'Payment Adjustable Rate Mortgages', 'No documents of income or assets', 'No independent property appraisal', 'Self-assessment mortgages', (known as "Liar Loans"), Ninja mortgages for those with 'No income, no job and no assets', and if you could walk and chew gum at the same time in the Land of the Free, you could get any kind of mortgage you wanted, OK, just like a Burger-King hamburger, 'any which way you wanted it'. Many of these mortgages had two years low starter rates, however, before they near-doubled in the third year, but mortgagors went for them like lemmings in the fond hope of flipping their extra condominiums at a tidy profit to the next mortgage mug in line, before the music stopped.

Then George Dubya Bush was cheering in 2002 for the 5.5 million subprime wannabe Americans who, blessedly, still didn't have a mortgage, as he went on in 2003 to enact the American Dream Downpayment Act, as in 'Dream on Baby', of up to $10,000.00 to help low-income earners with a deposit, to join the queue for the Carousel of leveraged one-way bets on future house price increases. And our man at the Fed, a year before that interview had already said on CBS: "I had no idea of how significant [structured securities] had become until very late. I didn't really get it until very late in 2005 and 2006". What? He didn't know what his President was up to, and couldn't see a nuclear mushroom of $1,300,000,000,000 of toxic mortgage gas emanating from Wall Street? Then a year later he's telling a different TV channel the crisis was *unforeseeable*!

Sir Alan now justifiably risked the same fate as Sir Walter Raleigh, who was also knighted for his services to global economic growth as he knelt before the first Her Majesty Queen Elizabeth I in 1584, but later found himself not just benighted, but beheaded as well in the 'Bloody Tower', for importing forbidden "toxic" substances. Greenspan soon admitted: "I made a mistake... the crisis has left me in a state of shocked disbelief". Sir Walter Raleigh's head would have been in "shocked disbelief" too, if at his execution his headless trunk had caught his own severed head, now staring back at where it used to sit, in "shocked disbelief". On the eve of the biggest financial crisis the world has ever seen, Sir Alan Greenspan completely lost his head as well and pleaded on television that "*no one, but no one*" could have foreseen this crisis of "toxic" assets, a crisis that was always bound to follow the explosion in 'Collateralised Mortgage/Debt Obligations' or CMOs/CDOs, wrapped up with 'Credit Default Swaps' or CDSs, an insurance wrapper that formed the equivalent function of the evening papers for preserving the heat and taste of Britain's sole contribution to the great global culinary*fest*, namely take-away Fish and Chips with extra salt and vinegar, as the bankers sought to turn water into wine; or as one software writer put it "You put chicken in the Grinder and out came sirloin". The Grinder? That's the computer loaded with the right software for dicing and slicing debts, but the sirloin had somehow picked up the stale smell of fish from the CDS wrappers, and there's nothing like the smell of stinking fish to close down the whole market overnight.

Bear Stearns in New York and Northern Rock Bank in Newcastle, North-East England, both suffered old-fashioned runs on the bank when the smell hit the street, and had to be rescued by JPMorgan Chase and the British taxpayer, respectively; American Home Mortgage had already filed for bankruptcy on 6th August, then Thornburn Mortgage in the Mid-West, next a Carlyle $960.0 billion Private Equity quoted entity in Amsterdam, then three mortgage funds worth €2.0 billion managed by BNP Parisbas suspended redemptions, and then the $1.8 billion Peleton Hedge Fund, all loaded with toxic mortgage assets, crashed and burned for the same "toxic" reason, while Goldman Sachs had to pump $3.0 billion into one of its global hedge funds and Countrywide Financial in the US and the Rams Mortgage business in Australia announced liquidity problems. The central banks in the US, UK and the EU and Japan all immediately hit the panic liquidity buttons in August and hosed the banking system down with gallons of money to try and put the fires out, with literally hundreds of billions of dollars, €uros and ¥en paid out and pledged. And the next year in dour Edinburgh, of all places, the two leading Scottish banks RBS and HBOS literally ran out of cash in early October 2008 and had to be rescued by a £62.0

billion secret emergency advance from the Bank of England.

The central bankers then accused the retail banks of having 'mis-priced the lending risk', whereas they had under-priced money for over a decade already, and had forgotten to take away the punch-bowl of excess, that's the legendary punchbowl of the 1950s/1960s Fed Chairman William McChesney Martin Jnr., who always removed the punch-bowl when the party was getting too lively, by raising interest rates in time. This time, however, with none of these proven old checks operated in time, or at all, the Party of Excess rolled on past midnight and well on into the wee' small hours. Remember Chuck Prince III, the ex-CEO of Citigroup, who said the music was still playing and that his bank was still dancing? He soon discovered he was the only one left standing, without a partner, in the last dance saloon.

Greenspan's autobiography was published in 2007 before the Bear Stearns collapse; it was republished in the Spring of 2008, with a new Epilogue dealing with that collapse, but just before the Lehman collapse, his second go at the unripe cherry of bad timing. In this new Epilogue, the upheaval in the financial markets in the Summer of 2007 was described by Greenspan as "an accident waiting to happen; this crisis was a psychological certainty". Greenspan happily tells us that he warned the Fed as early as November 2002 that the housing mortgage boom "cannot continue indefinitely into the future", but then did nothing about it for the next four years, as the boom went into overdrive with interest rates stuck at 1.0% for nearly two years. In May 2008 he saw a silver lining in the cloud in the republished edition, namely that house prices would stabilise as soon as the forced sales of houses had peaked!

His chosen metaphor was an artillery shell reaching the apex of its curved trajectory, but he still had not seen that the second half of the trajectory of this explosive metaphor would take it straight through the roof of the House of Lehman and flatten the global real estate and financial markets. Instead, he concludes that there was no democratic mandate for governments and central bankers to interfere with the boom, to "nip the budding euphoria", as he puts it, as there is little central banks can do to "direct or defuse them". WHAT? *Qui s'excuse, s'accuse!* Greenspan was then appalled and shaken that the financial system failed to protect itself from the euphoric boom he had created, by failing in the Fed's function to 'lean into the wind', but he himself had been blown along like a fully-reefed racer, shouting "Spinnakers away!" In 1998 there was a debate about regulating the CDS market: Greenspan's contribution was reported as 'We don't want any more regulating; we want deregulation; we're moving in the opposite direction, as markets take care of themselves'. Going, going, gone with the wind?

Then the *unforeseeable* crisis really broke just three months later, over the September week-end *that* began with that Greenspan interview: Lehman Bros was bust. It had assets of $639.0 billion and liabilities of $613.0 billion, implying debt leverage of around 25 times, which was an absurdly risky multiple of capital to debt; but $88.0 billion of the assets were a mixture of property-related loans and assets, starting with unsold 'Alt-A' mortgages, meaning mortgages of over $417,000 each, which accounted for $15.0 billion of the total, but the rest were mainly property and subprime mortgages, now all dubbed as "toxic" as they were unsaleable now that the music had stopped and no one knew their value, and they together represented nearly four times Lehman's capital: so without a bail-out, bankruptcy was inevitable.

Lehman also had total derivatives bought and sold of $729.0 billion with a fair net value of a possible $16.6 billion credit, which credit may prove to be difficult to collect in the course of its bankruptcy. Indeed, those former "bankers" left to wind down and tidy up the book were themselves demanding bonuses of £500,000 each for their work up to the end of 2009! The only winner in the collapse of Lehman were the liquidating accountants, or perhaps the manufacturer of the iconic boxes carried out by the staff as they left the offices, which were splashed across the front pages and TV screens all over the world as 'Iron Mountain', but in an apt metaphor were actually made of stiffened cardboard, like the supine board of Lehman that failed to control their CEO, or Chief Executive Officer.

As a major issuer of CDSs, ('Credit Default Swaps', or insurance for a bond or debt in case the borrower defaults or goes bust), Lehman's sudden collapse immediately hit the solvency of the biggest insurer in the world, and the biggest insurer in the $61.2 trillion CDS market, that's the $61,200,000,000,000 CDS insurance market. The mighty AIG, the 'American International Group', had

$1.0 trillion of assets, but with open 100% exposure to $441.0 billion of mortgage-related CDSs. Systemic risk was now a contagion blowing dangerously in the wind: on Monday morning 15th September AIG, the world's biggest insurer, needed $20.0 billion cash, then $75.0 billion by Monday evening and $85.0 billion by Tuesday morning and another $38.0 billion a month later, and another $30.0 billion the following March, until with a final $19.5 billion the total US-taxpayer support reached $182.5 billion, an utterly incredible amount to bail out a single company. AIG, the world's biggest insurer, had "forgotten" to re-insure or even hedge its own CDS exposure, as they were chasing profits around the world like a vulture that hadn't had a decent bite to eat since God-knows-when.

Amid the din, confusion, noise and dust a banker of the not quite-old-enough-school said: "I've had all the fun I can stand in investment banking", as he walked away from Lehman Bros. His next move the next day was not so wise, however, as he forgot his own dictum and thought he had spotted a good bargain in Merrill Lynch, who's CEO John Thain was clearly unhappy at the immediate prospect of the financial incinerator that had so readily turned Lehman into toast overnight. The 'Thundering Herd', now truly dubbed the 'Blundering Nerd', was quickly put out of its misery by Bank of America's Kenneth Lewis, who offered not cash but $50.0 billion of BoA paper, which looked like an opportunistic deal: "It didn't take but about two seconds to see the strategic implications or the positive implications of the deal", enthused the previously reluctant one, as he implicated BoA decisively in the future of Merrill Lynch, but the cash losses started the very next day. When the losses at Merrill had reached $15.5 billion two months later, including a mere $5.8 billion in potential bonuses written on the back of a fag packet, Lewis once again remembered that he had had enough of all this investment banking malarkey and tried to renege on the deal, as his $50.0 billion all-paper offer soon collapsed to $20.0 billion, and for good reason too: Merrill wasn't a bull at all, it was a dog.

BoA's Lewis was now lent on by a desperate US Treasury, bent on preventing a domino collapse, and was advised to get on and marry the bitch, and then send the bill in to 1600 Pennsylvania Avenue, Washington, where the new incumbent would pick up the tab on

Inauguration Day, as early as 21 January 2009, in the sum of $45.0 billion cash and a useful $118.0 billion loan-loss guarantee, which didn't need Congressional approval but was underwritten by the US-taxpayer. In the space of a year, Bear Stearns leveraged 33 times, down from a peak of 44 times, that's $525.0 billion of assets financed by just $12.0 billion of equity, Lehman Brothers leveraged 25 times and Merrill Lynch leveraged out-of-sight, had all gone, leaving just Goldman Sachs leveraged at 20 times, down from a 28 times peak, and Morgan Stanley leveraged at 17 times, down from a peak of 33 times, as the last outposts of a beleaguered so-called investment banking community: 'Geared Dealer-Brokers' (US), or 'Geared Stock-jobbers' (UK), would be a more accurate description for the lot of them. And within days of Lehman's collapse, it was no better with the commercial banks: Citigroup, WaMu or 'Washington Mutual', and countless other regional banks were all in trouble with losses and liquidity issues from toxic assets as well.

This monumental crisis of 2008 had been building for six years already, and despite the Bear Stearns' collapse in 2007, the man in charge until 2006, when the problems were being created, still couldn't *foresee* it? But then Greenspan was always a friend of the market and the market-makers, which is not where a central banker's sympathies should best lie. So why did Hank Paulson at the US Treasury let Lehman Bros. go to the wall? Various commercial banks had carried out due diligence and had passed, not least as the price demanded by its aggressive CEO was far too high. So the principle that public capital should not bail out private capital prevailed on that day; that and the notion that the systemic risk appeared to be an acceptable risk, albeit incalculable, even in view of Lehman's relatively small size. The next day, however, with the AIG mess on his hands, Paulson took a major non-democratic decision, that the state would now become the banker-of-last-resort and support the whole financial system. The US-taxpayer would bail-out the bankers, and discretely underwrite, in effect, their future bonuses. This was a quite different approach to what the Bank of England's Lifeboat, as lender-of-last-resort, had done in the 1974 banking crisis.

US Treasury Secretary "Hank the Hunk" Paulson must have questioned his own judgement since throwing Lehman to the wolves, but Lehman's top management had made appallingly bad misjudgements over the past three years and nobody liked the aggressive style of the CEO, or the way he dominated a supine board of directors. In appearance and behaviour, Dick Fuld Jnr. had all the charisma and instincts of Damien Hirst's shark, but on the same day that Lehman Bros finally went belly-up, at least the shark, safely marinated in formaldehyde and, like revenge, served up cold in a leak-proof steel tank, snagged a buyer at Sotheby's London saleroom for $17,200,000 cash.

Paulson's gut decision to let Lehman go to the wall was undoubtedly the correct one, to discourage banks from entering the 'Moral Hazard Territory', which certainly needed reinforcing. The problem was that the Moral Hazard card was played far too late in the day, as a result of earlier failures to act. If Paulson had bailed out Lehman, then the money mania would have carried on and created an even bigger bust down the road, whereas the reality was that the whole financial system was already one giant boil out of control that just had to be lanced without delay, and it was unfortunate that Lehman was the best available place for his scalpel to make the necessary incision.

Nevertheless, Paulson, or anyone else, could hardly have anticipated the next few days' events. Lehman's failure immediately set off a fireball across New York City, from 745 Seventh Avenue to One Pine Street, triggering the AIG crisis. So why did the US Treasury save AIG? Because it was just far too big to let it go bust, it would have affected the whole world, and anyway the US Treasury took an 80% stake that will yield it some recovery from its good underlying insurance business over time.

As the collateral damage from Lehman's failure spread ever wider across the financial sector, however, Paulson would have been less than human had he not doubted the wisdom of his original decision, but it was still the right one; indeed, there was a certain inevitability about it, whatever the consequences. Hank Paulson had no alternative but to reverse the dreadful indecisions of the Greenspan era, and time was no longer on his side, and yet in the heat of the crisis he made the most unpardonable and colossal error: he invested the TARP money, the Troubled Assets Relief Program money, without negotiating a single Subscription Agreement with any of the banks that received that money. Any investment comes with just such an agreement that regulates the investee company in a way that suits the investor, by agreement, in this case the US-taxpayer, such as agreed restrictions on bonuses, liquidity ratios, repayment terms and conditions. It was an unforgiveable lapse: Plato had a telling phrase for such a failure: *methienai tous kairous*, 'to let your opportunities slip'.

On the Monday of Lehman's demise, I happened to be in Paris. I approached the news-stand on Trocadero and asked the beret-clad, moustachioed and garlic-perfumed news-vendor if the English papers had arrived.

"Je veux lire au sujet de Lehman". I want to read about Lehman.

"La crise, c'est partout!" The Crisis is everywhere!

And his arm swept the Parisian sky from the Americas in the West right across to the East, in one enormous Gallic Gesture, that fittingly ended at the Eiffel Tower, having circumscribed the entire Northern Hemisphere. This was news indeed. And he was right. I had thought the crisis was an Anglo-sphere affair and had never imagined the contagion could spread everywhere else, which was still not appreciated on that day by the authorities anywhere. If only this news-vendor had been Greenspan's boss at the Fed, the crisis might have been *foreseen!*

In the short term the crisis quickly cratered credit and stock markets around the world and the dash for cash was now on in earnest, led by the banks themselves, insurance companies and mutual and hedge funds. Global Crunch was game-on and it wasn't sensible to be a loser, but losers there were wherever you looked: even the consistently-liquid US auction-rate security $330.0 billion market, for example, established in 1984 for long-term borrowers such as municipals and hospitals, seized up. The periodic rate-resets at auction turned them into short-term securities for the lender, but became illiquid as the banks withdrew credit, revealing that an instrument which is long-term to the borrower but short term to the lender was the first of many illusions to be exposed by Global Crunch.

Then the first signs of a global recession rapidly emerged in the fourth quarter, and in the most unlikely sectors such as minerals and oil, where the price of minerals had dropped by 60% and crude by 50% in just four months, as world trade fell off the cliff, and economies collapsed in the most unlikely places, such as Iceland,

Hungary, the Ukraine and across Russia and the Pacific. In the US in Q4, (the fourth quarter of 2008), on an annualised basis, consumer spending fell by 22%, private investment by 23%, and exports by 24%. In Q1 2009, US investment fell by another 49% and exports by another 31%. Overall, unemployment was up 3.3% (that's more than 5.0 million jobs) and GDP fell by 6%.

There were even reports of billionaires losing billions, of Russian Monopolygarcks retreating from their swish London Mayfair pads and their super-yachts on France's Côte d'Azur faster than Napoleon had retreated from Moscow in 1812, and with greater losses too. Bloomberg estimated in October that the richest 25 Russian billionaires had already lost £141.0 billion between them. The speed with which the crisis on Wall Street spread to Main Street everywhere was truly breathtaking, taking just six weeks post-Lehman to spread right across the globe, as the trail of US and local toxic mortgage assets was exposed in the most unlikeliest places, and revealed other economic excesses everywhere. One statistic shows how quickly the global recession spread out from the collapse on Wall Street: in Q3, the third quarter of 2007, Volvo's heavy truck sales were 40,000 units, but in Q3 2008 they were down to just 115 units. Try running a truck plant with those numbers.

On 27th October 2008 the Bank of England estimated that losses at that date on toxic assets were $1,577.0 billion in the US, £123.0 billion in the UK and €785.0 billion in the EU, an estimate of about $2.5 trillion, which shocked at the time but was to prove to be woefully under the mark: try around $10.0 trillion of equity, loans, guarantees and insurances and you'll be nearer the real total, according to the IMF in August 2009; and the biggest bailer-outer relative to GDP was the UK at £1,227 billion, or around 100.0% of GDP. This crisis went to the heart of the capitalist system and even questioned its morality and rationale. Mercifully, the communist system had been killed off in the 1990s so there was no competing system, just questions of how it had happened and how to control the future to prevent a repeat failure.

How could a generation of bankers, too young to remember the traumas of the 1974 and 1979 global oil shocks and their consequences and who blithely shrugged off the dot.com bubble of 2001 as a one-off aberration, which it was, have bankrupted the global system in a single decade? By using computer power and advanced mathematics to create new-fangled financial instruments, the implications of which their directors and regulators did not understand, to set up a twenty-four hour global round-the-clock trading casino, that they then milked mercilessly for their employers' burgeoning profits and for their own outlandish and obscene bonuses. This was the generation that broke the world economy through their short-sightedness, intent only on their own goals and driven by their sheer unbridled corporate and personal greed. The recession they seeded went on to affect every country in the world and every citizen in it, with the possible exception of the isolated loony state of North Korea, which blithely carried on starving its own people while letting off potential nuclear rockets into the Sea of Japan, in the name of advancing communications.

In February 2007, six months before the Bear Stearns debacle, I had been asked to write a leader for Spear's *Wealth Management Survey*, a UK quarterly for the mega-wealthy costing £25.0 a copy, but free on BA first class, if you can still afford the ticket. It was clear to me what the article should be about and I submitted a piece entitled *'Have the Central Bankers Lost Control?'* The editor nearly had a fit.

"We can't publish an article like that! We can't question the central banks!"

Well, we could and we did: we reached a compromise and the piece would be called *'Money Mania'* and my leading question would come at the end of the piece, but this was how it was originally submitted:

Have the Central Bankers Lost Control?

The global economy is producing wealth at the fastest rate ever, driven by the BRICs and other emerging markets, but no one knows how this new paradigm will react in a downturn: if the US slows, will this affect Chinese cheap exports? Would that impinge on China's massive purchases of US T-bills? How would the vast US budget deficit then be financed? What is the impact of this growth on inflation? This is the question that really worries the central bankers as they survey the asset-price bubbles popping up everywhere and the debt levels that drive them.

Hamlet mocked his mother with the notion that a great man's memory may outlive his death for fully half a year, but it's less than that, surely, since Milton Friedman shuffled off his mortal coil. Did monetarism die with him? It might as well have, as central bankers now monitor inflation indices rather than the growth in money supply, which is a surer guide to future inflation. And where is the UK money supply, as measured by M4? Well, it's hovering at thirteen percent...

The flesh is heir to a thousand natural shocks and any number of them are lurking in the global background: the triple US deficits may lead to currency turmoil; the vast pile of derivatives may contain some nasties; some hedge funds are not anything of the sort. The private equity market is borrowing up to six times EBITDA as the race to do the first $100 billion buy-out gains momentum. Private equity bidders have been running the numbers for a $20 billion buy-out of the UK's supermarket J. Sainsbury. Hold on, haven't we been here before, in the last boom with the UK buy-out of Gateway by the ineptly-named Isosceles, financed by Wasserstein Perella of NYC's first fund raised in Japan? Unfortunately, the arithmetic did not add up: the sum of the square of the other two sides in this wrong-angled triangle didn't add up to the square of the hypotenuse, and the deal went belly-up.

The old rules still apply: excess liquidity fosters inflation; asset prices are driven by debt; too much debt kills asset values; then confidence takes a bashing. Where is all this leading? Have the central bankers lost control of both inflation and more especially the money supply? We should be told, before the central bankers really do lose control.

This exhaustive survey seeks to record, examine and explain the greatest credit crisis the world has ever seen, which the authorities failed to foresee coming, and to investigate the causes and consequences of these extraordinary events, which have been building up slowly and methodically since the end of WW2, but at an accelerating pace from the early-1970s onwards. As at the scene of any major crime, all the evidence must be carefully sifted and weighed in the balance, and the failed structures, practices and guilty operatives must be fully exposed.

Her Majesty Queen Elizabeth II's brief and articulate question must receive the full and complete treatment and the answer it so richly deserves, and this loyal subject will do the very best he can, even keeping you going through this work by timely insertions of relevant humour – if you cannot laugh at it all, well, what hope is there in the face of human folly? I must keep her amused with this in-depth review of the economics of *Countdown to Catastrophe*, with the help of a certain Court Jester of my acquaintance, whose profession it is to make the Monarch laugh whilst imparting either unacceptably bad news or an important point of principle. So I must dive deep into the causes and consequences of this terrible crisis, maintaining humour, as I have no wish to hear my Sovereign say "I am not amused!", or I too might end up in the Bloody Tower.

And I can hear Her Majesty in the background with another one of those hat-pin questions: "If this crisis was started by all this money sloshing around and everyone getting into too much debt in the first place, why did the governments and central bankers think that pumping more money into the system and taking on all this debt themselves was the answer?" Hmmm; another very good question, Mam. I suspect that Her Majesty suspected that the banking crisis would go on to end up as a sovereign debt crisis – not Your Majesty's finances, Mam! – but national debt crises across the world.

PART II:

What Was Overlooked

Some Basic Principles of Economics

THIS sounds like a really boring way to start reading about the thriller white-knuckle ride called *Countdown to Catastrophe*, about as bad as going back to school, or worse. What you will read here, however, is very short and to the point. Many of this generation's economists, like the markets, have lost touch with reality: their training is data-driven, but the figures are mostly historic and but one-third of the bigger study, and leave out both the human and natural elements which account for the other two-thirds of the complete picture. It is not knowing these principles which makes economics so boring and at worse even irrelevant, and why governments, central bankers and regulators, not to mention businessmen, have made such colossal errors of judgement in recent years. So, if you want to know more than the central bankers did at the time of

Global Crunch, please bear with me for a few pages and resist any temptation to fast forward to Part III, to where the real action starts.

This study is focussed first on the Anglo-sphere world of America and Britain, where the two economies are intertwined by the English language and English law, but also by a shared history and heritage and by massive cross-investments, where some 40% of the income of the London Stock Exchange is Dollar-denominated, as Britain is the biggest foreign investor in America. For Americans, the study of Britain's history is essential to understanding their own history. It is almost as though Britain is in reality a State of the Union in economic terms, albeit moored offshore some three thousand miles away, but immediately adjacent to the even larger European economy.

The increasing globalisation of the last two decades, however, has meant that Anglo-sphere capitalist influences and practice have spread across the globe, accepted by some but resisted by others to varying degrees, and so this study goes on to look at the G20 world and how the Global Crunch came to affect every country and citizen on the planet.

Petty's Famous Dictum

The world's first econometrician, the English polymath Sir William Petty (1623-1687), formulated the first essential principle of economics in his *Treatises on Taxes and Contributions* published in 1662, when he wrote 'Labour is the Father and Active Principle of Wealth, as Lands are the Mother and Womb of Wealth'. The Austrian and Harvard economist Joseph A. Schumpeter (1883-1950), the author of *Business Cycles* who coined that memorable and significant phase, namely 'creative destruction', wrote of Petty's more memorable formulation: "This dictum put on their feet the two original factors of production of later theorists".

Petty's writings and his mathematical skills and his experiences of assessing the land values of Ireland in his Down Survey – so-called as it had to be written down – are collectively the first works on modern economics ever published. Petty sought to establish such new concepts as free trade, the factors contributing to and measurement of Gross Domestic Product, or GDP, which every economist now uses as a key bench-mark tool, the basis of taxation and public expenditures and debt, the velocity of money and money supply, which he interestingly stated should be held back at the level required just to keep the economy liquid, with monetary growth rising with the increase of GDP – try that one on Wall Street's bulge-bracket banks in the 2000s! He was the first pioneer of data collection as a necessary pre-requisite of political anatomy and objective economic analysis.

Adam Smith, GPLS, (1723-1790), author of *The Wealth of Nations* published in 1776, was the first economist who seriously studied Petty and also became tutor to his great-grandson, William Fitzmaurice-Petty (1737-1805), later the Second Earl Shelburne, who as Prime Minister of Britain (1782-1783) was the architect and chief executive of the fight for the Independence of America, and of the great wealth of Georgian England that flowed from that inspired decision and action, for which success he was elevated to First Marquis of Lansdowne. Towards the end of his great life, Lansdowne wrote about a five-day journey he had taken with his former tutor, from Edinburgh to London, in September 1761when he was just twenty-four: 'I owe to a journey I made with Mr. Adam Smith the difference between light and darkness through the best part of my life'.

Adam Smith was the champion of free trade, open markets and the liberalism that is implied in today's globalisation, and much else besides. After him, Marx, Schumpeter and Keynes all endorsed Petty as the originator of modern economic analysis. As Eliot Janeway, a former speech-writer for Franklin Delano Roosevelt, wrote in his last book in 1989: 'Petty died rich, ennobled, a legend in his lifetime, and the upstart aristocrat of talent who founded a long line of aristocrats of privilege, all powerful, a few of them also talented: a monument to the majesty that was [seventeenth century] England'.

So the first two principles of economics begin and end with Petty's 'Hands and Lands', with mankind and the earth, two very different aspects of creation. At a time when man's use, or abuse, of the earth is now under the international spotlight, and when the next techno-logical boom is likely to be ecology-driven, a few words to put them both in their proper economic perspective is compelling and relevant to this enquiry. And we shall see in due course, in an *exclusive* inter-view with Mr. Adam Smith himself, that the failure to appreciate the ramifications of Petty's famous dictum, of the relationship between Land and Labour, between "Hands and Lands", lay at the heart of Global Crunch and the naturally-repeating, but unnaturally-exaggerated by man-made error, boom-bust cycles.

"Hands and Lands"

The earth is a heavenly body which has her allotted station in the cosmos. She never ages or decays, and is never lacking in energy as she fulfils her role effortlessly. She requires no support, yet she supports all. Everything in the man-made world comes from the earth and returns to the earth, when its purpose is over. The earth is animate, full of life and gives birth to every living organism: mankind and the animals and birds, whether they live on the land, or in the sea or in the air, whether they are womb-born, egg-born, sweat-born or moisture-born, or flora and fauna born from seeds, they are all the offspring of the earth. And when they have lived their allotted span, they return to the earth, along with the rusted plough and all the garbage that each life produces, to be recycled in nature's own good time.

The earth is akin to a great spirit, but we are not in the habit of seeing it that way. We take her for granted, until someone threatens or attacks our bit of her, and then we fight for our lives to defend our patch, and even die for it. We take it for granted too, when those who pocket giant bonuses and think that it's *their's* because *they and no one else* earned it, as they forget the role of the rest of society and all that sustains it, beginning with the earth herself, which they have long lost contact with as a great spirit, and treat as so much real estate that they might, or might not, want to buy and sell, and mortgage.

Unexpectedly, in December 2009, a former economist at the New York Fed who had recently been appointed to the Bank of England's MPC, or Monetary Policy Committee, namely Dr. Adam Posen, stuck his head above the parapet and suggested a 'Bubble Tax' on buildings so as to smooth out the volatility of the property cycle, which he correctly deduced was the principal factor behind the boom-bust roller-coaster rides. Posen was basically reaching in the right direction as regards the endless property bubbles, but he had not got even halfway to the whole equation: his remarks showed that he had not appreciated the full subtlety of Petty's famous dictum, of how "Lands" relate to "Hands", and the role of the incidence of taxation as the balancing mechanism between them. This issue will be explored later, including in an interview with Petty's first and great disciple, Mr. Adam Smith, the voice from beyond the grave who understood the whole debate and its implications for today.

Unlike the earth, whose nature is forever giving without fear or favour, man's nature and personality are forever changing. Important characteristics of economic activity are driven by this dichotomy, namely the erratic nature of man in contrast to the constant nature of the earth. Human life and each individual are governed by the Principle of Change: whereas understanding the Principle is first and foremost a philosophic issue, nevertheless economists ignore the Principle at their peril. For example each economic cycle has its own distinctive style and characteristics, and what may have worked in the 1930s is unlikely to work in the 2010s, because the Principle of Change never serves up exactly the same situation twice. John Maynard Keynes put it exactly: "We do not know what the future will bring, except that it will be different from any future we could predict". And John Kenneth Galbraith wrote: "I believe the greatest error in economics is in seeing the economy as a stable and immutable structure". This perception of reality makes Economics interesting and important.

The Principle of Change

The Principle of Change affects every aspect of life on earth, and is a law well appreciated by philosophers and evolutionists, if one dare mention these two very different species of enquirers in the same breath. It is not possible to go into the details of the Principle here, or we will be up all night discussing the *Chitta* of the Vedantists, Herakleitos's "You cannot step into the same river twice", and even Plato's *Symposium* and Bhasho's Haiku verses and on to Werner Heisenberg's atomic Principle of Uncertainty. Instead, I will recount a very short story of the Principle of Change from the Sufi tradition, involving the engaging character of, yes my chosen Court Jester, The Incomparable Mullah Nasruddin, who had his own 'Shaggy-Dog Story' way of revealing the eternal verities.

One night the Mullah's wife said: "You no longer love me, you no longer kiss me, you no longer hug me. Remember when you were courting me? You used to bite me and I loved that very much! Can't you bite me once more?"

The Mullah Nasruddin got out of bed and started walking away.

"Where are you going now?" pleaded his wife.

"To the bathroom to get my teeth."

You can observe the Principle of Change in your own body and sentiments, which noticeably change every seven years: Shakespeare's seven ages of man was written in an age when 50 years was a good expectation of life, and indeed he achieved a bonus of two years when he died aged 52, but the point of this seven-year cycle is that it is the constantly recurring number $1/7$ which gives $142857'$, that is the master of the "mechanical" universe, and known as the Law of Seven for those who study the Enneagram. For those who prefer their scripture served up in a more orthodox manner, we have the *New Testament* and its even shorter phraseology to point to the Principle of Change: 'And it came to pass ...', and when the purpose clause is fully expressed we have "It came in order to pass ...", miraculously describing the whole universe and everything in this ever-changing play of creation in just one short phrase.

The economist does not have to be a psychologist or a philosopher, but must have a keen sense of the psychology of the archetype which Carl Jung called the 'mass-man'. For example, the terms 'bulls' and 'bears' are a broad psychological distinction and an important perception for economists and market observers and operators. As the world struggles with global recession in 2009, the solution is as much to do with human confidence, an intangible quality, as it is with anything else. As Greenspan declared: "Unless someone can change human nature, there will be another crisis ... No two crises have anything in common except human nature". Roosevelt knew the part played by human confidence, when in his inaugural address in 1933 he told Americans who had already endured four years of depression: "We have nothing to fear, but fear itself." And everyone who heard it felt better, or at least felt more confident. The effects of psychology in economics have been largely overlooked by many of those today who would call themselves economists; a notable exception was Vilfredo Pareto (1848-1923), an Italian econ-omist who swayed towards fascism. In his book *The Mind and Society* he wrote of the importance of psychology: "All conscientious observers of crises have noted the role played by the imagination. It is one of the principle causes of crises". And it goes without saying that it is one of the causes of ending the crisis, when despair turns to hope.

Professor Robert Shiller of Yale University said in early 2009: "This recession is by no means mechanical. People have lost a sense of confidence, a sense of trust in institutions and in each other. It is very hard for a central bank to address that just by cutting interest rates". Or in other words, what people are thinking is part of eco-nomics too, and as man is irrational, economics is just as much an art as a science. Economists today have tended to consider mankind as essentially rational beings who take decisions in their own best self-interest, but as studies in behavioural economics show, from Adam Smith's *Theory of Moral Sentiments* to E.R. Dodds' *The Greeks and the Irrational* to Richard Thaler's *Nudge*, that for every economic prob-lem, there's a behavioural insight that will make any solution more effective. These views may raise the hackles of economists who con-sider themselves as dealing with a branch of science, as mankind's inherent inconsistency must now be treated as being an essential, but unquantifiable, factor in economics.

Creative and Degenerate Economic Persons

In this book, the whole gamut of human nature in its economic ram-ifications is taken to fall between two poles, between those of Creative Person and Degenerate Person. You may not like my pre-ferred shorthand for human behaviour, and I would have to agree that Dr. Martin Luther King's brisk distinction between the light of creative altruism and the darkness of destructive selfishness is more elegant, but you should at least have some idea of what I am infer-ring by this terminology, in an economic context.

The Creative Person has an enquiring and open mind and is never greedy, gives regularly to charity, is always ready to help colleagues and friends and give what can be given, refines professional skills, craft or trade and delights in serving clients or customers, or producing quality products. He or she never knowingly produces shoddy work or poor-quality merchandise, for the client's or customer's satisfaction is their satisfaction and source of energy, while money is merely a medium of exchange. Such people are happy in their work and life. Such a man, for example, might be Tim Berners-Lee, the Englishman who invented the internet and gave it to the world without seeking any financial reward for himself; or Bill Gates, the brilliant software engineer and co-founder of Microsoft, who has pledged much of his fortune to third world philanthropy and the elimination of disease; or the garage mechanic who always knows how to get your car back on the road and charges a fair price.

The Degenerate Person, however, is greedy and lustful and thinks mainly of his own advantage. This person pollutes the environment without even thinking. They become governed by bad thoughts and engage in swindles, false accounting and ill-conceived hostile takeovers. They break securities laws, plunder employees pension funds, increasing their own remuneration while announcing massive employee lay-offs. The more the Degenerate Person gets, the more he wants. Such a man, for example, might be Bernard Madoff, the psychopathic Ponzi fraudster, who expressed no regret about all the charitable funds he had plundered, or Dick Fuld Jnr, the CEO who drove Lehman Brothers into bankruptcy through excessive greed. In the UK, the four directors of MG Rover bought the company for £10.0 from BMW, who were so anxious to be shot of what they called the 'English Patient' that they also donated a £500.0 million cash dowry, but these four directors then went on to bilk the company *legally* out of £42.0 million in compensation over the next four years, while the company went broke with the loss of 6,300 jobs; or the garage mechanic who says he's fixed your car when he knows he hasn't, and charges exorbitantly for the work he hasn't done.

The point about Creative and Degenerate Persons, however, is not that everyone is one or the other, as though they were mutually exclusive conditions, for each of these archetypes lives in each of us, with greater or less strength from day to day. Rather they express the gamut of potential economic behaviour in anyone, although tendencies towards the one or the other poles may become manifest in any of us over time, and at times individuals may well become irrevocably linked to one or the other extremes. The essential plot of Ayn Rand's novel *Atlas Shrugged*, a masterpiece in the psychology of human economic affairs, is all about the interplay between these two poles, between Dagny Taggart and her eponymous railroad network and Hank Rearden and his eponymous steel plants on the one hand, and Wesley Mouch and Orren Boyle on the other, between the creative force of private enterprise and the degenerate failure of the socialist Board of Unification. This tension is now reappearing in society in endless bureaucracy and arid ideas like 'Political Correctness' which threaten basic liberties such as freedom of speech, as encouraged by Degenerate Persons, just as Ayn Rand described it. In that book, as in business, everyone wants to know about the character and reputation of those with whom they deal, and very sensibly go to great lengths to find out exactly that.

In business the Hogan Development Survey, or HDS questionnaire, is increasingly used at the point of recruitment; it highlights eleven "proven" traits that can derail leaders, each named after the acceptable [creative] and unacceptable [degenerate] aspects of each characteristic, for example 'confident-arrogant', 'enthusiastic-volatile' and 'dutiful-dependent'. Apparently 85% of us have an economic dark side, 16% have three dark-side characteristics and these characteristics change as we get older, as the Principle of Change kicks in every seven years, and they tend to surface at times of great stress or success.

The Natural Cycles of Economics

So irrational man's existence is played out on this dependable planet, but is nevertheless governed by an important aspect of nature, which abhors a vacuum and rejects straight lines. So often investors, businessmen and politicians start dreaming of an economic graph that ascends from left to right, majestically and uninterruptedly, to the new economic promised land, the "new paradigm", until reality brings them back to earth with a crunch.

Britain's Prime Minister Gordon Brown even informed an astonished House of Commons in 2007 that he "had banished boom and bust forever", which is a very long time indeed, but it turned out inevitably that he was dreaming of Gordon's Fantasy Curve that just flopped back to earth within a year. Nature, as you will soon appreciate, only works in cycles. There are economic cycles, ageing, climatic, temperature, solar, warfare and cultural and stylistic cycles, and many others besides, and they do interact in unseen ways.

The Short Cycle

The short economic cycle was first perceived by the French physician Dr. Clement Juglar in 1860, when he observed that the human birth-rate rose and fell with the economy over what he defined as an eight-year cycle, although his followers have argued for nine and ten-year cycles. I prefer to think in terms of a nine-year cycle – (nine being the key number of the Enneagram) – before allowing for man-made and natural distortions of one or two years, such as Greenspan's running the US economy at a 1.0% interest rate from 2003 to mid-2004, for well over a year longer than was appropriate or even wise. Analysis of the short circle confirms the crisis points in Europe as follows: 1825, 1836, 1847, 1857, 1866, 1873, 1882, 1890, 1900, when America begins to follow the western cycles more closely, and on to 1907, 1913, 1920 and 1929. The Great Depression and WW2 were the man-made distortions that broke the pattern, which again reasserted itself after the WW2, as we shall see.

The cycles cannot be stopped by mankind, but it is possible to work knowingly within them. For example, the banker who lends most or all of the finance required for a 3-year commercial property development late in the short cycle and after values have risen strongly may find the bank's loan turns sour in the approaching downturn, as rentals decrease and the capital value of the project is exponentially reduced. The central banker or politician who eases credit and taxation as the economy booms, seeking 'a dash for growth', will find that it merely magnifies the existing upturn and the negative effects of the inevitable downturn. If they do this just as the Short and Long Cycles are both turning down, the results are likely to be near-catastrophic.

Well this, or something like it, was what we all thought Alan Greenspan and Gordon Brown had got the hang of, or so we hoped, or as they would at least have had us believe. What fools we all were to believe their rhetoric, or was it that their words did not tally with their own arithmetic? Consider the following graph and table, a UK Treasury favourite, taken from the Pink (formerly Red) Book for the 1993 and 2008 Budgets, the latter of which was promulgated on 12th March, just four months before the demise of Northern Rock and Bear Stearns, with the memorable strap-line 'Stability and Opportunity, building a strong, sustainable future', and then the heavens fell in, just as their own graph forecasted they would!

This Graph and Chart 1 shows the movement in the G7 (the Group of the US, UK, Canada, Germany, France, Italy and Japan) and their GDP (Gross Domestic Product) and world trade. It also shows how each Short Cycle is distinctly different, especially the

Graph/Chart 1:

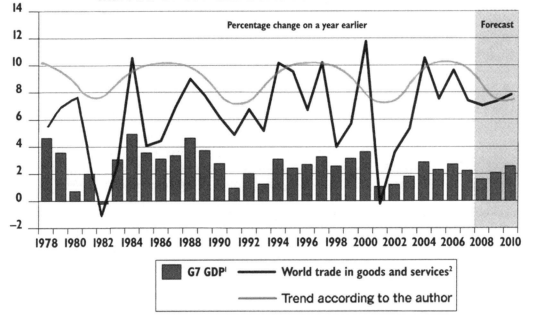

Chart BI: G7 GDP and world trade

Real GDP (major 7 countries) at constant prices
Treasury estimates based on OECD data

downturns of 1981/2 and 2000/1, while the Reagan/Thatcher recovery of 1984 was spectacular and basically sustainable for fifteen years, whereas the peak of the Tech Bubble in 1998/9 and subsequent fall in 2000 were just plain crazy, producing the oh-so-slow recovery in the new millennium.

If we go back to the same chart in the 1992-1993 Red Book, we can now produce our own summary table for Juglar's short cycles for the last thirty-six years. It should be no surprise that 36 divided by 9 gives 4 cycles, and the short cycles are the ones to be kept in mind whether as a private individual or investor, or banker or businessman or economist or politician.

Table 1:
The Short Cycles, 1973-2009

1973-1982
1982-1991
1991-2000
2000-2009

This graph spells out the cycles clearer than any other; and gives the best reading on the Anglo-sphere, G7 and world trade cycles. It passes the empirical test. Whereas the 1973, 1982, 1991 and 2000 downturns were fitting the Short Cycle with reliable regularity, it was not always the case immediately after WW2, nor were the downturns themselves regular in either duration or intensity. In the US, the downturn of 1953/4 saw GDP contract by 6.2%, then there was a short aberration in 1957/8 of minus 10.4%, whereas the two downturns in 1982 and 2000 each saw downturns of 6.4% in US GDP.

It could not have been more blindingly obvious from the above graph that from 2006 onwards it was time to take the foot off the gas, stop looking in the rear-view mirror at how much dust Alan Greenspan and Gordon Brown were blowing into the electorates' collective face, look through the front windshield instead and hunker down for the next cold shower on the way. It was already clear that the UK's M4, that's broad money in circulation, was going through the roof, past 10% and onto 13% in 2007, but nobody was watching the gauge – when did you last hear mention of this M4? The problem with the Treasury, however, is that they are always looking backwards at last quarter's tax revenues and the historic cumulative trends on receipts and expenditures and never see the brick wall in front of them until it's too late, when the inevitable sound of splintering wood and flying glass shatters our ear-drums, and we find ourselves in another fine old Laurel and Hardy mess. The Fed and Treasury boffins just pick themselves up as though nothing had happened – they're used to it by now! – dust themselves down and get ready to do it all over again, as though they were in some Ealing Studios serial comic-disaster movie.

The Long Cycle

Whereas Clement Juglar spotted the Short Cycle, another econometrician perceived the workings of a longer cycle: Nikolai Kondratieff, (1882-1938), studied the rise and fall of agricultural production in Russia and formulated the 'Long Wave', or 'K-wave', of thirty to sixty years, whilst himself focussing on fifty-four years, implying an average of forty-five years. Kondratieff placed the turning points as 1815, 1873 and 1918, but his work *Long Waves in Economic Life* was based on his observations during the years 1789-1926, but on a limited field of data, and for the last decade in Bolshevik Russia.

The importance of Kondratieff is that he first formulated the idea of a Long Wave, or K-wave, rather than his attempts at defining its duration; his title for his think-tank was, tellingly, the Institute of Conjecture. Personally, and based on ideas gleaned from the study of Vedic mathematics and cosmology where the number nine reigns supreme, I prefer to think of the Long Wave as ninety years, or nine (or ten) short cycles of nine years each, before allowing for man-made and natural distortions of up to ten years in the Long Wave. And beyond that there may well be a nine hundred year cycle, give or take an hundred years' distortions for man-made and natural distortions, a truly grand cycle that measures out civilisations.

The idea of a Long Cycle should not be lost sight of when considering the self-evident existence of the Short Cycle, as identifying the mutual crisis points could well be highly relevant. The 90-year cycles identified here are in **bold** type, while the 45/54-year cycles alternate between bold and normal type, dependent on your view, but my choice is for **bold**. America's Long Cycle is a separate study until she began to enter the emerging western world in around 1845, as railways and steam-boats began to open up international communications and trade, so the benchmark must be the British economy and her Industrial Revolution in the late Eighteenth Century, which America had caught up with fully by the time of WW1.

Beginning in **1650**, after the English Civil War (1642-1649) that was the man-made distortion of seven years in the Long Cycle that devastated the largely agrarian economy, which ended only with the execution of Charles I in 1649; then onto 1701, the year that Jethro Tull invented the seed drill and the War of the Spanish Succession commenced; then on to **1745**, the second Jacobite rebellion of Bonnie Prince Charlie in England, straddled by Frederick the Great's defeat of the Austrians in 1741 and the subsequent War of Austrian Succession until 1748; then to 1789 and the French Revolution and the year in which George Washington becomes the first President of an independent America, when the New World begins to grow into the cycles of the Old World of Europe; **1845**, when railway mania began in England and later spread to America, as England repealed the Corn Laws the following year while the Irish endured their worst potato famine, as Marx and Engels published their *Communist Manifesto* during the 1848 Year of Revolutions across Europe; then on to 1890 when the age of the motor-car was ushered in, both in America and Europe; which conveniently leads on to when America really had joined the European cycle, to **1930** and the Great Depression; then to 1974 and the first Oil Crisis; and, ominously, on towards **2020**, when the great Global Crunch of 2008/9 perhaps leads on to either debt-deflation or super-stagflation and civil unrest and wider conflict. So this author's view of the assumed ninety-year cycles, allowing ten years either way for man-made and natural distortions, goes from 1650-1745-1845-1930-2020, or perhaps 2010, bearing in mind the caveat of up to ten-year distortions of the Long Cycle.

Whereas HM Treasury's graph of the Short Cycles in the previous section deals with 1973-2009, the five previous cycles working on from the Wall Street crash of 1930, the bottom of the last Long Cycle, are now also shown, with the question of whether WW2 was the second Short Cycle or the man-made distortion of the Long Cycle left remaining unanswered, as follows:

Table 2:

The Short Cycles, 1929–2009

1929-1938	The Great Depression	1st Short Cycle
1939-1945	[WW2-'Man-made Distortion'	of the Long Cycle?]
1945-1952	The Post-war Recovery	2nd/3rd Short Cycle
1953-1963	The Gradual Expansion	3rd/4th Short Cycle
1964-1973	The Faster Expansion	4th/5th Short Cycle
1973-1982	The Rudderless Decade	5th/6th Short Cycle
1982-1991	The Greed Decade	6th/7th Short Cycle
1991-2000	The Tech Decade	7th/8th Short Cycle
2000-2009	The Noughties Decade	8th/9th Short Cycle

Graph 2:

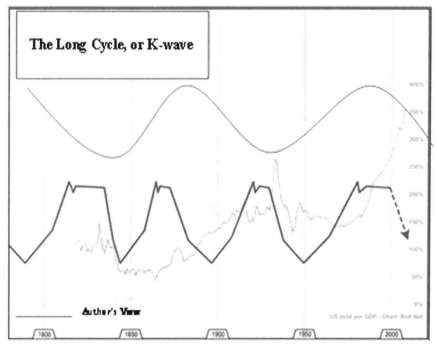

Source: Longwavegroup.com

Is 2000-2009 the 8th Short Cycle, or is it the 9th Short Cycle – perhaps the last in the current Long Cycle? We do not know yet but time will soon tell, as the effect of WW2 is the unknown that could fall into the bracketed [Man-made Distortion] category. Within the parameters of this partially subjective but also exploratory argument, it could be argued that WW2 was perhaps the second Short Cycle of the recovery from the Great Depression, where armaments drove the German and Japanese economies, huge house-building drove the UK economy and Roosevelt's New Deal drove, or did not drive, the US economy, but the war itself definitely did send the US economy into overdrive and delivered up the technologies for the post-war world's expansion. In this case, the 2000-2009 Short Cycle might well be the eighth rather than the ninth Short Cycle, and possibly coinciding with the bottom of this Long Cycle. Or perhaps the current Short Cycle from 2009-2018 is the last in its Long Cycle, before the excesses of the 2000s lead to possible either debt-deflation or super-stagflation in the run-up to 2020, and possibly Great Depression 2? Who knows in 2009, but either way it feels like the end of this particular bumpy road is in prospect, or woe betides us in the next few years if we do not put in place the right structural and regulatory checks and balances in this current Short Cycle: another failure of the global banking system, Banking Crisis 2, is likely to be catastrophic.

So we might even be approaching the crisis point where both the Short and Long Cycles reach their down-points together between 2010 or 2018, especially if the effects of the 2009 global recession, beginning with deflation and possibly ending in stagflation, drag on for up to ten years. The Longwavegroup.com chart shown above confirms this possibility, as it shows US debt soaring while the economy plunges in 2009, indicating a severe bout of stagflation could be in prospect, exacerbated by the wholesale implementation in 2009 of Keynesian stimuli and Friedmanite monetary reflation by the western democracies, which will be discussed in the Noughties Decade in Part III below.

The longwavegroup.com in Canada has made a serious study of Kondratieff's long wave theory, as exemplified in Graph 2 above, which tracks US private plus public debt, i.e. US total debt, per GDP against their interpretation of the theory in the context of the US economy. It is interesting to note that a comparison of the UK's and US's Long Waves first coincide in 1845, when transcontinental transport links began to develop across the Atlantic too, and again in the run-up to 2020; the fact that they do not coincide at the obvious date of 1930 is, in my opinion, that the 90-year cycle is just that, and exists without being divided into the hiatus of the 45/54-years of two halves. The Long Wave Group, I am sure, will stick to their football game of two halves theory, (always allowing for extra time of up to 9, so making 54, or with 45 a total of 99), which at least gives them the added advantage of sucking on lemons at half-time! Nevertheless, the delineation of the K-waves into 45/54 or 90 years makes little difference as we approach 2010/20, as this decade is ominously at the bottom of both interpretations.

The Longwavegroup.com has also compared this chart revealingly against the graphs for US stock prices on the S&P 500 and US prices generally since 1789, and US Treasury bond yields since 1800, as can be reviewed on their eponymous website. Their 45/54-year cycle line is not calibrated, as it is a formulaic line, beginning with Kondratieff's Spring as the first leg of the up-line, followed by Summer for the second leg of the upswing, with Autumn across the top and Winter is the down-lines, where the last down-line is made to fit the key down years which may vary by nine years. It seems that the number 9 holds the key one way or the other in either interpretation of the Long Wave, just as it surely holds the key to the Short Cycle.

The Inter-action of the Short and Long Cycles

At least one serious economist has raised the possibility that the current crisis will lead to a longer downturn than usual. Robert Shiller, Professor of Economics at Yale University, who predicted the end of the internet bubble, said in January 2009: "We could have many years of a very weak economy. Big recessions are followed by years of weakness and typically unemployment keeps rising. To say this will last years is not a dramatic statement. What is happening now is much worse than 1990. We could be facing a decade of real weakness. This is no ordinary recession. There are signs that people see this as a different story. People are talking about a depression, something that we haven't seen previously".

Shiller is clearly picking up on the Principle of Change in these comments. The important point is that both the Short and Long Cycles do exist, so the Short Cycle is not operating between parallel lines, as it were, but between bent lines with on average ninety year troughs, always allowing for the up to ten-year distortions caused by natural or man-made causes. These distortions include natural disasters, such as volcanoes and hurricanes, floods and droughts, plague and disease; and man-made disasters such as protectionist policies, massive bankruptcies and credit crises, insurrections and wars, and political crises which distort the cycles, and often change the course of history quite dramatically.

The Cycles are Nature's way of resting and purging the economy. If excess has poisoned the system, then Schumpeter's "creative destruction" kills off the bad loans and unproductive assets, shows up greed and incompetence, and rebalances and re-energises the productive resources for the next upturn. It is as though Nature's Cycles are her way of pruning back the old growth to allow for next season's recovery. Nor are these economic cycles the only cycles that impact the economy: there are temperature and climatic cycles, and cycles of migration and warfare, that have very big influences on economic activity, as we shall see.

The Styles of Economic Cycles

And finally there's an important final point to note about the cycles, and the Principle of Change, namely that each cycle from bust-to-boom-to-bust has its own styles and characteristics. These govern the preferred methods and structures of financing, the emerging technologies that capture the mood and meet the needs of the times, the fads in the stock markets and even the manner in which business is conducted and consumers spend their money. All these styles appear and change and disappear, just like ladies' hemlines and camisoles, and motor car designs. And each cycle always ends in a different manner, with its own variety of mega-frauds.

Some aspects of the operation of the cycles are common to most of them. For example, stock exchanges tend to rise as the cycle bottoms out and long before the real economy sees any sign of a pick up, so the exchanges are seen as a leading indicator, with house prices in the US hitting bottom only after the stock markets have already been rising for six months. Conversely, unemployment is a lagging indicator, and starts to rise after a downturn has already set in. As the inevitable upturn kicks in, liquidity is already rising and then excess liquidity transfers into higher asset prices, as happened in the dot.com boom of the late-1990s.

In the first decade of the third millennium, for example, the particular *Zeitgeist* for banking models moved on from 'narrow banks' that lent to their customers at the risk of their own capital, to 'casino banks' that originated loans and then sold them onto investors at a profit but now at the investors risk, with the aid of risk-transfer credit insurance instruments, which volumes of business drove the bonus culture beyond the capacity of 'narrow banks'. The 'narrow banks' proved the more enduring model, however, while the originate-to-distribute model of the 'casino banks' brought the house down, not with their winnings but with the losses they created both for themselves and their client-investors. It pays to observe closely the emerging styles of each new Short Cycle.

The Problem of Corrupt Data and Forecasts

Not many central or retail bankers, economists or politicians or businessmen saw the "unforeseeable" crisis of 2008/9 coming. Why was this? Well, economics is not a science: mathematics is a science, the science of number, and economics quite rightly makes great use of mathematics, but that doesn't make economics a pure science, particularly as the exact nature of number and its expression can never quite be made to fit all the moving parts of the living economy, and the more complicated the maths the more divergent from reality it becomes. If Economics is not a Science, what is it then? Some hood or other once described Hollywood as a "Copulation of Ideas and People" and to this intuitive one, Economics is indeed a 'Copulation of Words and Numbers'. Or to put it in more acceptable vernacular terminology, Economics is a descriptive branch of Anthropology: it is primarily an intuitive Art, not a prescriptive Science.

In fact, one reason why so many did not see the crisis coming is that there are too many numbers, but most of these numbers are historic and drag their users' vision backwards, to looking at past numbers, and away from the present. As Hector Sants, the Head of the UK's regulator the FSA put it in a BBC documentary: "We are backward-looking, we won't think about looking at the future in respect of business model risk". And when they do look to the future, the computer can only mechanically extrapolate the past, based on assumptions supplied by humankind. "Complexity, transparency, liquidity and leverage have all played a huge role in this crisis. And these are things that are not generally modelled as a quantifiable risk," said Leslie Rahl, President of Capital Market Risk Advisors, speaking to the *International Herald Tribune* in 2009.

In the build-up to Global Crunch, each innovation in financial instruments added complexity to the system for the obvious reason that complexity, encouraged by the regulators' emphasis on complex modelling, sold and made the most money. "Innovation can be a dangerous game," however, as "The technology got ahead of our ability to use it in responsible ways," echoed Andrew Lo, of MIT's Sloan School of Management. Financial economists relied on EMH, or the 'Efficient Market Hypothesis', as in the notion that markets regulate themselves, as if financial innovation was always beneficial. Mathematics in economics assumes perfect rationality and produces the perfect abstract market paradigm every time, but the only trouble is that it is asymmetric to the actuality. This really shows up on macro-economic forecasting models, because computers cannot be programmed to anticipate a market collapse any more than they can be programmed to make predictions about the Mullah Nasruddin's Teeth. How do you programme for counter-party risk, systemic risk, human folly, market illiquidity, or when market stress renders assets previously uncorrelated with other risks to being suddenly correlated, as happened in the LTCM debacle, as we shall see.

The Bank of England operates the DSGE computer model, the 'Dynamic Stochastic General Equilibrium', in case you didn't know. 'Stochastic' is a Greek word with an implied *double-entendre*: it means 'to aim at a mark, and therefore, to enter into conjecture and guesswork'; and as for General Equilibrium, I have no idea in which campaigns he fought or whether he won or lost. This DSGE model, however, does not include financial intermediaries, such as banks, which sounds like more than a minor omission likely to cause General Disequilibrium, as this was exactly the area that went illiquid in Global Crunch and caused the collapse of a raft of banks. In September 2007, after Bear Stearns' crash, the distinguished academic economist and a governor of the Fed, Frederic Mishkin, gave an analysis of simulations from the Fed's FRB/US computer model at the annual symposium at Jackson Hole, Wyoming. He declared that if house prices fell by 20.0% over the next two years, the slump would only knock 0.25% off GDP and add 0.1% to unemployment, because the Fed would respond "aggressively" by cutting interest rates by 1.0%. Since his presentation, US house prices have indeed slumped by 20% or more, but unemployment has risen by over 5.0% to 10.0% and GDP has dropped by 5.5%, while interest rates were cut not by 1.0%, but by 5.0%, to 0-0.25%. Clearly, these projections were an extreme case of the Mullah Nasruddin's Teeth Syndrome, that things can change over time by far more than you thought possible or computers can ever predict. Just ask the Mullah's wife!

The problems of these computer limitations, however, are greatly magnified when it is impossible to input any reliable assumptions at all, as in the summer of 2008: whither oil at $147.0 per barrel, producing an unheard of $4.0 per gallon at US petrol pumps, food inflation in double figures and mineral prices soaring, interest rates in the US and UK at over 5.0%, and a Dollar/Pound exchange rate at 2.0? Within four months oil would be at $38.0, wheat and minerals off over 50%, interest rates headed for zero, and 1.48 Dollars to the Pound. Then so many of these numbers, particularly those generated by governments and their agencies, are "lies, damned lies and statistics," and that was before the new mischief of spin came in with President Clinton and New Labour's Blair and Brown, who kept on moving the goal-posts, on whose certainty comparative statistics must rely.

Take inflation for example. In 2008 UK inflation trended along at around 2.0% according to the government. This calculation was based on the EU's criteria of the Consumer Price Index or CPI, which excludes the cost of housing, a much higher cost in the crowded space of the UK than on the Continent. The previous basis for this calculation was the UK's own Retail Price Index or RPI, which was running around 2.0% higher than the CPI, at 4.0%. In the crisis, in

February 2009, the CPI rose to 3.2%, but by then inflation was the least of the Bank's worries as interest rates were falling to just 0.5% to make way for monetary reflation. Actual inflation tracked by independent economists was running at over 5.5%, however, while indices compiled by Morgan Stanley and *The Daily Telegraph*, which were based on what consumers actually needed, were running at over 6.0% and 8.0%. These indices were much nearer the real mark than the government's, as over the last decade of the second millennium prices visibly rose by around 100.0% or so, especially housing, conveniently not included in the CPI.

Take unemployment as another example. These statistics are capable of all kinds of manipulation, as categories of unemployed persons can be altered by any statistician's passing whim: those students finding their first work, those on special leave for maternity or paternity or eternity – that's the bone idle – those claiming disability and other benefits, those on short-time working, those made redundant for the first few months, those in hospitals for X number of days, those deemed to have taken early retirement and those in training, the list of possible exclusions is endless.

In August 2009, *The Daily Telegraph* reported on major anomalies in the UK's unemployment figure of 2.6 million, until in Q4 2009 HM Treasury, always looking backwards as ever, spotted that Income Tax receipts were off 20%. Investigation revealed that 1.7 million had opted for part-time work rather than risk formal unemployment. This 2.6 million "actual" unemployed, which was effectively well over 3.0 million in adjusted real terms as evidenced by the fall-off in income tax receipts, compared with the UK's Department of Work and Pensions press release in February 2009 stating that 5.8 million people were claiming benefits on Social Security, including 1.4 million claiming Job Seekers Allowance, (which used to be called Incapacity Benefit, you see), and others claiming benefits as lone parents, carers and for actual disability.

The UK Treasury's projection for gross income tax receipts for 2009/10 was £140.5 billion, but Social Security Benefits were projected at £164.7 billion; so everyone in the UK receiving and paying taxes on salaries, wages, bonuses, interest, dividends and rents were only paying for 85.3% of the cost of all those scroungers, well half of them at least, on Social Security. In both the US and UK the Social

36

Security and Medicare/NHS budgets are under-funded and essentially bust. One English couple were actually caught out claiming benefits when they posted a picture of themselves on the internet, 'Wish you were here' and all that, lounging on the sun-deck of their yacht!

And what about GDP, that all-important statistic which tells you how big the pie is, and whether it's growing or shrinking? The US GDP in Q3 2009 was up 0.9% and you could hear Ben Bernanke begin breathing again, as this signalled to him that the global recession was at last over, and the US was back to 3.6% annual growth rate. But is it? GDP comprises consumption + investment + net exports + government spending; and inflation. So if government increases spending, GDP will go up, although production probably will not to the same degree. When you strip out the US government schemes for rusty old autos and shiny new home buyers, which ended in this Q3 and adjust down by the effect of Helicopter Ben's doubling of the monetary base which is worth around 7% in GDP terms, the plain fact is that the US private sector was still contracting. Governments, you see, can manipulate GDP, and cynically too: interesting that Gordon Brown's return to full VAT at 17.5% will add to GDP in Q1 2010, just-in-time for the UK General Election, and that he is determined to keep government spending going until then. You now see why.

Economics is much more than just statistics: it takes in the natural cycles, the erratic nature of man, mass-man's psychology and the styles of the times, all within the political, legal and structural conditions pertaining at any time and place, that so drive the conditions wherever "Hands and Lands" meet. And the economist needs to have a *feeling*, or a gut-reaction based on experience, to interpret and second-guess the data for how all these variables are headed and are inter-acting, and to take in anecdotal evidence that presents itself on the street and in conversations and from the ether, in the practice of an art that requires both the thinking and the feeling that produces good judgement. And any number of computer models cannot do this for you, as they are mechanical and cannot reflect the nature of man and the Principle of Change. A mandarin in the UK's HM Treasury said in the 1980s: "Computers are governed by GIGO – garbage in, garbage out," and they always will be, as computer "intelligence" is no replacement for human intelligence honed over time. "Computer models were built on the false assumption that risk can be calculated properly, carefully quantified and thus contained. That has been one of the major causes of the current crisis," said George Soros, Chairman of the Quantum Fund, speaking at a panel discussion hosted by BigThink.com, an online forum. A Big Rethink is clearly called for.

I had just finished writing this section, when a Creative Person friend, knowing I was engaged in this in-depth survey, sent me a copy of George Soros's 2008 book *The New Paradigm for Financial Markets: The Credit Crisis of 2008 and What It Means*. It consists of two halves: the first half finds the author dragging an old bone of a philosophic theory before the reader, while the second half deals with the actual crisis the world faces, which the author tries to explain by reference to the theory. The first half is nonsensical, while the second half poses some key questions despite the theory.

The philosophy Soros espouses is old Aristotelian recycled thinkery-thunk on the distinction between theoretical reason and practical reason, with which he tries to understand the boom-and-bust cycles as something arising in the human mind, which he proposes consists of the cognitive function which seeks to understand the market, and the participating or manipulative function, which tries to change the situation. This duality of the Soros mind works in opposite directions and they can interfere with each other, which interference Soros calls 'reflexivity', but which is just an old-fashioned headache, which leads to the market participants and regulators not knowing what they are doing because knowledge is absent, so uncertainty enters the equation, and Soros then invokes Newton's *Principia* to support his view, while the rest of us swallow a couple of Aspirin.

If you have read enough of this nonsense already, I can inform you that Soros has not lost his humour as he relates that his recurring back-pain has informed his investment decisions better than his theory, before he fast forwards those readers to Part II who have had enough of it. Aristotle's theories were consigned by David Hume's *Enquiry Concerning Human Understanding* to the dustbin as long ago as the eighteenth century, while Hume's disciple Albert Einstein confined Newton in to the same receptacle with a single word, "Superfluous", in the twentieth. In Part II Soros detects a super-bubble beyond the property bubble, which I will return to.

In this essay on forgotten economic principles, Soros's duality of the Aristotelian mind is deposed by the distinction between Creative and Degenerate Persons' economic *characters* which work either way in a continuum, but have no inherent clash within each of their own respective minds, but between them as persons; so any of his reflexivity concept is not in any mind but is in the clash between the opposite ends of the continuum, between the characters, as in *Atlas Shrugged*, whereas the actual economic clash occurs in the politico-economic conditions where "Hands and Lands" meet, and where the Principle of Change is also always operating; and the boom-bust short cycles are not in any human mind but in Mother Nature's, which is a given condition that the human mind has to foresee, cope with and learn to work within. As the Mullah Nasruddin observed: "If you follow Aristotle's philosophy, you are likely to find yourself in galoshes right up to your eyebrows!" Follow Plato was ever the rule.

PART III:

Who's to Blame

Bretton Woods and the Post-War Recovery

As WW2 entered the beginning of the end after D-Day, the stability between nations and their currencies was rightly perceived as a condition precedent to get international trade moving again on a fair exchange basis, in order to begin mending a broken world. At the Bretton Woods Conference in New Hampshire in 1944, when the Allies victory was only a matter of time, all currencies were aligned on a fixed basis with the mighty Dollar, the strongest currency in the world, and the Dollar was convertible into gold at $35.0 per ounce by governments, on demand. There was no need for any exporter-supplier to be concerned about the value of their international receipts and they had control over their own prices in their local currency, which were pegged within a 1% band to the Dollar, which was backed by gold. This neat arrangement, however, was the launch of the dollar as the reserve currency of the world, which was to have some unforeseen ramifications.

Bretton Woods was both necessary and successful in its day. The conference also established two institutions that were fundamental to the stability of the post-war era, namely the World Bank and the International Monetary Fund. The IMF's function was to bail-out those countries, with the capital provided to it by the subscribing nations, that got their economies out of balance, and its loans came with strict criteria for recovery and repayment over time, which almost invariably meant the reigning in of public sector expenditure. The IMF has had a remarkably good track record of success, and in 2008 was fully deployed in East Europe and the Ukraine, providing over $68.0 billion in emergency loans, and far more in 2009 as the crisis spread.

The first and worst post-war recession was in 1958, but by 1960 the warring nations in Europe and the Far East had recovered sufficiently for a boom in world trade between the developed countries, and a sense of well-being returned to their citizens, and by 1965 the US economy was bowling along at 6.0% p.a. The beginnings of the safety-net of the Welfare State were now established across the free post-war democracies, and in Britain the National Health Service, established in 1946, soon became that country's most-loved and respected institution, which President Obama wishes to emulate with universal healthcare in the US sixty years later. Taxes were still high for many years after the war, but years of slowly increasing prosperity beckoned.

Commercial companies' focus, after six years given over to war production, was on volume production of consumer goods, and the old pre-war manufacturing bibles from the likes of Ford Motor were good enough for the times: everything that was made was easily sold, with the new emphasis on management tools required for steady expansion. This wasn't enough for the stock markets, however, and the style of the conglomerate and the takeover came to the fore: the rationale was that earnings would be smoother and larger if a company consisted of four divisions, including a gushing cash-cow, one former cash-cow still throwing off cash, one coming out of development and about to start throwing off cash, and a fourth still in development for the future and funded by the other three cash-producing legs of the corporate stool. This new mantra created absurd structures, such as North American Philips buying top-of-the-line Baker Furniture so that their TVs could be sold with a handsome cabinet; Goodyear Tyre bought a hotel chain on the logic of tyres = travel = overnight stops; Exxon's massive pre-electronic bureaucracy inspired a drive into office furniture; and Mobil Oil bought a store chain which seemed pretty pointless, so they topped it with a Big Top and bought a circus. Needless to say, Wall Street got fat on the fees as M&A, 'Mergers and Acquisitions', became an addiction and an established revenue stream for bankers. Conglomerates were in style and were good for you, whether you were the taxman, a banker, a corporate M&A advisor, a shareholder, manager, employee or pensioner.

So Wall Street in the US and the City in the UK became pivotal in the post-war structure with banking, stock-broking and fund management, now with M&A or Corporate Finance added. The US economy expanded effortlessly, achieving 5.0% annual growth under President Johnson, while Prime Minister Macmillan could lord it over a recovering UK that "You've never had it so good!" Taxes were high, especially in the UK, but there was no capital gains tax until 1965; credit was available for expansion and the banks were as solid as rocks and the stock markets of New York and London purred along at a steady clip and oil was cheap; and every household not on actual poverty was living the American dream of a house, an auto and the latest electrical devices in the kitchen and the ubiquitous television, and the UK was only, as ever, a few years behind. And it was the "Swinging Sixties" in London that set the new *Zeitgeist* of personal licence and freedom of expression, that gave rise to the cult of celebrity, with Mary Quant's mini-skirt modelled by Twiggie, the Mini car, the Pill and the Beatles from Liverpool setting the world alight.

The reconstruction of Europe, financed by the US Marshall Plan, in turn augmented by the repayment of UK war debt to the US, and then spurred by the Treaty of Rome in 1957 and the drive towards the Common Market across Western Europe, was proceeding apace and Germany was emerging again as an industrial powerhouse and exporter. In 1948 the German recovery took off when Ludwig Erhard, the Allies' Economics Director, following much of the conservative parts of the Colm-Dodge-Goldsmith Plan of 1946, boldly abandoned all price and production controls over-night, a shock therapy that initially caused prices to rise sharply, which encouraged production, so that as the black markets dissolved, so prices fell back and the shops were soon full of goods. Germany's GDP for the next quarter-century was a dynamic 6.0% p.a., the economic miracle known as the *Wirtschaftswunder*. And the Far East was still not yet part of any economic equation that affected life in the West.

The same old economic skeletons, however, both man-made and natural, were ready to jump out of their cupboard and give anyone around a nasty turn. It was also to be the age when the new developments began to drive the sharp distinction between Creative and Degenerate Persons. The fraudsters of the age were overshadowed by Bernie Cornfeld's Investors Overseas Services, or IOS, headquartered in Geneva and selling US mutual funds across Europe, when he wasn't bedding Heidi Fleiss in his LA mansion. Cornfeld pioneered the concept of the 'Fund of Funds' with great success throughout the 1960s. When IOS got into trouble in the 1969 bear market, however, another mercurial financier Robert Vesco rode to his rescue, but he embezzled $224.0 million of IOS's money to bail out his own company, before he fled to the Caribbean; Cornfeld was eventually acquitted of any wrong-doing before a Swiss Court, but his name became synonymous with the playboy Degenerate Person who lived a lavish lifestyle as he master-minded what looked like a giant international scam.

In Britain, the Ceylonese immigrant Emil Savundra shocked the City when his Fire, Auto and Marine insurance company collapsed and he went to prison; and the super-salesman John Bloom's Rolls Razor washing machine company went bust through over-trading and he ended up doing a spot of porridge too. All these financial disasters captivated the public and appalled the City at the time, but only involved sums that would hardly make a headline half-a-century on, in today's world of mega frauds. It's a sober reflection on the Noughties Decade and an example of the Principle of Change, that if the morals and punishments of the 1960s prevailed today, many of those still working on Wall Street and in the City would now be behind bars.

In 1969 I became a qualified professional in the City and my salary rose to the then dizzying height of £4,500 per annum, plus 10% bonus. As I lay in my bed in my house in London's Notting Hill, purchased in 1965 for £4,500 but now worth over £14,500 just four years later, the strange realisation dawned on me that my house was now earning more than I was at work, and free of tax too. Forty years later, this same phenomenon has continued unabated throughout five decades.

The 1970s: The Rudderless Decade

So far, so good. In President Nixon's second year, however, this benign US economic recovery was moving to the end of an expansive Short Cycle, and in 1970 US growth fell to zero as inflation reached 6.0%, gold reserves as required by Bretton Woods were dropping alarmingly, the French had been converting their dollars into gold since 1965, and the need to raise US interest rates was clear, but Nixon was wary of the inevitable recession as he headed towards his re-election year in 1972. In the UK, Heath's Conservatives came to power, and Chancellor Tony Barber's first budget in 1971 started the liberalisation of the banking system under the title 'Competition and Credit Control', which assumed that the Bank of England's pricing of credit would control bank lending.

Richard Nixon embodied the whole gamut from Creative to Degenerate Persons, from encouraging China's market economy to authorising the Watergate break-in, tendencies that had already won him the sobriquet of 'Tricky Dicky'. But in 1971 the Degenerate Person in Nixon came to the fore, as he put his own re-election prospects ahead of what the situation demanded: as US prices were rising and interest rate rises were clearly in the air, Nixon introduced a wage-price freeze in the summer, which was promptly lifted in 1973 when re-election had been won, and he suspended the Dollar's convertibility into gold at $35.0 per ounce, thereby solving, or deferring, the pressing inflationary issues in the US economy ahead of the 1972 elections. Nixon had pulled a master-stroke of personal politics, but with unforeseen consequences to the global economy and the established post-war world order.

The dollar soon fell to \$100.0 per ounce of gold, losing two-thirds of its value by 1973, which didn't please the oil producers in the Middle East much at all, whose income in Dollars was consequently down by two-thirds as well. Their organisation OPEC, the 'Oil Producing and Exporting Countries' started in Baghdad in 1960, declared price increases of 400.0% in the Winter of 1974, to get back to the former value for their oil. This was such a shock to the western economies that they plunged into an abrupt and deep recession, at the same time as inflation let rip, creating the phenomenon of stagflation, of rising prices in a stagnant economy, with the necessity of high interest rates to curb the inflation, which in turn further choked any chance of economic growth. In America, inflation rose to 11.0% and unemployment to 5.6% in 1974, but rising to 9.0% at its peak. In Europe, the brutal shock of the oil embargo on Rotterdam led to an immediate collapse in the booming property markets and caused mayhem in the banking sector, while in the UK the Barber Boom of credit had not gone into the industrial base as the government expected, but straight into the property markets which went rapidly bust, triggering the secondary banking crisis.

The Bank of England had to launch a "Lifeboat" to rescue the UK's secondary banks which had lent lavishly to the tertiary banks that had in turn lent on to the property developers, most of which were almost now hopelessly bust overnight, but everyone was amazed when the Lifeboat hauled in Nat-West, one of the Big Four London clearing banks, as it was about to go bust just five days before Christmas 1974. Then the UK's third largest oil company, Burmah Oil, was rescued by the Bank of England buying it for just £1.0, which later floated it out for a cool profit of £130.0 million. It wasn't long before the IMF, in 1976, was called in to straighten out Britain's finances.

The Rudderless Decade was the true cost of Degenerate Person Nixon returning to the White House, from which he soon had to resign in total disgrace as he stared impeachment in the face, over the anti-democratic break-in at Watergate that was also designed to bolster his campaign, with inside information and ammunition against his Democratic opponent Barry Goldwater. Nixon's economic legacy was to unleash inflation for the rest of the 1970s and beyond. And the slide in value of all paper money, or fiat currencies, has continued ever since: by early 2009, as gold breached $1,000.0 an ounce in February and again in March and September, the Dollar had lost 97% of its 1944 Bretton Woods' value, some loss indeed. Nixon's lasting legacy had been to unleash the hounds of unsound money across the world.

An unintended consequence of Nixon's unilateral cancellation of Bretton Woods was that any notion that world trade was constrained by being linked to the availability of the finite stock of gold no longer pertained. This supposed limit to growth in world trade was now replaced anyway by the virtually limitless amount of post-Bretton Woods inflationary dollars, augmented by recycled petro-dollars from OPEC, that flooded the world with dollars as the US became a mammoth importer, and exporters to the US, which includes the rest of the developed world, now had to recycle their dollars too, not into their own domestic currencies which would then have risen and caused their export prices to rise and thus reduce their exports, but mainly back into US dollars. Some commentators have suggested that this process has led to the continuing US trade deficits which have caused asset price bubbles around the world. It undoubtedly created increased global money supply and therefore the fuel for bubbles, just as it increased world trade, but is not in itself the primary cause of asset bubbles, as we shall see. In 2006, the US trade deficit was still only 6.5% of US GDP, and the foreign exchange markets are a natural market regulator in this process, as they can devalue and revalue any currency over-time, and even over-night, as they do.

As the oil-driven stagflation of the 1970s gathered pace in both the US and UK, so did the power of the Unions develop as inflation set in and prices kept rising, and so the demands for increases in wages became a never-ending negotiation to the point where continuous battle was engaged, but management increasingly found themselves with their backs to the wall on all fronts: profits slumped, markets slumbered, interest rates rose, as did input prices, so working capital requirements rose, as banks also became reluctant to lend. In the US, President Ford's deregulation of many key transportation industries certainly helped, but Industry was still caught in a terrible jam: its cash flows produced profits that were insufficient for a time to purchase the new raw materials required to replace those that had just been shipped, so no one was making money, just shipping it and losing it, and so inflation accounting had to be introduced. There was only one way out: government expenditures had to decline and taxes rise, and until a balance was restored in the public finances, interest rates would have to remain depressingly high. Paul Volcker, Carter's appointment as the Chairman of the Federal Reserve Board, stuck through thick and thin with high interest rates until mid-1982, when Nixon's oil price-inspired inflation genie was safely back in its bottle, ten lost years later.

Britain adopted a very different approach before the Oil Crisis turned the problem into a stag-flationary super-disaster. Prime Minister Heath came to power in 1972 and his Chancellor, Tony Barber, set his sights on a mad 'Dash for Growth' at the end of the early-1970s boom, in defiance of the Short Cycle itself, which was due to turn down anyway. Barber's ill-judged budgets from 1972 to 1974 were based on the British economy achieving a whopping 5.0% growth per annum, a Degenerate Person's target that had never been achieved or even imagined before. Then the Oil Crisis with its massive inflationary twist pricked what little air was left in Barber's loose credit-driven balloon, as the economy fizzled down and wallowed in high inflation and practically zero growth for the next seven years. Barber's appalling timing and plan led to money supply growth of 30.0% and consequent inflation of 9.7%, 16.5% and 26.1% in the three years 1972 to 1974. The Degenerate Person's gamut in the 1970s embraced Nixon's self-serving isolationist tactic and Barber's boomerang boom, but the rest of us paid for it.

This failure in the UK led to the return of Harold Wilson's socialist left-wing government that immediately re-embraced the Unions who, while enjoying their sandwiches and beer sessions at No.10 Downing Street, plotted to put the heads of British industry in a half-Nelson and demand much higher wages for no productivity gains whatsoever, so that 'cost-push, wages-pull' inflation became the slogan and order of the day. And in America, the Auto Workers, the Teamsters and lesser Unions added healthcare and retirement demands to their compensation negotiations, costs from which the mass-employment industries such as auto manufacturing never recovered, as they continued to carry these burdens for three more long decades of decline, which became ever more unaffordable in an

48

unforgiving competitive yet expanding global marketplace.

The stagflation unleashed by these Degenerate Persons, the architects of the misfortunes of millions, persisted for the rest of the decade, producing low growth with high inflation and high unemployment. In the US the election of President Carter was a triumph of hope over disaster, epitomised in the disastrous attempt to free the Americans held hostage in their embassy in Tehran, with helicopters nobly but impossibly led, which were not even properly 'desertised' and so their rotors drove the sand into their own engines and downed them, a perfect metaphor for Carter's presidency and the 1970s. In the UK the Labour government went from bad to worse, and mercifully collapsed into the saving embrace of the IMF in 1976. This macabre scene was reminiscent of an unsuspecting James Bond in those seventies movies, when he falls into the hands of the Manichean villain: "Welcome, Mr. Bond, we've been expecting you!"

The hallmark of the Rudderless Decade were the images of Prime Minister Callaghan's London in 1979, when Britain was on an enforced three-day week as a result of the coalminers go-slow and when the Unions came out in sympathy, when the dead lay unburied in the cemeteries and even dead tax inspectors couldn't get to the head of the queue for a decent burial, the uncollected rubbish piled up high in Leicester Square, and the stylish restaurants of the West End were only lit by candles. The Rudderless Decade of the 1970s showed up governments and management as out of control of their own destinies and of their national economies.

Everyone was glad to see the back of the Seventies, the Nixon-Carter/Heath-Wilson-Callaghan decade whose style was failure writ large. As the 1980s approached, it was clear that if western capitalism was to be rescued from the sclerosis affecting it on all sides, that firm leadership with practical policies addressing the real issues of inflation, productivity and the power of the Unions were vital for survival and renewal.

The 1980s: The Greed Decade

The US and UK had emerged from the Rudderless Decade in terrible shape, with inflation out of control alongside zero real growth, domestic budgets out of balance and the power of the organised Unions seemingly in control just about everywhere, but especially in the UK. In 1980 US interest rates went to over 20.0% and by late 1982 unemployment was over 11.0%. Cometh the hour cometh the man, in this case with a certain transatlantic lady accomplice, as these seemingly intractable problems on both sides of the Atlantic were tackled head-on and solved by a formidable pair of political heavy-hitters. These Creative Persons worked in harmony together, apart from the day the US invaded Grenada, not realising it was a so-called UK protectorate! His best/worst line, after being shot in an attempted assassination, was "Honey, I forgot to duck!" Her best/worst line was "There's no such thing as society!" His truest saying was "There's nothing does so much good to the inside of a man as the outside of a horse!" Her truest was: "This lady is not for turning: there is no alternative!" which earned her the sobriquet of TINA.

Ronald Reagan was a Hollywood B-movie actor from Iowa who went on to become a successful Governor of California, before entering the White House in January 1981 as the fortieth President of the United States. Margaret Thatcher was the daughter of a Methodist lay-preacher, whose father's day-job was as a grocer in Grantham, Lincolnshire, who became Prime Minister and First Lord of the Treasury of Great Britain and Northern Ireland in June 1979. They beat inflation by cutting government expenditures, they beat the power of the Unions by standing up to them and passing legislation that curbed them, they then cut taxes to boost their economies, they lifted the restrictions on banks to let credit flow, and flow it did until their decade itself hit the buffers of excess. Unquestionably, however, their days in power were extraordinarily successful, if not without the inevitable detractors of their failings, but that's politics for you. President Jefferson said, with candour and realism, at his first inaugural address: "I have learned to expect that it will rarely fall to the lot of imperfect man to retire from this station, with the reputation and favour which brought him into it". The 1980s buried the failings of the 1970s, but set up many of the elements that led to Global Crunch in 2008/9, so it deserves a fuller account and analysis of what really happened, more so than any other post-war decade.

The transatlantic recession that got underway towards the end of 1979 peaked in 1981. Shortly after Reagan's election, the US prime rate hit 21.5%, its highest level ever, and the UK's base rate hit 17.0%. Both economies were suffering from runaway inflation. When Thatcher took office, inflation was already soaring through 10.0% per annum and heading for over 20.0% in 1980, but she had no hesitation in removing foreign exchange controls in 1979: the message was simple, Adam Smith's free markets would be the arbiter of price and individual liberty. The late 1970s had also seen the advance of the monetarist theories of Professor Milton Friedman of the Chicago school: he coined the phrase that 'there is no such thing as a free lunch' to underline his basic tenet that monetary growth was the root cause of inflation. In simple terms, the more the money in circulation, the higher prices will go and the more lunch will inevitably cost, as finally determined by freely floating exchange rates. The flip-side of this discipline was that then you could let free markets work out the rest.

Both Reagan and Thatcher determined to counter the runaway inflation by adopting the monetarists' favoured approach of raising interest rates, encouraging productivity by tax cuts and by cutting government expenditures; and by curbing the monopolistic-like power of the Unions and their Degenerate Person leaders which had grown unchecked, and the realisation that increases in wages beyond increases in productivity were the prime force driving the inflationary spiral. Reagan wasted no time in tackling the Unions in 1981: at great political risk, he sacked the nation's entire force of over 30,000 air traffic controllers, whose strike was paralysing the nation's key coast-to-coast transportation system and the economy. It was a bold move and it worked, as no planes collided or crashed and controllers drifted back to work and signed new contracts. Thatcher's government introduced new legislation to curb Trade Union power, by introducing democracy onto the shop floor: days lost through 'wildcat strikes', when no ballot amongst workers to take a vote on a Union's strike call was allowed, disappeared almost overnight. Thatcher's real fight with the Unions came in 1984-1985, when that most Degenerate Person Arthur Scargill, the head of the UK's Miners' Unions intent on fighting the battles of the previous decade's Short Cycle, once again led the miners on a year-long politically-inspired strike, but Thatcher stood firm and saw Scargill off. It was important that Reagan and Thatcher broke the back of the Unions' monopoly of labour and the tyranny of inflation, as otherwise the real economic progress could not be achieved that was to set up their subsequent successes.

One of the first seeds of financial destruction had been sown by President Jimmy Carter in October 1977, when he signed the Community Reinvestment Act, which made it illegal to refuse mortgages to lower income groups and minorities, which was reinforced in 1991 by the Home Mortgage Disclosure Act that demanded racial equality by lenders. The next was in March 1980, when Carter signed the Depository Institutions Deregulation and Monetary Control Act, as though the salutary message of the UK's Barber Boom and Inflationary Bust of the 1970s had not crossed the Atlantic. This legislation was the first attempt to unpick the US's Glass-Steagall Act of 1933, which had mandated that low-risk deposit-taking commercial banks could not be jointly-owned with risk-taking investment banks or insurance companies. Carter's new act allowed commercial banks to merge and repealed Glass-Steagall's Regulation Q, so that the Fed would no longer set interest rates on savings accounts, in an effort to counter the wide swings in deposit rates that had persisted through the post-Nixon 1970s, American banks could now set whatever rates they wanted on checking and savings accounts. US Savings & Loan Institutions (S&Ls), equivalent to the UK's ubiquitous building societies, were forced to offer higher rates on deposits than they had traditionally earned on mortgages. The same legislation also raised Federal Insurance on S&L deposit accounts from $40,000 to $100,000, thereby swelling the S&L deposit base, just as the S&Ls were forced to pursue higher-risk lending that they didn't understand, building skyscrapers and operating mines and airports and other nonsense, with entirely foreseeable and dire consequences for their future.

Reagan and Thatcher were also determined to reduce income taxes in order to put more money in consumers' pockets, so that consumer demand would haul their economies out of the recessions they had inherited. Reagan cut income tax by 5.0% in October 1981, by a further 10.0% in July 1982 and by a further 10.0% in July 1983. He also granted tax incentives for the construction of office and apartment buildings, just as Thatcher had done a year earlier with the creation of 'Enterprise Zones' in derelict urban areas, where private investors could deduct the cost of their investment from their taxable income. Thatcher had also reduced the higher rate of income tax from 83.0% to 60.0% as a first step, a dramatic reduction which boosted confidence. She also abolished the investment income surcharge of 15.0%, which meant that the top rate of tax on all income was effectively cut from 98.0% to 60.0%. And in October 1981 Reagan also signed a Bill raising the level of Federal Debt above $1.0 trillion for the first time, which he announced optimistically was 'a monument to the policies of the past, policies which as of today are reversed', as he engaged fast-forward. He and Thatcher were both going for lower taxes and lower government spending as the way back to posterity, coupled with easy credit.

Mrs. Thatcher also determined to break the bankers' monopoly by deregulating the financial services industry in the UK as well. In 1986 she followed the peanut farmer's suit and authorised building societies to broaden the scope of their lending away from their traditional business of providing mortgages to home owners. In effect, the Building Societies Act replaced the 1874 Act and societies were free to become banks, and the banks did their best to enter the home mortgages market in a competitive free-for-all. The building societies had traditionally only made new advances as their deposits and repayments allowed and they did not borrow from banks, but now these super-conservative not-for-profit mutual societies were exposed to the full blast of public status exposure and competition, and like the S&Ls in America they soon found themselves conducting business they did not fully understand. Then many of them succumbed to the lure of de-mutualisation and floated themselves onto the London Stock Exchange as limited companies, where increasing profits are the rationale and aim, as they dispensed free quoted shares to their loyal depositors and the usual array of Degenerate Person carpet-baggers who turned up at the last minute.

Unwittingly, Carter and Thatcher had unleashed the credit boom that would drive the spectacular growth of the 1980s but end in bust in the early 1990s, but also create the momentum of easy money and rising property values that eventually ended in Global Crunch thirty years later. During the 1980s the credit supply revolution was led by the investment banks and stock market operators with their new financial non-bank instruments, bonds for corporate and individual investors, that yielded higher returns. These developments, which created disintermediation in the credit markets, however, subtly shifted central banks' control as exercised through the commercial banks to one of mere influence in the bond markets. The trend that emerged, contrary to the intuitive perception of Sir William Petty, was that aggregate credit growth was now consistently ahead of GDP growth, which is inherently inflationary. The problem with this latter trend was that, with the increasing globalisation of trade and its extended supply lines, the central banks were also losing control of the ability to wrestle with domestic inflation as well, as it was now increasingly arising overseas. In the brave new world of open credit, the main instrument of control left for central bankers was interest rates, while governments thought that regulators would police the permissive financial system. When both these controls failed at the end of the Noughties Decade, Global Crunch was inevitable.

In 1982 interest rates had declined further and economic activity picked up, although unemployment, which in America reached nearly 11.0%, failed to respond quickly. Then Mexico had defaulted on $80.0 billion of foreign debt, its first Tequila Crisis, which crisis cascaded down through Latin America, turning the sub-continent into a bankers' graveyard and a lost decade or two for the borrowers. Already in early 1982, however, the US National Savings and Loan League asked Congress for $15.5 billion to insure deposits of ailing S&Ls, as the problems brought on by Carter's pen in 1980 were surprisingly quick to appear, losses which were a mini-trailer for Global Crunch and which would eventually cost the US-taxpayer $87.0 billion to $150.0 billion by 1995, the estimates vary by a mile, from 744 busted S&Ls. Nevertheless the reduction in interest rates and the economic recovery fed directly into the housing market in both America and Britain and prices started rising strongly. This surge in house prices sucked in buyers, and first-time buyers saw prices rising beyond their reach and they became desperate to get on the home-owning bandwagon. Then in March 1983 OPEC cut the price of oil from $34.0 to $29.0 a barrel. This had a beneficial effect on inflation and enabled both governments to hold interest rates down, thereby contributing to the credit boom and directly causing property values to rise still further. During the 1980s decade, house prices in the US and UK economies rose in real terms by up to an unsustainable two-and-a-half times.

In 1983, attracted by the size of the growing domestic residential mortgage market, bankers at First Boston led by Larry Fink and others at Salomon Brothers created the first CMO, or 'Collateralised Mortgage Obligation', but they were constrained by the lack of computer power then available. They had realised that the mortgage trusts and pass-throughs that Freddie Mac and Mae were serving up to the US market did not meet investors' demands on risk and reward and that CMOs needed to hold different classes of each segment of mortgages, by dicing and slicing the underlying mortgage assets, as diversity of risk was the new mantra. They realised massive databases would be required to track every mortgage, analyse home-owners repayments and predict repayment rates and defaults. And they needed the internet to interact with the client investor and model the final bespoke bonds to fit investors' exact needs. In 1983 it was very slow work, but in 1988 the self-styled guru of the software for this market, Michael Osinski, went to work for Lehman to write the sophisticated software the market needed for securitising home mortgages on the huge scale now available. In 1983 those that set out to pioneer the CMO were Creative Persons working for an important social and economic goal that was meant to make mortgages more available to both mortgagors and investors, by removing the wrinkles that lay between them and their different aspirations and specific needs.

The merger boom was now getting into its stride too, and in 1984 Standard Oil merged with Gulf Corporation in an unheard of $13.3 billion deal, which dwarfed Du Pont's $7.5 billion earlier acquisition of Conoco in August 1981. The message was clear: big is beautiful, and funding was available. As the merger boom took off on the back of easy credit, Michael Milken, a fixed-interest dealer in Drexel Burnham Lambert's West Coast operation, began to peddle his high-yielding junk bonds to the S&L and insurance industries, which now required these higher yields in Carter's newly deregulated market-place. The management buy-out (MBO) syndrome was spawned and the era of the highly leveraged transaction (HLT) put the merger/MBO market into top gear. These new financial structures soon found their way across the Atlantic and became a major feature of the deal-driven 1980s. The MBO movement was originally intended by Creative Persons to enable existing managers to acquire the businesses they ran from their larger corporate owners, thereby replacing corporate shackles with management freedom and incentives, and in effect reversing the dead hand of the conglomerate model of the 1960s and 1970s.

The HLT characteristics and structures, however, were soon adopted by Degenerate Persons to enable corporate raiders to go on a hostile takeover binge. MBOs and HLTs were financed on wafer-thin permanent capital. This high leverage or gearing, of high levels of borrowings in relation to permanent capital, at times reached 1,000.0%, or ten times or more of the permanent capital, as opposed to the more normal 50.0% to 100.0% level. The theory was that disposal of non-strategic operations would be made quickly by the new owner to reduce the burden of the borrowings, but as the decade wore on the dealmakers forgot their own mantra, and used the HLT structure to buy businesses which had no surplus assets of any size to sell off. Worse still, when a major retailer which had been financed by junk bonds went bust, Michael Milken confessed that his team had never factored a sales decrease into their sums. As soon as sales inevitably turned down in the Short Cycle, this and many other over-leveraged transactions were bankrupt. Michael Milken was considered by many a financial wizard at his peak, but he and his team were clearly unaware of the existence of business cycles, the first lesson for any financier, as they were driven by the deal and the fees on the table with no thought for the morrow.

At about this time in the 1980s, it was worth asking if anyone knew where this out-of-control and immoderate financial orgy was headed. In fact as early as 7th June 1984 the Chairman of the SEC, the Securities and Exchange Commission, Creative Person John Shad, had warned in the clearest terms that 'the more leveraged takeovers and buy-outs today, the more bankruptcies tomorrow'. These prophetic words fell on the deaf ears of the raging Bull market of 'Get Rich Quick' Degenerate Persons, where the markets were producing much more money for Wall Street's workers than the real economy of increased production was for the rest of the workforce, as the MBO and HLT boom went into overdrive. In 1985 the Chairman of the Federal Reserve, another Creative Person Paul Volcker, warned in February that corporate debt was growing too quickly on account of the "huge volumes of mergers, leveraged buy-outs and stock repurchases".

Paul Volcker and his successor, Alan Greenspan, repeatedly voiced their concern, but this did not deter Macy's, the New York department store for example, from being privatised later in 1985 in a $3.6 billion management buy-out, but there were no surplus assets of any value to sell down to reduce the massive debts the MBO had taken on. This deal collapsed into bankruptcy in the ensuing Short Cycle in the early 1992 recession, following hard on the trail of similar errors at Bloomingdale's. It never occurred to the dealmakers involved with these transactions that a store chain in a falling market will have weakening sales seeking to serve a stubborn cost base, now increased by massive interest charges on the MBO acquisition debt.

Astonishingly, the US Treasury Department was enjoying rising receipts from this boom and on 6th December 1985 came out in favour of the excesses of Degenerate Persons and stated that it was "adamantly opposed" to a Federal Reserve recommendation for curbing hostile takeovers financed by high-yield, high-risk junk bonds, a clear example of the loss of power of the central bankers, as the bond markets took over from the commercial bank lending. Over at the White House, meanwhile, Reagan one week later signed the Gramm-Rudman-Hollings Deficit-Reduction Amendment that was designed to bring the budget into balance within five years, by 1991, which was bound to be right at the bottom of the Short Cycle: unsurprisingly, the deficit in that year turned out to be $269.0 billion. This boom was now pulling US government policy in two completely different directions. In May 1987 the Governor of the Bank of England publicly warned bankers about the seriously over-heated property markets in Britain, and again in 1989 at a summit in Paris. Thatcher was so alarmed at the level of personal debt that she symbolically returned her own credit cards and warned the banks against mail-shots soliciting borrowers for their expensive plastic loans. But the market-players didn't listen, and the Government in its own de-regulated economy had no means of making them listen, or comply.

In 1986 the price of oil, already down from $34.0 to $29.0, and then to $25.0 at the beginning of the year, crashed to $10.0 per barrel, and the oil-driven Texan economy took a severe plunge. Texas was the first state where the property bubbles collapsed and the state's S&Ls started going bust by the day, followed by the rest of the country, as the excesses and frauds popped up everywhere: a notable Degenerate Person, Charles W. Knapp, seized control of the L.A.-based American S&L, the nation's largest, and ran its loan book up from just under $2.0 billion to over $40.0 billion before he was rumbled, when these loans were worth just $500.0 million, a loss of an unbelievable 98.0% on what were meant to be secure loans. This tale proceeds from gross delinquency to outright larceny: a similar Degenerate, Charles Keating, another west coast entrepreneur was sent to prison for racketeering and fraud; his Lincoln Savings S&L sold sham property deals to investors, at an eventual cost to the US-taxpayer of $3.4 billion. Before the inevitable Short Cycle recession had even taken hold of the wider economy in the early 1990s, every single commercial bank in Texas defaulted as well, putting an enormous strain on the already overblown Federal banking system.

The year 1986 also saw the first insider dealing scandal spawned by the booming stock market. When a broker-dealer at Drexel Burnham Lambert was arrested, he pointed the finger at a fellow Degenerate Person, a Russian émigré so-called financier, Ivan Boesky who, in a practice known as arbitrage, bought shares on the NYSE just before they soared on take-over announcements, but it was simply on inside information, 'arbitrage' merely its grandiose epithet. Boesky was also arrested and the American authorities tipped off British investigators about share-dealings ahead of the Irish brewer Guinness's takeover of Scotland's Distillers Company earlier in the year, which was the biggest hostile takeover ever seen in London. Interestingly, the merchant bank advisor to Guinness and the major M&A advisor in the City at the time, Morgan Grenfell, started the 1980s boom decade with just sixteen partners and a capital base of only £14.0 million, but it ended the Greed Decade being sold to Deutsche Bank in 1989 for £900.0 million, so quick is the growth in financial institutions operating at the heart of markets, and yet the fees they charged were as flat as piss on a plate compared to the astronomic fees charged in the next two decades.

Meanwhile in Japan, their version of Degenerate Persons favoured politicians with cash and shares while using criminal tactics to put the squeeze on incumbent managers and shareholders by strong-arm market tactics, a distinctly Sumo-version of western so-called arbitrage; no wonder the Nikkei rose to 38,000 as it was throttled by Sumo wrestlers, only to collapse to 8,500, as if James Bond had dealt the Sumos something nasty and, no wonder again, then languish there at around 8,500 for over twenty years and more. Scandal and criminality destroy any confidence in markets, which is why it must always be rooted out and punished severely: 'Degenerate Person Transgressors will be prosecuted' is ever the rule.

Whereas the NYSE had quietly moved to screen-based trading in 1973 with the early technology available, when the London Stock Exchange followed in 1986 with the latest digital data-delivery and trading and back office settlement systems it was code-named 'Big Bang', as the change-over would be implemented in a single day, and which heralded the introduction of the new regulatory authorities in the UK. Practically every major bank in Britain, America and Europe scrambled to get a seat at the table of global securities trading, where London is in a strategic time-zone latitude that linked Tokyo, Singapore and Hong Kong with London, and on to New York, Chicago and Los Angeles in the same day.

A must-have designer item for the new trading floors and offices were smart brushed-aluminium time-zone digital clocks, showing the local time in each of these key trading cities. Venerable stockbrokers, with their old wooden railway-station time-pieces in their dark smoky offices recording only GMT on their giant white dials, were offered vast sums by competing buyers falling over each other for their franchises and were enticed with guaranteed salary and bonus packages and other perks, regardless of the results. The older partners could not believe their luck, and as soon as their 'golden handcuffs' were off, they retired to the country as BOBOs – 'Burnt Out But Opulent', but their departure also saw the back of the old values and dependable virtues of 'My word is my bond'. Needless to say, much of the consideration paid for these partnerships found its way into the property market.

The boom continued into 1987: between January and August the Dow Jones Industrial Average rose by over 40.0% and the London FTSE 100 by over 33.0%, both fuelled by annual growth running at over 4.0%. Reagan started the year by having to submit the first trillion dollar budget deficit, which paradoxically helped to fund the current account deficit as the exporting surplus countries reinvested their dollars back into US dollar assets, rather than into their own currencies, which would have raised their own currencies and therefore their own export prices. The increased leverage provided by the banks to the hedge and buy-out funds increased the credit expansion, particularly when these funds started playing the carry trade. (This phenomenon reached a peak in the late 2000s and is dealt with below in 'Cash and Carry' in Part IV).

In the second half of 1987, the new Chairman of the Federal Reserve, Alan Greenspan, stated: "It is absolutely essential [that the Federal Reserve's] focus be on restraining inflation because if that fails, then we have very little hope for sustained economic growth", which was central bank-speak for arguing interest rates had to rise to curb the boom and inflation. There was no similar perception in Britain, however, where interest rates were declining from 10.0% to 8.0%. Then, quite unexpectedly, the Dow Jones Industrial Average plunged 261 points between 14th and 16th October, as thirty-year Treasury Bonds soared 2.0% in four months to 10.2%. These higher interest rates were immediately followed by 'Black Monday' on 19th October, when there was a worldwide stock market meltdown and the Dow and the FT-SE 100 both fell by over 500 points, while in a strange parallel Southern England experienced a rare hurricane that the Met Office failed to see coming, rather like the central bankers with Global Crunch twenty years later. This extraordinary melt-down was very unsettling, as no one could quite put their finger on the cause of it: was it Greenspan's warning of higher interest rates? Or of higher inflation? Or bond prices falling? Was the party really over? Worse still, was there a hidden systemic risk or basic fault in 'Big Bang' and electronic trading? Whatever it was, 'Black Monday' showed the new-found awesome power of 'post-Big Bang' 24-hour electronic global trading.

'Black Monday' reflected all of the above questions about future conditions, but the fact that there was a basic fault-line in the electronic system in New York was not revealed until much later. What basically happened was this: as the market started to fall, the market-makers, futures traders and arbitrage traders, who trade on an instant for minor pickings, started to sell but there were not enough real equity buyers to halt the flow of stock, so the sellers dropped their prices to try and create a buying frenzy, which then developed into a flood of stock hitting the market, as programmed sell orders as the latest widespread wheeze of portfolio insurance kicked in as well, and buyers stood back in disbelief as the market went on plummeting. What was not appreciated at the time was that the instant trader-sellers in the animal pit of the NYSE were operating on broadband, while the cool equity buyers, the suppliers of real liquidity to the market, were in portfolio meetings in tranquil boardrooms quietly assessing the unexpected and unfolding situation and only operating, if at all, by analogue telephones.

It was the asymmetric timing between digital and dial-up that had never been appreciated before, in its effect on the market's immediately available minute-to-minute liquidity. The fact that the sellers had marked prices so low and so quickly to attract in the buyers made the situation worse; they had shot themselves in the foot and had nowhere to run. The solution for the future was simple: if the market fell too fast, a circuit-breaker was triggered to allow the market time to clear itself, and at a higher price than pertained on 'Black Monday'. And the moral to be drawn from that day's crash is? Financial innovation comes with unforeseen and unexpected consequences.

The unforced error of the 'Black Monday' melt-down, which saw the Dow lose 22.6% or some $500.0 billion, was the authorities' decision to keep the bull market running. One short glance at Graph 1 would have shown them that this Short Cycle was not yet spent, but at the very moment that they should have taken their foot off the peddle, they stepped on the gas as the market melt-down stayed uncomfortably in their rear-view mirror. The worst offender was Britain, where Chancellor Nigel Lawson formulated the most disastrous budget cocktail since WW2: he reduced base rate to 7.5% in May 1988, having already reduced the higher rate of income tax from 60.0% to 40.0%, and then gave a totally absurd boost to the housing market by allowing double tax relief on mortgage interest for two people buying a property together, which gave a bugger's muddle of a boost to the bottom rung of the booming housing ladder. In 1988 bank lending in Britain rose by a quarter and the following year interest rates were forced back up to 12.0% as demand for credit soared and the annual increase in M4, or broad money, reached £90.0 billion. Lawson's budget was hailed by Thatcher as the most successful budget ever, but he later claimed in 1992 that his budget interest rate reduction was made at the suggestion of Thatcher herself: "To my eternal regret I accepted the poisoned chalice", he wrote. Catastrophe in the UK was now only just around the corner, with the Short Cycle downturn coming over the horizon.

In the US, the Spring of 1988 saw Donald Trump, the New York property developer, announced that he would buy the famed New York Plaza Hotel for $410.0 million and add yet a third casino in Atlantic City in 1989. These transactions were mainly financed by bank loans and junk bonds. The credit-financed boom had turned Trump into a billionaire, but he still owed a billion, as there was very little of his own capital in these deals. The perceptions of the Fed on where the economy was heading had not communicated themselves to the financial markets. Amazingly, the largest banks both in America and Britain decided to raise more capital and in 1988-1990 went on a final binge of lending into the already overblown property markets. Citigroup, then Citicorp, raised $560.0 million in Preferred Shares, convertible into 15.0% of the bank's capital, from a Saudi Prince, Al-Waleed bin Talal. Flush with cash and new borrowing power, the bank continued lending aggressively in the North-East corridor between New York and Boston even as the market was falling. In 1992 Citigroup's non-performing loans were about $15.0 billion, mainly in property, compared with shareholder's funds of $13.5 billion.

As if in a game of me-too or catch-up, Britain's Barclays Bank raised £920.0 million in the London market in late 1988, most of which was soon lent to property developers. Barclays 1991 accounts confirmed that it had lent £5.4 billion to commercial property companies, as compared with its capital base of £5.7 billion; if all the other lending against underlying property assets is taken into account, that is to the working capital facilities of both large and small companies, farm and personal overdrafts secured on property, the bank's effective lending on property probably amounted to over six times the bank's capital. Taking the disclosed new lending against pure commercial property only, Barclay's lending was £1.0 billion in 1988, £1.3 billion in 1989, £800.0 million in 1990, but only £132.0 million in 1991, when reality had belatedly dawned. When such visible institutions carry on lending after the game-over whistle has been blown, their misplaced domestic enthusiasm proves infectious and foreign banks were quick to follow their lead into disaster, particularly the Japanese banks in London and New York.

By 1989 the era of the HLT was going berserk. Two transactions will serve to indicate the sheer hysteria which overtook the market. In the Autumn of 1988 the management of RJR-Nabisco, a tobacco and cookies giant originally from North Carolina comprising the R.J.Reynolds tobacco and National Biscuit companies, a strange left-over of an amalgamation from the dinosaur age of the conglomerate, announced that the management, yes – the management, were organising an MBO at a transaction value of around $17.0 billion. Instead of buying an operation out from a larger corporation, the management were now using the MBO structure to buy the whole corporation from its own shareholders off the New York Stock Exchange, which was a total conflict of interest between the managers and the shareholders! The New York financier Henry Kravis of the leading MBO firm of KKR felt that the RJR-Nabisco management was "stealing his franchise" to finance this most highly leveraged and highly priced deal of the century. KKR under the direction of its founder Creative Person Jerome Kohlberg had always acted as a 'White Knight' rescuer of companies on the wrong end of unwanted hostile bids. Now the firm was considering launching a bid against management's own controversial bid, in effect a hostile bid against the management, but for the potential advantage of the share-holders. The older Kohlberg disapproved of these Degenerate Persons tactics and the lack of perspective of proper interests and resigned from KKR

Kravis went boldly on his mission of … of what exactly? To ensure the shareholders had a competing bid, but how did that square with his duty to his own investors? Or to protect his own supposed fran-chise, using his investors' cash? Or because he thought he could bring in better management into two industries that he had little experi-ence of? He eventually bought the entire company for $25.1 billion, financed almost entirely by several tiers of debt. A syndicate of two hundred banks – yes, two hundred! – lent $14.5 billion and received fees of $325.0 million. Drexel provided a $3.5 billion bridge loan and received fees of $227.0 million. These borrowings totalled $18.0 bil-lion, but the cash portion of the deal was only $0.9 billion of capital to finance a transaction valued at twenty-five times that amount. The old rules were well out the window, all right, but what was Kravis trying to achieve? What was the grammar and the syntax of the new KKR now? Was he trying to serve up the whole meat, two veg and potatoes of a vast fortune overnight, at the future expense of those who built these businesses patiently over time, but especially for KKR itself and its advisors?

Kravis didn't forget the HLT rule book, however, and swiftly paid down part of the acquisition debt by selling the Del Monte canned and fresh fruit business to the Anglo-Turkish Polly Peck, the best-performing share on the London Stock Exchange, which itself collapsed in 1991 as a result of a decade-long fraud over conversion of year end foreign exchange rates. At the closing dinner in New York, however, for the four hundred professionals on the KKR deal, the host quipped: "To think it only needed a billion dollars to get us all together this evening!" Kohlberg would have groaned. When KKR finally exited the deal years later, they had made no more money for their investors than if they had invested in the NYSE and saved everyone else the bother, apart that is from all the fee earners who didn't create a single new job or product. And at the end of it all, a puff on a Camel and a bite out of an Oreo cookie tasted just as good or bad, but cost an extra dime or two to pay for Degenerate Persons fees and closing dinner.

Not to be out-done, the newly-formed New York corporate finance boutique Wasserstein Perella raised an MBO fund from Japanese and American institutions and invested much of it in a single leveraged buy-out of a supermarket chain in Britain, where Wasserstein Perella had no real prior experience. The buy-out vehicle, Isosceles plc, purchased the loser Gateway supermarket chain for nearly £2.0 billion in 1989. The transaction went wrong from the start as Gateway's operations could not compete with well organised and conservatively run chains like J. Sainsbury, Tesco and Marks & Spencer, even before Gateway took on massive debts of £1.4 billion under the MBO structure. Its 1991 profit scarcely covered the annual interest costs of £160.0 million, but worse was to come when the funding strategy went hopelessly wrong: the plan to sell off its American subsidiary Herman's Sporting Goods chain failed to attract any realistic offer, as its profits had somehow collapsed quicker than an athlete spiking his foot on the starting block. In the Isosceles deal, the square of the hypotenuse of debt didn't add up to the sum of the squares of the other two sides, Gateway and Herman.

Bruce "Bid-'em Up" Wasserstein, one of the barbarians at the gates in the KKR-RJR profitless deal, also advised on the 1988 $13.0 billion Philip Morris acquisition of the soft-cheese manufacturer Kraft Foods and the Time-Warner acquisition by AOL, all of which failed and ended in divorce, something he went through three times in his own personal life, while he twice sold himself for several hundreds of millions, once to Deutsche Bank and once to Lazard's, where his presence proved disruptive at both houses. He advised on 1,000 M&As "worth" around $250.0 billion, deploying his brash and unkempt style to great purpose but little effect, other than to generate huge fees as he left countless companies floundering in debt, as he delivered his "Dare to be great" tirade before his clients made their final over-priced offers. Wasserstein wielded a solitary power and was the apogee Degenerate Person, the quintessential child of the misguided debt-driven era. Having failed in his messy recipe of mixing cheese with tobacco, he was advising the US Kraft Foods once again in an attempt this time to mix cheese and chocolate, on its 2009 hostile take-over offer for the UK's Cadbury's chocolates business, when the grim reaper tapped him on the shoulder with his bony digit and summoned this particular Barbarian to the Pearly Gates. If Kraft's unlikely bid for Cadbury's succeeds, will they strike a bar of chocolate-covered cheese in his honour, I ask myself. I am surprised, come to think of it, that he wasn't advising Philip Morris instead, as there used to be actual chocolate cigarettes as I remember them in Christmas-stockings long ago.

The point about many of these LBO/HLT transactions was that they were not the workings of the capitalist system in the sense that that term implies. Firstly, the capital in these HLT deals was purely 'transactional' money and was not 'investment' money. They were transactions that changed the ownership but not much else, and were driven by the greed of Degenerate Persons and not the real investment of Creative Persons like Bill Gates who develop new businesses like Microsoft, with new markets and new jobs and timely products. These transactional deals created their own side effects in the general economy, as assets which had been relatively unencumbered were now supporting debts for most of their value, although no new assets had been created, which phenomenon must be inflationary.

It is quite different in a stock market transaction, where the seller is paid out by replacement capital from the buyer, whereas in an HLT the seller is mainly paid out by debt put onto existing assets. Secondly, the feverish activity in transactional capital was creating millionaires as never before, and much of the financially-engineered profits from the successful transactions were translated into a further boost for the property markets. Thirdly, the HLT mentality triggered the greed factor that percolated through all levels of society; a mentality of borrow now to buy into the rising stock and property markets took firm hold and became the style on both sides of the Atlantic, as everyone wanted a piece of the action, regardless of their ability to afford it, whether they were consumers bingeing on plastic until they were maxed out, buy-out merchants paying too much for vanity, or corporate raiders chewing off more than they could swallow.

In this climate of unbridled greed major takeovers were announced almost daily in the 1980s. Some were financed by sound companies and for good strategic reasons. In June 1989 Time Inc. bought Warner Communications for $14.0 billion to create the largest media company in the world, which was one of "Bid-'em Up Bruce's" better deals, until he advised them to merge with AOL at far too high a price. For each logical, sensible and soundly financed takeover put together by Creative Persons, however, there was generally one which was illogical, unnecessary and a monument to the ill-judgement of Degenerate Persons. To take a British example, the conservatively run Trustee Savings Bank (TSB), a century's-old commercial bank mainly for individuals and small corporates, decided it wanted to enter the totally different world of investment banking and launched a £750.0 million bid for Hill Samuel, a medium-sized player in the London market, just before 'Black Monday' in October 1987. Despite the worldwide stock market crash, TSB insisted on pressing on with its now expensive and increasingly illogical acquisition, for 'reasons of strategic growth', meaning 'because we're fed up with just being a mere utility and want to join the real action in the City which we don't understand yet'.

Upon acquisition, TSB shovelled a billion pounds and more into its new corporate 'show-off' must-have toy, but Hill Samuel itself was now greedily eyeing the burgeoning property sectors and had taken its old eye off its main franchise of medium-sized quoted industrial companies, with the result that its satellite office in exclusive St. James's Square in London's fashionable West End pumped all the extra money into the property market and lost the lot. TSB had lost its investment twice over in just a year and had nothing left of Hill Samuel to show for its so-called growth strategy. Fittingly, it was itself soon put out of its misery and gobbled up by Lloyds Bank, which itself went on to make some illogical acquisitions in the 1990s before shooting itself in the foot with the most stupid banking acquisition of all time, in 2009.

Several major British public companies also managed to make absurdly priced` acquisitions in America that were financed almost entirely by debt. They all paid the ultimate price, insolvency. That archetypal Degenerate Person, the late Robert Maxwell, the one who fell overboard and allegedly found he couldn't swim, bought the publisher Macmillan Inc. and then three days later the Official Airlines Guide for over $2.0 billion on borrowed money, all in the same week. His company, Maxwell Communications, was bust by late 1991, but not before he had raided the pension funds of his employees for cash to try and stay afloat before mysteriously dying before the law caught up with him. Then Blue Arrow, a recruitment agency that came from nowhere in the 1980s, launched a record fund-raising in the City in 1988 to buy the much larger Manpower Inc. in Milwaukee, for close on £1.0 billion. The price of Blue Arrow shares collapsed in the aftermarket, amid allegations that the stock market had been deliberately misled. Next Ferranti, the electronics concern, bought International Signal & Control of Pennsylvania, but its accounts were fraudulent and included non-existent defence contracts with Pakistan. Ferranti lost £400.0 million on the deal and was sold off. All these deals were driven by Degenerate Persons intent on corporate aggrandisement with the easy money available to boost their already swollen egos, but they would have made more money by staying at home and doing nothing, just counting the pounds from their existing operations.

A final wild idea was promoted in the summer of 1989 for the pilots and management of United Airlines (UAL) to buy out their highly-cyclical, asset-intensive, debt-strapped, fuel-dependent, price-sensitive business for $6.8 billion. Luckily for the prospective buyers, which were going to include British Airways as a major investor, an earlier HLT got into financial difficulties and saved everyone the bother and the inevitable losses. Canada's Campeau Corporation, which was also advised by Wasserstein & Perella of Gateway fame, got into serious difficulties paying the interest on the C$6.0 billion junk bonds and debt they had raised for an HLT to acquire Allied & Federated Department Stores in America. Campeau went bust in September, and UAL could not get its debt money in October, as the Japanese banks pulled back. This failure marked the end of the HLT boom and the Dow dropped 190 points on the day, dubbed 'Friday the Thirteenth'. At the time of the collapse of the UAL transaction, Donald Trump was still stomping around the banks trying to borrow and buy AMR Corporation, the holding company for the respected American Airlines based in Texas, also for around $6.0 billion, but the banks had woken up to this nightmare in time.

The seal was also set for the final collapse of the property markets. In January 1990, the US Comptroller of the Currency, Mr. Robert Clarke, realised that property lending by banks and S&Ls was so out of control that such lending practices had to be curbed. In February Drexel Burnham Lambert, that snake-pit of self-imploding debt instruments, false prospectuses and market rigging of Degenerate Persons, mercifully filed for bankruptcy after defaulting on over only $100.0 million of short term loans. At the same time Trump failed to meet interest payments on his massive loans, even without AMR. Oh! How they must have laughed in Dallas! The Treasury Secretary announced that the S&L fiasco would cost $300.0 billion in the 1990s alone, which would push an already Federal deficit even higher, although the eventual cost was less than $100.0 billion.

As 1990 developed it became clear that the economy would not achieve the soft landing that Alan Greenspan, the Federal Reserve Chairman, was hoping for. By November he had to announce that the economy was in a "meaningful downturn", but he concluded that "recession may still be avoidable"! It was not until January 1991 that The White House conceded that the economy was already in recession. By this time twenty-eight states of the Union faced budget deficits, and on 6th January the Bank of New England was taken over by regulators as it was bust, brought down by the collapse in the property market. Developers and owners defaulted on their loans by simply handing back the keys of hundreds of properties to their mortgagee banks, a ritual that soon attracted its own epitaph of 'Jingle Mail'. In his State of the Union address at the end of January, President Bush Snr. still managed to say that growth would be resumed soon, but by now the banking and S&L crisis had been triggered by the biggest collapse in property values the world had ever seen at that time, and the Federal Deficit was rising remorselessly. The President had already reneged on his 1988 promise of no new taxes in 1990, so now he had little option but to slash interest rates, letting the Dollar plunge, and grab what work was left in a recessionary world.

In Britain, the early 1990s saw the property markets start collapsing, just as in Texas and in New England, as interest rates rose, tenants disappeared and rentals dropped. The collapse of the prestigious Canary Wharf project in London's former Docklands was not the only major collapse. Even in the heart of the City of London, which had not experienced a significant collapse in rentals since WW2, vast losses were incurred as demand dried up and the market became a buyer's paradise and a seller's nightmare. At Paternoster Square, adjoining St. Paul's Cathedral, an Anglo-Japanese consortium invested a total of £215.0 million to acquire an out-of-date 850,000 square foot office block. The redevelopment had not started, but in August 1992 was 80.0% vacant, but was valued by experts (advising the *Daily Mail* newspaper) at only £40.0 million, indicating a loss of over 80.0%. There were many other stricken developments all over London as a result of the seemingly sudden downturn. Nor was there any better news from the residential sector, where prices declined by 30% to 40%, as annual repossessions approached 85,000 dwellings. The number of borrowers overdue with mortgage repayments exceeded a further 330,000 in 1992/3.

The property and stock markets had been badly hit by the high interest rates imposed as a result of Britain having joined the EU's Exchange Rate Mechanism at too high a rate, which required Britain's interest rates to rise to a hopelessly high 12.0%. Britain had joined the EU's ERM in October 1990, but at the impossibly high fixed rate of 2.95 Deutschemarks to the Pound Sterling, and was only too pleased to be blown clean out of the ERM on "White

Wednesday" 16th September 1992 as interest rates rose to 13%, 14% and up to 15% before lunchtime, when George Soros' Quantum Fund had taken a $10.0 billion position in the FX market against the Bank of England's support for the Pound and earned his fund a £1.0 billion profit. The Chancellor of the hour, Norman Lamont, sang in his bath with joy at this merciful deliverance, and the UK was once again free to determine its own interest rates by reference to the needs of its own economy, which began recovering in 1993 as interest rates went all the way down to 6.0%, too late to save the property market, but better by far than held captive to the 'One-Size-Fits-All' notion of the single €uro-currency. One EU Commissioner was so taken by this deeply-flawed concept, Herr Martin Bangemann of the Economic Commission of Europe, that he started to pontificate about the 'One-Size-Fits-All' for bananas, cucumbers and his design for a universal EU condom!

As the stock and property markets went into reverse from 1990 onwards, so the stockbrokers and realtors that had been acquired in the rush to buy from 1986/87 went into decline. About 150,000 jobs disappeared on Wall Street and about half that number in the City of London. There were still about thirty securities houses trading in London in the summer of 1992, with only enough volume to support half-a-dozen. The UK's mighty Prudential Corporation sold off the realty business it had acquired only a few years before for a cumulative loss of over £200.0 million. Then the British insurance industry found itself staring at a potential £2.0 billion loss on new-style policies granted to insure property values to mortgage companies, the forerunner of the CDS that was to dominate the 2000s, many of them rashly written at the top of the boom. And losses at the Lloyds insurance market, which was scandal-ridden in the 1970s, compounded by inefficiency during the 1980s, produced losses of over £3.0 billion between 1989 and 1991 for its Names, or the individuals insuring the risks.

The 1980s ended much as they had begun, in recession, with high inflation and high interest rates, with a long and slow haul back to growth. Reagan's adherence to deficit-funding maintained strong growth for seven of his eight years, while Thatcher had saved Britain's economy and hauled it out of the mire. Reaganomics and Thatcherism had achieved much in the early years, but the freeing up of the financial and credit markets had ended in a giant bust. The warning was now well and truly in the system, but went unheeded and uncorrected. How could this be? Economists had retreated from empirical analysis into the new paradigm assertions, or repeated assertions, but it was more a case of Paradigm Lost.

Thatcherism and Reaganomics was a gallimaufry of Adam Smith, F. A. Hayek and Milton Friedman, and consisted of privatisations, lower taxes, the abolition of exchange controls, housing for as many as possible, a reduction of the power wielded by organised Trade Unions, and monetary deregulation supposedly balanced by new-style regulation. The mixture of Thatcherism and Reaganomics's massive spend on the military and 'Star Wars' destroyed Communism and in 1989 the Berlin Wall came down. It was the decade, however, that set up the background conditions for Global Crunch twenty years later, which nearly destroyed Capitalism. No new school of economics has yet emerged from the wreckage to light the way forward.

This portrait of the 1980s is a rewrite from a piece that I published in 1992; it ended with the following assessment: "The boom of the Greed Decade took place on the back of rising property values and it ended when those values went into freefall, caused by natural market forces. The boom in property values attracted a massive availability of credit, which credit was also used to change the ownership of industrial assets without adding anything much to real investment. It is unlikely that anyone alive today will see such excess in financial markets again in their lifetime … Capitalism has got to re-examine its basic structure, methods and ways of doing business. In particular the incidence of taxation on the two primary factors of production must be radically overhauled, before industry dies of financial and fiscal starvation and before another boom in property values and attendant borrowings brings the financial system nearer collapse.

"It is said that there are two kinds of idiot, the one who gets out in time and the one that doesn't. President Reagan, a prototypical escapee who could always read the lines that were written for him, got out at the top and donated Vice-President Bush as his successor, but Bush was always his own economic epitaph. Prime Minister Thatcher stayed on just too long …In the 1980s, the bulls and bears that got in and out in time made money, but the pigs went broke".

Well, that would have been a pretty good ending as long as you had died some time before about 2005, well before the even more catastrophic collapse of 2007/8! The style of the 1980s rightly won it the accolade of the 'Greed Decade', as it left Thorstein Veblen's *Conspicuous Consumption* of the 'Roaring '20s' well and truly spinning in its slipstream. And as you look at the Global Crunch at the end of the first decade of the third millennium, the seeds of much of that decade's tumultuous problems were already sown in the 1980s, whose eventual millions and billions of losses would become billions and trillions in the 2000s.

What I hadn't realised at the end of the 1980s was that the West, having allowed the good money concept to be driven out in the 1970s, was now skirting with a new trajectory for a massive future debt-deflation, which if uncorrected would inevitably lead to Great Depression 2 at the end of the current K-4 Long Cycle, somewhere between 2010 and 2018. The debt binge had really started in the 1980s, however, as is evident from Graphs 2 and 3.

The 1990s: The Tech Decade

The style of the '90s began quite differently from the 'Greed Decade', which had been far too raw and vulgar in its expressions and had collapsed in such an appalling and unsightly way: at the start of the new decade, people kept their wallet out of sight and didn't talk about house prices; behaviour at work and in the office took on the dull conformity of political correctness, no drinks at lunchtime, in the gym before work began, women in suits not skirts; and everyone on their computer with their heads down, as though the cotton-pickers of yore had migrated into the skyscrapers: there was a conscious effort to be efficient at work rather than happy at work, to be a cypher in this post-80s clean decade, where there would be no dishonesty and sharp practices, at least not as it began, but no one had any idea what the new decade would bring, or especially what it would develop into, just as long as it was distinctly different from the 'Greed Decade'.

The 1990s had begun with all the nasty recessionary factors that existed at the beginning of the 1980s, all except the power of the

Unions, a big exception to be sure. Inflation all the same was back in double-digits and interest rates and unemployment were high and the property markets were on their back, along with the stock markets. In the US, Greenspan cut interest rates to 3% which enabled the banks to buy Treasuries yielding 6%, thus recapitalising the banks and creating further liquidity for the recovery, as equities soared while bond yields fell. When interest rates had to rise in 1994, as the banks had monetised so much government debt/Treasuries that there was a bond market rout and 10-year bonds collapsed, yields soared and liquidity was sucked out of the system, halting the recovery, which may well be a harbinger of how 2010 unfolds. In 1991 the UK's GDP declined by a significant 1.4%. It wasn't until 1992 that the first signs of recovery appeared and the stock markets moved up, with the Dow through 2,000 in late 1991, but it wasn't until 1993 that the real economy began to revive, three long years since the downturn, and then in 1996 the property markets woke up again, got out of bed and resumed their upward march.

Clinton had won his first election in 1992 on a great one-liner: "It's the economy, Stupid!" Thatcher had already been pushed from office for mainly the same reason in November 1991; if only she had resigned in her tenth year along with her political soul-mate Reagan, that would have been so appropriate, but she ended up as the second type of idiot who didn't get out in time and the recession floored her, as she was bundled off in an appalling manner from the office she had won three times in general elections, by her own cabinet. The matricides didn't think to realise that by doing this they had over-ridden the choice of the electorate, who were not impressed.

In the autumn of 1991, a little-noticed event also took place that portended future events: Sweden suffered a banking crisis hang-over from the excesses of its 'Greed Decade' brought on by its property crisis, caused by lax lending after credit markets were liberalised. The top three banks were nationalised for 65.0 billion kronor/£5.7 billion in 2009 money, and gave guarantees to two banks it already controlled, but only after they had all marked their assets to market before any help was offered: a government-appointed valuation committee was established, so at least there was a commonality of valuations. Assets were sold off by an all-party Bank Support Agency. Directors of failed banks were prosecuted and paid fines of £4.4

million, while their future pay was also docked for two years. The medicine worked, the banking system was saved, while the rest of the world hardly even noticed.

The stock markets, meanwhile, soon told us what this Short Cycle was all about: focus. The conglomerates, like Hanson Trust with its multi-sector operations in the UK and US, with its strapline 'The company from over here doing rather well over there', dismembered themselves before the markets did it for them. The market's focus soon picked up on a burgeoning sector, technology, that was changing the world from analogue to digital on the back of the internet, with new markets for just about everything from e-mail to e-commerce to mobile phones and flat screens for computers and televisions and CDs, and countless other products. This was just the *Zeitgeist* that was required after the 1980s, a new direction that would develop new clean products that served man's needs and didn't harm the planet. At the centre of it all was the new medium of the internet which was destined to change human life as we knew it, as Bill Gates's vision of "Frictionless Capitalism" took centre stage. And on the stock markets the TMT stocks forged ahead: Technology, Media, and Telephones. The 'Cyberspace Decade' was on in earnest, and it wasn't long before companies like Netscape, Cisco, Lucent, Vodafone and Nokia were the new names and the new industries leading the next Bull market.

In 1995 there was an aberration in the financial sector that should have been a wake-up call for bankers and regulators alike: Degenerate Person in the form of Nick Leeson had busted Baring's Bank of London, but he was working several thousand miles away, out of their Singapore office, which had delivered shed-loads of profit back to its parent in London, which fuelled handsome bonuses all round. Then after a major earthquake in Japan, Leeson began shorting the Yen, but he was soon losing in the market, so he chased his losses until they were an astronomic $600.0 million or so, but no one back in London spotted anything untoward as his fellow Degenerate Person-Wife Mrs Leeson worked in the back office in Singapore and was hiding the losses. When the scandal broke, no one could assess the extent of the losses or the liabilities, so the Bank of England had no choice as a result but to rule out a rescue. Ing Bank of Holland offered £1.0 for the whole business and made a lot of money as a result. The lessons were numerous: any unit making abnormal profits should exercise top management's attention and more than normal; deals delivering huge bonuses are similarly suspect; the electronic control systems could not detect fraud but could be used to hide it, with complicity; and in the modern electronic world, the greatest losses often occur at long distances from head office, as Barings discovered, and as AIG would discover in 2008.

By now the 'Cyberspace Decade' was getting into its stride and the phenomenon of the dot.com boom was beginning to pop up everywhere. A strange idea took hold of entrepreneurs, investment bankers and investors: Cyberspace was the new real estate, only different. This realty was not like buying land for which you paid the price agreed and your lawyers made sure you got what you paid for; for this one was in the ether and belonged to the first pioneer who captured the new franchise in the sky for whatever they wanted to peddle via the internet. An aerial re-enactment of the gold-rush to San Francisco in 1849 was on in earnest, and as the new panhandlers wrote their software with pens and keyboards, they developed their own vocabulary and strange phraseology: 'first mover's advantage' meant getting in quick to capture a franchise, a good line for getting an investor to part with his money without delay; if the first movers got their money, and the 'Burn Rate' of cash expended didn't beat them first, they were soon creating the 'New Paradigm', a new world where computers would spin away making money 24/7 and the old world of boom and bust would be replaced by a straight line going up forever, while investment bankers raised their arm to the sky to herald the new graph, in the manner of a Nazi salute; and then a fanfare of trumpets and spreadsheets would sound and destroy the walls of Jericho of the 'Old Economy' and herald the glorious sunrise of the 'New Economy'. If this sounds crazy, well that's exactly what it was. And it took off on 9th August, (a date that keeps recurring in this edition), in 1995 when Netscape's browser software company IPO'd, in an Initial Public Offering on the Nasdaq stock exchange, with no profits and little revenues, at $28.0 per share and promptly shot on its first day to an incomprehensible $71.0 per share.

Something new was in the air alright. And the craziness did enter the soul of one Mary, and she did lift her head and saw the coming of the 'New Economy', and she did follow her fixed star in the firmament that would lead her, and all who followed her, to the holy grail known as the Internet galaxy, and she would people this new galaxy with millionaires and billionaires like no other galaxy in eternity, and she would be named Vice-President of all that she surveyed. After Morgan Stanley had surprised themselves and the markets by sponsoring two highly successful internet IPOs, Netscape and Cisco, in 1995, Mary 'Air Miles' Meeker took off from their San Francisco office to repeatedly criss-cross the United States of America on the mission of the Degenerate Person to supply some rationale to all this nonsense, especially the astonishing market values attained by these start-ups, which had little revenues, which were anyway exceeded in most cases by huge losses in establishing their franchise in Cyberspace, and needed incalculable sums to reach their first docking platform in the sky, known as Point Break-even, also known as EBITDA. This acronym – Earnings, before Interest, Taxation, Depreciation and Amortisation – was useful for earthbound companies as it represented gross cash-flow. Unfortunately this definition didn't work in outer space, but EBITDAM did the trick as it now included the biggest expense of these internet companies, namely Marketing back on earth, which was essential in establishing their new franchise in the ether back onto mother earth, which was ground-zero for where the punters with the wallets were, but it was all costing much more in marketing than anyone had ever imagined.

Mary would deplane at the next internet sighting and rush to meet the geeks. (Warren Buffett coined the phrase 'Beware the Geeks bringing new formulas'). Mary had a simple test for wannabe dot.com zillionaires: people, product and potential. If the team had these three essentials, Mary sprinkled her holy waters on their project. Then the next P was the hardest: Pricing for the IPO, where Mary's employers would hit pay-dirt. Here Mary had to stoop so low she went out-of-sight into the dark bowels of the earth to come up with her new recipe of total nonsense: as there were no profits, the basic rule on stock market quoted companies would just have to go. So what was there to value? Aah! There were revenues, weren't there? And revenues could be divided into subscribers and clients and "hits" on the website, with average spends and minutes spent dawdling or browsing on the internet, while paying advertisers winked at them from the sidelines of their screens, hoping to sell them tangerine flake streamlined toothpaste and slam-dunk chicken nuggets and pay-before-you-go funerals, and other must-have consumer items.

So revenues would have to be valued based on what had been achieved, but in most cases these were an unhappy negative multiple of the losses! So losses would have to be relabelled as the necessary one-off cost to get into Cyberspace and achieve your franchise. So now the valuation needed to address the breakeven point of EBITDA, after allowing for the -DAM bit too, that expensive suffix of the 'New Economy'. Well these revenues of a few months, or even a year if you got lucky, made a graph and any upward graph can be extrapolated into a fantasy curve of the future with valuation multiples attached, based on *assumptions*, as in the Assumption of the Virgin Mary Meeker, wow! Assumptions are useful, along with Risks, as they only get read in a prospectus in Bear markets, and here was a raging Bull out-of-control where all the punters just wanted to smell Mary's holy waters! And that's how the Degenerate Person Mary tore up the rule book, fooled the markets and created the biggest stock market bubble of all time, which made tulip-mania look like a pleasant afternoon in the garden, as she ascended into Cyberspace on her virtual personal star, Icaruspace.con.

As the market mania raged on, Alan Greenspan as chairman of the Federal Reserve, weary of an incipient market bubble, deemed it was not the Fed's function to burst the bubble by raising interest rates, especially as the real economy back on Planet Earth was beginning to tick along nicely, inflation was stuck around 2.0% and interest rates settled at a sustainable few basis points above 5.0%, unemployment was down, property markets were beginning to rise again and President Clinton's plan to balance the budget was even looking achievable. Even so, Greenspan warned the markets of their "irrationable exhuberance" in late-1996, the Dow dipped below 6,500 for a day or two, before renewing its inexorable upward march. Greenspan's view was that addressing the stock market boom "directly and pre-emptively" was out of the Fed's reach, and that resources would be better employed in mopping up any crash. This perception was the source of the subsequent mistakes in the next boom to follow, the property boom of the 2000s. New internet IPOs, meanwhile, took place every day, sometimes several, including no less than ten on 11th February 2001, and they all went to first day premiums to the issue price, 25.0%, 50.0%, 100.0%, 150.0% and 200.0%, and even higher. It was irrational and definitely exuberant, but it didn't look like stopping, and it didn't, until it did.

In 1996 the US Telecommunications Act opened up another leg to the Tech stool, namely the internet and telecoms equipment providers like Cisco and Lucent Technologies, the former development and engineering arm of Bell Telephone. Licences for mobile telephony were granted and companies like Verizon came to the fore. Because of America's sheer size, the cost of installing networks meant that for once in the Tech Decade the Europeans were ahead of America in the mobile sector, as Britain's Vodafone picked up 45.0% of the US Verizon network, in its ambition to provide the first worldwide cellular 'phone service. These companies soon went to very high multiples and their market capitalisations somehow connected with internet company valuations and drove them higher too, hauling them into a new stratosphere. This is where the CDS market took off, between 1998-2001, when CDSs were used to spread the risk of $1.0 trillion in loans to rapidly expanding telecoms networks; many of these ventures defaulted, but there was no overall market collapse, as a result of the use of CDSs, which began to look like a good idea. And the internet bubble had now crossed the Atlantic and these companies were beginning to be floated on Europe's junior markets.

When Morgan Stanley agreed to float Britain's Lastminute.com, a start-up online discount ticketing vendor, on the London Stock Exchange, the advertising budget must have blown the M clean off the EBITDAM, as every high-rise bus in London had Lastminute.com splashed all down the length and height of it, and in seductive pink lipstick too, the dot.com equivalent of the tramp of doom with the sandwich board declaring: 'The end of the world as you know it is nigh'.

Then in 1998, the Asian Crisis broke and unleashed currency devaluations, which in turn triggered the Russian devaluation of the rouble and the repudiation of her $40.0 billion of debt, which unleashed a wave of extreme volatility on foreign exchange markets across the entire globe, costing banks and investors billions of dollars. Greenspan was now in an impossible quandary partly of his own making: having decided for two years not to raise interest rates when he could and probably should have done, he now had to reduce them to fend off a panic spreading from the other side of the world. Already, the waves were lapping on to the shoreline of Greenwich, Connecticut and on up to Steamboat Alley and swamping the magic black box at LTCM, 'Long Term Capital Management Inc.', a hedge fund manager with two Nobel Laureates on the board.

LTCM was managed by its proprietary Black Box, wasn't long term and it didn't have much capital either, not at least in relation to its borrowings, which soon went down from 55 to 33 times its capital, when the floodwaters arrived. LTCM's strategy was based on simple 'relative value' spread trades, accurately described by Warren Buffett's partner Charlie Mungo as "a stick with shit on both ends". The profits were small but perceived as safe, but there were two types of instrument to each trade, and a third risk in the form of currency risk, which was where the Russian rouble upset the apple-cart. LTCM had also prided itself on being global and so also had a large portfolio of Russian bonds, GKOs and MinFins, which didn't help when they defaulted in August 1998. LTCM was caught wrong-footed in the currency turmoil, a risk that the black box was not programmed to deal with, which oversight affected practically every one of its 30,000 hedged transactions, as LTCM quickly lost $4.6 billion and had to liquidate everything in an increasingly skittish market.

The pace of asset sell-offs now required LTCM to sell quickly to repay its repo debts in the market, which put LTCM into a downwards self-liquidating spiral that the rest of the market knew all about. Its repo debts? A repo is a repurchase agreement, where you sell a bond to a bank and agree to repurchase it in the near future for a specified price, which includes the bank's interest and costs. This releases cash to the seller, but if the bond's value declines the seller is the loser, but the next risk for the seller is that when the repo is repurchased it would be unlikely to be replaced if the seller had suffered financial impairment in the meantime. When repos unwind, they can unwind fast. Imagine, would you think of buying a $3.4 million house with just $100,000 capital and borrowing $3.3 million on a monthly roll-over basis, to be renegotiated in all weathers? The Fed had to broker an immediate $3.625 billion rescue by thirteen NYC banks, including the UK's Barclays Bank, who had moved fast to assess the risks they were undertaking, as they jointly took over LTCM.

LTCM's business model was flawed in two essential ways. First, structurally, its potential margins on its 'relative value trades' were reducing under the pressure of its own and its me-too rivals, to the point where insufficient returns on its capital now required impossibly high levels of gearing, or borrowing, which in turn increased its risk exponentially, so that its capital evaporated like ice cubes left out in the sun when the crunch came. Second, its 30,000 trades were not deemed to be exposed to any collateral risk, but they were all suddenly collateralised by the Russian default which affected exchange rates and markets across the world. LTCM's Black Box, like all computer models, couldn't cope with a sharp bite of that man again, the Mullah Nasruddin's Teeth Syndrome, which delivered a lesson in the fallibility of leveraged hedge funds. As the Mullah would say: "Money for old rope generally leaves you in the end with just the old rope", as he knowingly surveys his false teeth.

The stock market, however, was encouraged by the masterly operation that had saved LTCM from a disorderly wind-down and, now that interest rates were lower, the internet mania engaged top gear again and now went into overdrive. The market was now learning about the differences between online companies: first, there were purely virtual companies like e-Bay the auction website, which were highly profitable, but there was only about one of them; secondly, there were information companies, which was where the internet had set out from, such as the search engines and worldwide web browsers, where most of the real money was made, in companies like Yahoo!, America Online (AOL) and Netscape, which was taken over by AOL, and Google in the next decade, but that was just about all of them in that segment – I mean, how many search engines do you really need, exactly? And thirdly, there were the vast number of upstart companies that wanted to exploit e-commerce and become e-retailers and sell you something real and tangible directly, cutting out the retailer/wholesaler and his profit and costs, like Amazon.com with its book offerings and Boo.com with its fashion and clothes offerings.

The Creative Person Jeff Bezos had thought through e-commerce carefully and early on had decided to focus on a simple product that sold in droves, the humble book, which the buyer identifies and can be packed and posted, requires no product training or warranties or after-sales service, but even he was astonished when he outgrew the giant Ingrams International fulfilment operation down the road in Seattle, and had to invest in his own terrestrial facility as his website took off. Amazon, as he called his company so that its' name began with an A, then moved into CDs and now sells many lines of consumer goods as the internet continues to gain ground amongst consumers learning to live and work increasingly with the internet.

Boo.com, formed in London by three Swedes, was unfortunately a different story of Degenerate Persons. They chose a product line that simply didn't lend itself to e-commerce, namely fashion, where customers need to check colour and feel the cloth and try the garments on for size and fit and look, and smell the coffee and enjoy the retail therapy. Boo.com raised $185.0 million, opened offices in the usual fashionista capitals, flew between them in private jets until they had burned through the money in eighteen months, an absurd burn rate of over $10.0 million a month, selling precisely $1.1 million's worth of garments via their dysfunctional website, before declaring bankruptcy. These Nordic would-be raiders were not the Creative Persons they hoped to be, worse luck for them and their investors, but the speed and style in which they burnt through the cash put them firmly at the top of the Degenerate Persons category of the failed dot.com entrepreneurs.

Extraordinarily, most of the money in what was left of the late-1990s went into this third category of e-commerce, where massive losses eventually piled up. Interestingly, the main problem for these start-ups was that they didn't own the real products they were seeking to sell, but they opened the eyes of those that did have them. E-commerce worked well for those manufacturers and retailers with their own products and catalogues and they took up the running on the internet. By 2000 the first supermarkets were offering an online service and the idea caught on quickly: why drive downtown to pick up a packet of the kids favourite cereals that taste like radioactive cardboard and ruin their appetites, when you can order them online in a couple of clicks and have them dropped off outside the front door? Then businesses with ticketing systems, such as airlines, trains and shows and events moved their booking systems online, which meant you didn't have to go out and queue, only to be disappointed.

Buying or selling a house, check out the internet first. Slowly the internet was entering everyone's lives.

The New Economy reached its corporate apotheosis over the Old Economy as 2000 had hardly begun: a confident and suited Steve Case of upstart AOL walked onto the stage at NYC's Equitable Centre on 10th January and announced his company was buying the open-necked Gerald Levin's venerable Time Warner Inc. for $165.0 billion – in AOL paper! AOL had twenty million subscribers and over half of all American internet users at the time; its latest twelve-month profit was $879.0 million, but its market cap was an incredible $163.0 billion, which is a measure not of AOL's real value but of the sheer stupidity of investors and the hype generated on Wall Street; and AOL's revenues were just $5.2 billion, compared with Time Warners' $26.0 billion and market cap of $83.5 billion. It appeared that the world had gone upside down, where present content was worth less than future distribution potential.

Levitt's apologia was succinct; "The new media stock market valuations are real ... AOL's valuation is real, and I am attesting to that". Instead of being hounded by the press for selling out his venerable company stuffed with media assets for paper, not cash, the reaction was almost laudatory: He, Levin, "has grasped what many casual observers, especially older and wealthier ones, just can't believe: for the old media, now, it's go digital or die," gushed a scribbler in *The Wall Street Journal*. The merger never worked, AOL's subscriber base was under constant assault from upstart competitors and in 2008 a divorce was effected, that left AOL looking for a new bride that could enhance their distribution with real product offerings. Gerald Levin should have worn a sober suit that day in New York in 2000, one that stopped him dreaming.

I will never forget the day in 1988, standing in line for the 'Power Breakfast' at The Regency Hotel at 61st and Park, when I found myself behind Dr. Henry Kissinger in the queue and observed: "Sorry to see that my Swindon Town beat your Leyton Orient on Saturday", which caused some good-natured banter between us. For this was the day that the *Wall Street Journal* ran a recruitment advertisement on a whole page for a New York bulge-bracket bank: a bald egghead with a single strand of hair was looking quizzically at the reader, under the caption "We're looking for Eggheads with

Attitude". This spelt and smelt of trouble down the road, I felt certain. The Eggheads eagerly designed new products around ever-sophisticated mathematical models that were driven by computer-power and labelled with three-letter acronyms, ending with CDSs. And remember, 1988 was also the year that the software writer Osinski had joined Lehman to perfect the CMO systems for the 'Collaterised Mortgage Obligations' market.

The generic name for these inventions was 'derivatives', as they arose as a result of an actual transaction that these new inventions were meant to be derived from, for example to insure a debt (Credit Default Swaps – CDSs), or an exchange rate (Exchange Rate Swaps – ERSs), or an interest rate change (Interest Rate Swaps – IRSs) or a share price movement (Contracts for Difference – CFDs), or whatever. Then the Attitude kicked in as the Eggheads sold these new-fangled financial instruments to other Eggheads in other banks and institutions. At first it was slow work to build these new electronically-driven shadow markets as it all depended on the target counter-party also feeling the need to recruit his own Eggheads with Attitude, but the directors and shareholders came to love these Eggheads as they were developing new revenue streams for the banks and all in the name of greater financial security, or so they thought, and was at the time indeed the case. While the internet mania bankers crashed to earth in a deflating vortex of valueless paper, these eggheads quietly worked on the sidelines to develop these new instruments that shadowed the bank's primary transactions, and they were blameless in the 2001 downturn.

As the year 2000 dawned President Clinton was able to boast that his second term was ending with inflation and unemployment at very low levels, with interest rates at 5.5%, with stock and property markets at all time highs, with the budget balanced and with the national debt forecast to be paid off by 2015: "It was the economy, Stupid!" Not many Presidents have been able to say that at the end of their second term, but Clinton was a master of spin, governing in the space between the square brackets where major problems don't exist, right up until he shut the door of The White House for the last time. With only eleven months to go to the election, could Clinton make it to the exit in time, before the internet bubble was well and truly pricked? In February the US economic expansion had continued uninterruptedly for over nine years and was beginning to defy the 'Short Cycle'. As Greenspan now saw it, the continued and strong expansion was storing up future inflation as demand was outstripping the ability of the supply side of the economy to deliver. So interest rates were raised by a quarter percent, but the markets continued on regardless, as the Nasdaq rose through 5,000 in early March, up 2,000 points in just four months, and the Dow Jones Internet Composite Index went through 500, up 130.0% in the past year.

As usual, the UK's interest in high-tech closely followed America and in March the tech market was tangibly about to crack, when I won a mandate to manage out a very small internet fund for The Royal Bank of Scotland plc. After the closing meeting, I flew back from Edinburgh to Southampton, about an hour-and-a-half, and read all the latest reports on investee companies in the fund. There were some good, even excellent, ideas, but the valuations were completely out of sight: one company had sold just one system of its indigo-vision technology, albeit to The White House, and was on the market at a valuation of £8.0 million, based on just one prestigious sale! On landing, my strategy was already clear, start selling everything on Monday. And as we started selling, the markets started sliding, but we were first in the queue for the exit and by the summer just about everything was sold, the bank got its money back and some, earning a compounded return of 27.3% per annum. Even a month later and it would have been a very different story.

The markets on both sides of the Atlantic were scraping the peaks in the first quarter, and in late February US interest rates were raised to 6.0% in reaction to another strong set of consumer spending figures, and the sell-off of Internet stocks started and continued in a slow motion crash for five weeks until Black Monday II on 4th April. The demise of the dot.com mania was gleefully recorded on gloating websites called FuckedCompany.com, Dotcomfailures.com and other such sites, which attracted their own ghoulish cult-like followings. The internet market collapse affected sentiment, in turn affecting all technology stocks, then spreading into the markets generally, and then the whole economy began to slide as the interest rate hikes cut confidence again, all the way down to an economically dismal Christmas and a bleak New Year, with many dot.com bankruptcies, but Clinton had spun out of office with Japanese-style just-in-time perfection.

The 9/11 terrorist plane attacks in 2001 on the Twin Towers and the Pentagon drew a severe line under the absurdities of the 'Tech Decade' of the1990s. As is usual in each Short Cycle, the busts are accompanied with a raft of frauds and malpractices. A month after the Al Qa'eda attacks on 9/11, a wired energy trader called Enron in Houston announced that it was taking a $544.0 million post-tax charge in relation to an investment partnership involving its own CFO; another month and Enron announced that it had overstated its profits by more than $500.0 million over the previous four years. In December it filed for bankruptcy. Its auditors Arthur Andersen were prominent in the 1990s for their questionable advice on growing profits by accounting subtleties, but were now under investigation themselves for their advice on setting up a whole slew of offshore vehicles for Enron, until the audit partner concerned sent a highly damaging e-mail around the firm ordering all e-mails relating to Enron to be deleted, and that was the end of Arthur Andersen for good.

And then the other scams at Global Crossing, Tyco and WorldCom came to light, and thus ended the decade that had started out determined to be different and not end up like the 1980s. How the as-yet untainted Eggheads with Attitude must have grinned at the denouement of all this Pie in the CyberSky: the next Short Cycle would surely be their time in the sun, dealing in money only, with their new-fangled three letter acronyms, called derivatives, a conglomerate market that would reach $600.0 trillion in the next Short Cycle.

The 2000s: The Noughties Decade

The 9/11 attacks on the Twin Towers and the Pentagon in September 2001 were the man-made distortion in the Short Cycle that lengthened the recession in the US by over a year, until growth unexpectedly resumed at 5.0% in the first quarter of 2002, only to level off in the second quarter. Greenspan had already reduced interest rates from the beginning of the year to 9/11 from 6.5% to 3.5% to mitigate the recession, but after the attacks the Fed reduced interest rates by 0.50% in each of the next three months and a further 0.25% in

December, down to just 1.75%, fearing a long downturn was in prospect, and on down to just 1% in early 2003. As mortgage rates hit historic lows, the real estate markets came alive and started the economy growing again, but in a way that was set to create the next unsustainable and most damaging boom in the 90-year Long Cycle, given another upward twist by the Fed's rate cuts from 10th August 2007 with an unprecedented 0.75% cut on 22nd January 2008. The collapse of the stock market bubble was set to give rise to the property bubble. In this sense Al Qa'eda's attack was to achieve far more than they had dared hope for, and certainly much more than they or anyone else realised at the time.

The Eggheads with Attitude, meanwhile, had made steady progress in the 1990s, but by 2000 they were morphing into Quants, so-called because they were doing Quantitative Financial Maths. By 2001 the CDS market, for example, was worth $900.0 billion, enough to feed a large number of Quants; by 2005 it had reached $14.0 trillion, up to $42.6 trillion by June 2007 and by December 2008 it had exploded to $62.0 trillion, according to the Bank for International Settlements in Basle, and every young Wall Street hopeful with mathematics wanted to become a Quant and earn million dollar-plus bonuses. As the complexity of these new instruments expanded exponentially, however, the directors and auditors were left trailing and not really knowing what was going on in these unregulated and non-transparent markets, but what the hell, as the 2000s unfolded the banks were making so much money nobody bothered to think of the consequences if something went wrong.

2007: The Crunch Sizzles

At this point several disparate but emerging strands of the US economy came together, or rather collided, in the most unexpected ways. First, the perception of Greenspan at the Fed, reinforced by his view that the Fed had been right about not disturbing the real economy by raising interest rates to prick the dot.com bubble from 1996-9, which proved a correct call as the money in that bubble did not imperil the overall economy and fizzled out as a result of its own absurdities, which blinded Greenspan to the starkly different threat posed by the next bubble, the property bubble, created by interest rates that were left far too low from 2002 to mid-2006. This anomaly created, unwittingly, the real estate boom and bust which did affect the real economy very badly, and indeed, as a result of the new innovations developed by the Quants, nearly bust the world's financial system, while the low interest rate environment also perversely drove the need for higher yields generated by the mortgage and debt securitisation process. Greenspan couldn't have created a better double-whammy of a sling to bust the system and bring Capitalism to its knees if he had tried.

Secondly, since 1992 Congress had pushed the government-sponsored Fannie Mae (the Federal National Mortgage Association) and Freddie Mac, the mortgage underwriters chartered to ease the flow of mortgage credit, to increase their purchase of mortgages to middle and lower income borrowers, thus giving such mortgages the governmental seal of approval. Then in 1996 the department of Housing and Urban Development, or HUD, gave these agencies explicit origination targets of 42%, rising to 50% in 2000 and 52% in 2005, with increases in these targets to 20% in 2000 and 22% in 2005 for 'special affordable loans', which target was increased to 28% in 2008. In addition these two government-sponsored agencies were buying subprimes for their own portfolios.

Thirdly, the accelerating origination and securitisation of US subprime mortgages into CMOs/CDOs from 2002 onwards and their sale throughout the financial system, including overseas, spread the toxicity throughout the world: in 2006 the level of mortgage originations reached an incredible $3.0 trillion, of which 20.0% was subprime and 20.0% was Alt-A, which were often interest-only mortgages and granted with no proof of income, so the poor performance of this combined 40.0%, or $1.2 trillion in just one year, rendered these securitised packages toxic.

Fourthly, the inclusion in this securitisation process of CDS insurance wrappers, which had grown on the back of corporate loans, were now transferred across to higher risk personal loans, which were becoming increasingly toxic, but the buyers were blinded by the false AAA ratings in one eye and by the presence of the CDSs in the other. The heavy buyers of AAA-rated securities, like UBS, RBS, Citigroup and Deutsche Bank, seemed unaware that an AAA-rating only referred to the likelihood of the principal and interest being repaid on maturity and took no account of any leverage applied by the buyer to its purchase in the meantime, often over thirty years.

Fifthly, the rating agencies AAA-ratings required CDS insurance wrappers, so BBB or worse was argued up to AAA, provided they came with that wrapper, and up to the end of 2005 they were readily available from AIG, which accumulated these CDS risks on its own balance sheet for 100.0% until 2005. It never occurred to anyone that a national decline in the US house market would occur as had last happened in the 1930s, as declines had been in specific markets like Texas in the 1980s when oil prices went south, or in California in the 1990s when the Peace Dividend sent the defence industry west.

The first signs of the coming credit crunch came out of the US in the first half of 2007: three announcements came close together which pointed out that CMOs/CDOs and mortgage funds could not meet their interest payments; HSBC's US subsidiary Household Financial was experiencing impairment provisions on delinquent accounts way above the historic average; the US LBO specialist Carlyle Group had formed a subsidiary Carlyle Capital Corp., CCC, which had entered the mortgage market with a $960.0 million equity CDO mortgage fund listed in Amsterdam, which was leveraged so many times over that when the market moved down a fraction the capital was wiped out and CCC collapsed in March, and its assets were liquidated as it could not meet its margin calls, with the real problem for Carlyle being that its core investors from the Gulf took a total bath in this fund and are now threatening Carlyle's future funding; then finally, BNP Paribas experienced the same situation with its three funds with $2.0 billion invested in CMOs, which were then closed for redemptions.

The first sign of trouble in the UK was the sudden appearance of long queues in September 2008 outside the branches of the Northern Rock Bank, the UK's fifth largest mortgage lender based in Newcastle, which had been a Building Society before it went public in 1997, as depositors now sought their money back. It had abandoned all its former mutual society conservatism and joined the hunt for bigger profits by tapping the short-term three- and six-months inter-bank capital markets and lending out long-term on thirty-year mortgages, often at 125.0% of valuation of the property offered as security. Borrowing short and lending long is the quickest way to bankruptcy for any bank and, as the inter-bank lending markets ran dry and closed for business, so did Northern Rock, the first bank failure in Britain for over one hundred years. The Government decided to bail out the bank, despite an offer from Lloyds-TSB Bank to rescue it with a three-year HM Treasury guarantee for £30.0 billion.

The bail-out for what was now popularly known as Northern Wreck cost £27.0 billion cash and the bank was put into run-off mode, with £15.0 billion repaid to the government by end-December 2008. In Q3 2009, the EU Competition Commissioner ordered that the bank be split into a good/bad bank and that the government should pump in another £8.0 billion, at which point it looked as though Brown's failure could cost the UK-taxpayer several billions. Northern Rock was the first of many failures of former building societies, originally liberated by Thatcher in the 1980s to join the brave new world of the great big banking free-for-all, that was intended to help owners acquire their own homes, not have them shoved out if things went wrong.

The valuations for the US and UK property markets both left the realm of reality for the same reason, namely interest rates were left far too low for the wrong reasons, but caused by entirely different perceptions. In the US, Greenspan's Fed wanted to help the real economy over the double-whammy of the dot.com collapse and 9/11, and just simply left interest rates far too low for far too long, thinking from 2005 onwards that the increasingly evident real estate boom was just like the dot.com boom and wouldn't affect the real economy that was chugging along nicely. This misperception nearly bankrupted the world: a real estate boom affects the real economy as it affects man's third basic requirement after food and water, and clothing.

In the UK, Gordon Brown instructed the Bank of England, as we have seen, to stop dealing with bank supervision and stop watching the M4 gauge of 'broad money' expansion and to pin their noses to the EU's CPI gauge of inflation instead, and as we have seen this gauge did not fit the conditions of the UK economy as it omitted the cost of housing and under-estimated inflation by at least 50% and probably more, so that, as in the US, real interest rates were also left far too low and for too long and monetary expansion went far too high, with the same result as in the US, that real estate prices went too high on the back of too much easily available credit on even easier terms.

It so happens that Bear Stearns, the first bank, or investment bank, to collapse on 9th August 2007, was the major player in the US real estate mortgage origination and securitisation business, that went into overdrive from 2002 onwards, and then onwards and upwards until finally bust, with the Fed just standing by, watching and wringing its hands saying "It's nothing to do with us", while the boffins at the Bank of England reported that their CPI gauge wasn't moving, "No, we're watching it like a hawk, Sir, it hasn't budged an inch or we would have rung you, Sir!" While behind their backs the M4 gauge was cruising through 13% and the RPI gauge was jamming up against 4.5%.

Systemic fraud was operating in the US mortgage markets from origination well before securitisation on Wall Street. The CMOs/CDOs of mortgage debts, insured by CDSs, were the first drivers of this US-led crisis. The trail from Sunrise Avenue at the base of this layer-cake was lined with shady ethics and greedy villains, and at every level these Degenerate Persons were in the mood to steal from the system, especially at the top level of Wall Street. From the would-be homeowners who falsified their ability, or did not have to disclose their inability to repay their mortgage, from the realtors who published upbeat valuations that assumed future growth, to brokers and bank executives who pushed these flawed proposals through the system, to the originating banks who sold these mortgages on up the system so that their bonuses went up as they churned the bank's capital, to the rating agencies who gave out-AAA ratings on this toxic mixture, and on to Wall Street where the so-called bankers – hustlers would be a better description – diced and sliced these mortgages into packages that were then sold on at a final profit and a bonus to themselves.

Henry Ford himself would have admired the efficiency of this mass production line, if not the end-product: "You can have any mortgage you want, as long as it's toxic." At the heart of the production line was the Grinder, the computer software that diced and

90

sliced the mortgages into CMOs or CDOs, before they were wrapped up in their CDS insurance wrappers. The dicing operation mixed mortgages up from different regions, at different valuation levels, with different types of mortgage terms and with varying levels of affluence amongst the mortgagors. The slicing operation involved cutting the resultant CMO/CDO into different slices for different types of investor, with the Senior tranches paying more for the first claim on the underlying cash-flows, the Mezzanine paying less for the second claim, and the Junior tranches paying much less for the right to mop up the scraps. All this met the prime requirement for diversification in investment portfolios, until that is, the US housing market went into a deep national slump across the whole country and at every price level.

Michael Lewis, of *Liar's Poker* fame, put it like it was: "Long Beach Financial, a subsidiary of Washington Mutual, was moving money out the door as fast as it could, few questions asked, in loans built to self-destruct. It specialised in asking homeowners with bad credit and no proof of income to put no money down and defer interest payments for as long as possible. In Bakersfield, California, a Mexican strawberry picker with an income of $14,000 and no English was lent every penny he needed to buy a house for $750,000...What was underestimated was the total unabashed complicity of the upper class of American capitalism." Standard & Poor was asked what would happen if house prices fell, to which the answer was: "Our computer model has no ability to accept a negative number". Washington Mutual, or WaMu, the fourth largest bank in America, was soon seized by regulators in September 2008 and sold to JPMorgan Chase for just $1.9 billion; in this transaction WaMu's Senior Debt was given a major haircut, and after the losses incurred by creditors of the failed Lehman, damaged sentiment for all bank paper was now a major factor in the ensuing credit contraction.

Keysha Cooper was a senior mortgage underwriter at WaMu, whose job was to spot fraudulent loan applications, and her evidence at the origination level is damming: "At WaMu it wasn't about the quality of the loans...it was about how many loans did you guys close and fund. They started giving loan officers free trips if they closed so many loans, fly them to Hawaii for a month. One of my account reps went to Jamaica for a month because he closed $3.5 million in a month. If a loan came from a top loan officer, they didn't care what the situation was, you had to make that loan work. You were like a bad [read 'Degenerate'] person if you declined a loan."

One loan file was filled with so many discrepancies, however, that Keysha felt certain that it involved mortgage fraud, so she turned the loan down, only to be scolded by her supervisor and told to restructure the loan to make it work: "How can you restructure fraud? This is a fraudulent loan." She was placed on probation for 30 days and her Degenerate Person team manager approved the loan, which was in default within four months without the borrower having made a single payment. "They tried to hang it on me but I said 'No, I put in the system that I am not approving this loan' ".

On another application, Keysha became suspicious when a photograph showed a street address which was different to the one in the application file; after unsuccessfully alerting the appraiser twice, some Degenerate Person approved the $800,000 loan, which was in default within six months and the property proved to be an empty lot. Brokers often offered her bribes, including one of $900.0 to send her son to football summer boot camp, which she as Creative Person naturally declined. Hidden fees, she said, meant brokers could easily make between $20,000 and $40,000 on a $500,000 loan. Keysha was eventually laid off, aged 35. A partner in Bernstein, Litowitz, Berger & Grossman, stated that the CEO of WaMu, that's Kerry Killinger, "pocketed tens of millions of dollars from WaMu, while investors were left with worthless stock." As Keysha tells it, Degenerate Persons were all around her at every turn and at every level. Now, how many mortgage processors/underwriters are there in the mortgage system? My guess is there are at least around 1,000 per state, or 50,000 across the states, or possibly double that number in the boom; now, multiply Keysha's experience by just a percentage of 50,000 and you can begin to see why the nation's finances became horribly toxidified.

In this questionable manner, many too many toxic mortgages arrived on Wall Street to be diced and sliced into CDOs and CMOs and ABSs, or 'Asset-Backed Securities', to be sold off around the world to financial institutions looking for above average yield, in the low interest rate environment sponsored by Greenspan's Fed and Brown's BoE. Then Wall Street developed a new derivative, CDO^2s, which was a CDO combining other CDOs, termed a synthetic CDO^2, and soon there were – yes, you guessed it – CDO^3s concocted out of CDO^2s, but now consisting of 90% nylon and sliced to satisfy the huge global appetite for yield. The main player in this merry-go-round market was Bear Stearns, the wannabe catch-up kid that couldn't keep up with its four more successful peers, Goldman, Morgan, Merrill and Lehman, who all had dicing and slicing operations, but not to anything like the same scope as Bear's, although envious eyes were caste in its direction whenever the mortgage market was booming. And the latest CDS wheeze is the Sovereign Credit Default Swap, which is used for protection against government bond defaults, a market that has grown fivefold since Lehman's demise.

These diced and sliced CMOs/CDOs were toxic for the following reason. If you buy six loose apples and put them in your fruit bowl and one goes rotten, you can see it and remove it and know you have a value of 83.4% left. If you buy your apples in a barrel where you can't see your apples, as with CMOs/CDOs, you don't know your value when you open the lid and detect a tell-tale smell. You have no idea of the value. In the debt markets, a mere fractional change of yield can be devastating on the value, as the markets price such instruments to three decimal points. At this point the ratings applied to the fresh apples are now completely out of quilter. Worst still, they had been led on by the 60% of prime mortgages in the pack and by the presence of the CDS insurance wrapper, so they gave the package AAA-rating. And then the subprimes started smelling in the barrel.

Bear Stearns had entered the mortgage securitisation business in 1981, was seventh in the league table in 1998, but ousted Salomon Bros from the No.1 spot in 1989, with turnover of $7.1 billion in MBSs, 'Mortgage Backed Securities'. By 2001, almost half the loans originated by US banks had been securitised and sold on to non-bank entities. Bear Stearn's me-too strategy was to develop a vertical production line for mortgages, from origination, servicing, bundling or securitisation into CDOs, MBSs and ABSs for onward sale. To this end Bear Stearns acquired Encore Credit Corporation, a subprime mortgage originator, for $26.0 million and in 2005 acquired Beardirect.com which originated mortgages online in 29 states, and acquired EMC Mortgage Corporation, a loan acquisition and servicing firm. In 2006, Bear Stearns originated 31% of the loans it securitised, double the amount in 2005.

In 2003 Bear Stearns established two hedge funds for AAA-rated and AA-rated MBSs, to be managed by Ralph Cioffi and Matthew Tannin. The funds had 40 profitable months until things went negative in early 2007, as the subprime crisis started sizzling. Then Bear Stearns made a terrible mistake, to back the funds with a total of $150.0 million in equity and then to lend to them $3.0 billion on top when the repo market turned sour, for a total in-house bail-out exposure of $3.2 billion. In taking that decision, the bond traders at the company, paid annually $15.0 million each on average, couldn't come up with a valuation of their own two in-house funds, but the decision to support them was taken in the belief that the maximum hit to the company would be $200.0 million, which was less than the cost of the certain litigation. That decision cost Bear Stearns its independence as the calculations of value were wrong by over a billion dollars. When the short-term financing evaporated, Bear Stearns was sold to JPMorgan for $2.0 per share, later raised to $10.0 per share, with the US Treasury guaranteeing JPMorgan a $30.0 billion facility, under Section 13.3 of the Federal Reserve Act provisions of "unusual and exigent circumstances".

JPMorgan had long wanted to emulate Bear Stearns' mortgage production line for many years, but could never figure out how super-prime mortgages on a low yield could ever be turned into much higher yields – how could sirloin come out of the Grinder if you only put in chicken? – and so they wisely stayed out of the business. They soon found out how it was done in the two Bear Stearns' hedge funds, however, when Cioffi's communications to the investors stated that only 6% of the portfolios were invested in subprime, whereas the true figure was 60%. In June 2009 Cioffi and Tannin were indicted by a federal grand jury on charges of conspiracy, securities fraud and wire fraud. The subprime market became toxic toast in the first half of 2008 and by September 2009 the world's intermediary financial markets seized up with billions of dollars of now unsalable CMOs/CDOs, ABSs, and CLOs, or 'Collateralised Loan Obligations'. When the music stopped, the banks sitting on the unsold and now toxic pile of securities and mortgages and buy-out loans were either going to have to be bailed-out or taken over or go bust. After Lehman went bust, it was clear that the others, like Citigroup which was bailed out and WaMu which was taken over, would not be allowed to fail. Hank Paulson had quickly decided to underwrite banks and auto manufacturers with taxpayers' money, and the rest of the world followed suit.

In the UK, the damaging effects were approximately the same. The difference was that the Brits actually believed that their property rises really were for real. Living in their crowded little island of 62 million souls, of whom 25 million live in and around London and the south-east, the cyclical rise in property values is an absolute fact of life, as is the fact that ever since around the 1960s practically every wage and salaried worker has earned more from the annual untaxed rise in their house prices than they have from their taxed income at work. Only in the 2000s, however, the banks started lending 125.0% of valuations in anticipation of future rises in values and forgot to check people's income and their ability to repay, as they recklessly relied on self-certified incomes. It was the subsequent heady but real rise and real fall in property lending that did the real damage for the British banks and its economy, on the back of low interest rates and under-priced lending risk.

In the UK, some of the milder issues raised by Keysha at WaMu, such as over-valuations, anticipating future rises in values, overstating income on self-assessments, undoubtedly occurred. The real difference in the UK, however, was that whole criminal gangs involving bogus estate agents/realtors began to milk the mortgage gravy train for all it was worth, especially in new-build hot-spots such as Manchester, Birmingham and Liverpool. Chelsea Building Society has written off £41.0 million as a result of fraud involving third parties, whilst Bradford & Bingley Bank, a former Building Society that is now part of Banco Santander of Spain and which operates more in the Midlands and North of England, has written off £271.0 million in the first half of 2009 on account of external fraud. The Police are investigating several of these organised scams and the arrests are beginning. The other important difference in the UK, however, was that the City had not set up securitisation production lines on anything like the scale of Wall Street.

2008: The Crunch Explodes
Lehman, AIG and CDSs

Lehman was brought down by toxic securitisation packages of CMOs/CDOs, but it had a gross exposure to the CDS market of $729.0 billion. This particular counter-party had gone bust, but no matter, these things were insured, weren't they? They were indeed, down the road at American International Group, acronym AIG, where 'Anything Insurable is Good'. The net pay-out on Lehman's CDS auction ended up at $5.2 billion.

The AIG Financial Products unit that built the bulk of AIG's CDS position was based in London's No.1 Curzon Street in fashionable Mayfair, and most trades were executed between Banque AIG in Paris and Lehman's London office, so it was beyond the reach of the US insurance regulators and the UK bank regulators, and fell within the regulatory scope of the US Office of Thrift Supervision, no less. The figures are interesting: by 2007 AIG FP's London office had a CDS portfolio of $500.0 billion, generating $250.0 million annual premiums; but by the September quarter 2007 this had led to a $352.0 million unrealised loss; this unit's income of $737.0 million in 1999 had risen to $3.26 billion by 2005; by the June quarter 2008, this AIG FP unit had racked up losses of $25.0 billion and the whole of AIG FP had losses of $45.0 billion, and AIG as a whole, including CDS trades executed by the Head Office managers and losses at its standard mortgage-insurance unit United Guaranty in North Carolina, had losses just on CDS insurances of nearly $100.0 billion by the time of the TARP bail-out in October 2008. It's simple arithmetic: if you earn a $1/_2$% premium on a 100.0% exposure and the deal goes wrong, your losses are $99^1/_2$ times greater than your income, before the expenses of having got your shareholders into that position in the first place. Interestingly, Banque AIG S.A. was the only AIG name on the roster of tenants shown at No.1 Curzon Street.

If the AIG position on Monday 15th September 2008 appeared to dwarf the problems at Lehman, by March 2009 the loss exposure racked up by this AIG unit in London was reported as nearing $500.0 billion, or half-a-trillion dollars, but there was only $2.0 million cash left in the kitty. The American Degenerate Person boss of this twelve man crew, Joe Cassano, had been remunerated with $203.0 million over eight years. In 2007 he told an analyst: "It is hard for us, without being flippant, to even see a scenario within any kind of realm of reason that would see us losing a Dollar". On Friday the 13th March 2009, AIG formally pointed the finger at the Sicilian features of Joe Cassano's face and blamed him and his unit for its own near demise, referring to it as the 'Ground Zero' of Global Crunch. AIG FP began in 1987 insuring IRSs, the now $325.0 trillion 'Interest Rate Swaps' market that accounts for over half of all derivatives markets in 2009, and also other plain vanilla derivatives, and by 2001 was contributing profits of £300.0 million, or 15% of AIG's group profits. Then Cassano, a tough-talking trader from Brooklyn, took over at the end of 2001, and ran the unit as his fiefdom, would not brook discussion and humiliated his staff to the point where one said: "The fear level was so high that you presented to him what you did so as not to upset him", the very indictment of the unacceptable face of Degenerate Person, whose threatening style often leads to massive losses, just as it did with Dick Fuld at Lehman.

These staggering losses at AIG FP also arose because AIG did not hedge or reinsure its CDS book. When clients asked AIG to post collateral to support their contingent CDS liabilities, AIG argued that AIG itself was triple AAA-rated and so had no need to post collateral, but when its rating fell to AA, clients such as Goldman Sachs immediately and quite legally and necessarily demanded collateral, effectively meaning cash, and astonishingly had the right, with the lower AIG rating and under their CDS contracts, to value the underlying assets of the CDSs involved, which meant that the likes of Goldman could within reason write their own cheques, but there wasn't any money left in AIG to meet its horrendous liabilities.

That is where the TARP entered the stage, courtesy of a reluctant Congress at the second attempt, on behalf of the now-powerless US-taxpayer pinned against the wall, as in Wall Street, to pay out billions as a result of their immigrant/ex-patriot Degenerate Person Joe, as in 'Nice Guy', Cassano. And who got the TARP money? Goldman recovered $12.9 billion at 100.0 cents on its dollar claim on its $20.0 billion CDS exposure to AIG, but much of the rest went overseas: in descending order, if that is the right way to put it, SocGen of France received $11.9 billion, Deutsche Bank $11.8 billion and the UK's

Barclays $8.5 billion, and so on, all at 100% of their self-adjudicated claims.

Goldman had seen the writing on the wall in April 2008 as a result of their daily VaR assessment, on which more later, which showed losses on their mortgage portfolio for several days running and so they started dumping these assets on the market and shorting the ABX Index, which had been created in the last days of the property boom in January 2007, with a series of CDSs related to subprime mortgages, which was effectively Goldman's bet that subprimes would lose value. The rest of the CMO/CDO factories on Wall Street kept going for profit right up to the crash and lost billions, but Goldman Sachs only lost $1.7 billion on its mortgage book, compared for example with $58.0 billion losses at its rival UBS. As a troubled and grievous Ben "Helicopter" Bernanke opined, without the US-taxpayer funded TARP bail-out, the world's financial system would have doubtless collapsed, and of that there was not the slightest doubt.

Lehman had been trading on Wall Street for 158 years; AIG had been started by an American missionary in Shanghai in 1933, collecting weekly pennies for life assurance policies. The much smaller Lehman was the biggest bankruptcy in history and now threatened the much bigger AIG with the same fate – entirely because of CDS exposure. It is reckoned that the whole CDS market has contracts roughly three to four times greater than the underlying debts issued, which would mean that up to $400.0 billion CDSs may have been written on Lehman's own bonds alone. So Uncle Sam had no option but to bail out AIG with an initial $85.0 billion and take 79.9% of AIG, which may even yield a profit over time from AIG's good underlying insurance businesses.

The TARP Bail-out

The crisis forced the US government to go to Congress to seek a $700.0 billion "Troubled Asset Relief Program", termed the TARP, to purchase toxic mortgages or CDOs from banks. The US had been down this road before, with the Savings & Loans crisis of the 1980s, which saw the creation of Resolution Trust Corporation. This agency took over 744 S&Ls holding $400.0 billion of assets; when the S&L assets had been sold and the crisis had abated by 1995, the total cost to the taxpayer was $87.0 billion, or a "respectable" 21.8% loss. That is beginning to look a cheap number this time round, because in those days the species called 'Eggheads with Attitude' had not emerged from the Darwinian womb.

The TARP legislation came before Congress the day Lehman Bros. filed for bankruptcy and, in a moment of democracy at its finest, was rejected, and by a majority of Republicans during the election campaign too. Congress felt it was being pushed too far and too quickly by Paulson the former famed Wall Streeter, who had been to Congress a few years earlier to argue for greater bank freedom to lend on lower capital ratios, which had led to the Financial Services Relief Act just two years earlier, and they didn't like handing unlimited control with no checks whatsoever to one man, armed with signed blank cheques to go on the street offering to buy toxic assets off his former buddies, at unknown prices and terms. Congress was leery of the tee-totalling ex-CEO of Goldman Sachs, with the non-existent smile and starring eyes of a Genghis Khan on a mission to save his world as he knew it; after all, he had just let a former rival bank go into bankruptcy with untold consequences that very day, and the fact that he sported the deadly earnest look of a sadist who wouldn't do a masochist a good turn didn't help at all. The interesting point, however, is that Paulson had got his sums broadly right, as the figure of $700.0 billion, an absolutely staggering sum, was pretty much the exact sum required to stabilise the system and avoid immediate meltdown, but then he did call Lloyd Blankfein, CEO of Goldman Sachs, 24 times in the first 6 days of the crisis, as in the help-card of 'Call a Friend' when you're stuck on a question in that BBC TV quiz game, "Who Wants to Be a Millionaire?"

Paulson must have wondered since, and even to this day perhaps, if he took the right decision over Lehman on *that* fateful week-end. On the side of the decision for bankruptcy were some powerful factors: the banks were out of control, the economy was way overheated and Lehman was both out of control and overheated, and bust. Under its existing management, it would probably stay that way too, even if rescued. And following the Bear Stearns collapse six months earlier, hadn't everyone got their positions in the market into better shape? If the boil had to be lanced, then this was the smallest pimple of a bulge-bracket bank left and its bankruptcy would therefore create the least systemic risk, surely? The trouble with this apparently reasonable view was the last bit, the threat of systemic risk: what was not foreseen by Paulson and his advisors was the effect of Lehman's non-transparent derivatives book, and especially its large CDS portfolio, as bankruptcy unleashed counter-party and insured risks on a huge scale, which had a far bigger impact on confidence worldwide than anyone could have foreseen. In fact, global panic set in the very same day. On that basis, Paulson might continue to rue the day, but he could, however, always justify his decision in the certain knowledge, that if it hadn't been Lehman, it would have been another bank, somewhere, and sooner rather than later. And in the UK, as soon as the 6th and 7th October, RBS and HBOS, the two leading Scottish banks, were completely bust, literally out of money and unable to survive another day, without an undisclosed emergency cash injection of £61.6 billion from the Bank of England.

The TARP came back to Congress with an extra $150.0 billion of pork-barrel schemes attached – it was election time after all – and a much broader range of implementation, including investing in banks directly. Paulson's initial idea of buying out toxic assets from their banks was seen as best suited to the banks, which was how it had been designed; the politicians, however, were concerned by the pricing issue, of how much the taxpayer would be paying for these assets of doubtful value, and the fact that the bankers who created the mess in the first place would still be in charge and commanding their outlandish bonuses. Where was the element of punishment and moral retribution for their moral and business failings, the penalty for their greed? And they wouldn't even have to do the work-outs on their own assets, and how could the government perform that function? In the S&L fiasco, the government had bought up the whole of failed institutions to perform that function, so that management sorted out their own mess. So investing in shares, with attendant terms including restrictions on executive pay, seemed a better political solution, and quicker and easier to implement, as the $850.0 billion TARP and PIG (as in pork-barrel) passed Congress and the House of Representatives on its second attempt.

Then on 25th November the Fed announced another $800.0 billion in two new lending programmes that did not require Congressional approvals: $200.0 billion would be allocated to buy up loans to consumers and small businesses, and $600.0 billion to buy up "debt tied to home loans guaranteed by Fannie Mae, Freddie Mac and other government-controlled financing companies". The US Government had now taken on at least $47.0 trillion in direct and indirect financial obligations, equivalent to 50% of GDP. As Laurence Meyer, a former Fed governor, wisely said: "They are doing whatever it takes. The problem is the more you go in this direction, the harder it is to turn around and the harder your exit strategy is". On the same day Paulson abandoned his attempts to remove the toxic assets from the banks, the change of administrations led to some non-joined up government, and it was not until four months later that his successor re-addressed this most vital issue, when Timothy Geithner proposed his cumbersome Public-Private Investment Programme (P-PIP), but this idea also failed over the transfer-pricing issue of toxic assets.

By the end of 2008, half the TARP's money, around $350.0 billion had been dispensed into nine major banks and many smaller regional banks, with $17.0 billion allocated to Motown. The first half of the TARP achieved nothing of Congresses hopes for new lending and preventing home foreclosures, as no conditions at all were put on the recipient banks. They viewed their hand-out as 'insurance' or 'stabilisation' or 'survival money', and some as 'acquisition money, a kind of subset of 'stabilisation of the system'. Anyway, that was probably what Paulson intended in the first instance: any idea that banks would go out and make new loans, in a gathering recession, was wishful thinking, as banks naturally draw in their horns in a downturn in order to avoid further losses.

At the end of Q1 2009, the total money pumped out by Uncle Sam in rescue cash amounted to $6.8 trillion, and $2.1 trillion in insurance exposure, comprised as follows:

Table 3:
US Bail-out Packages at End-Q1, 2009

Investments:	Sectors:	$-Trillions
TARP	Banks and Autos	0.7
Other Investments	Including AIG, Bear Stearns, etc.	0.7
Federal Home Loans	MBSs/Loans from Fannie, Freddie & Ginnie Mae	1.5
Commercial Paper	As buyer of last resort	1.6

Loans:

TALF	Consumer and small business loan securities	0.9
Term Auction Facility	Short term loans to financial institutions	0.9
Other Loans	Incl. line of credit to AIG	0.5

Insurance:

Bank Debt	New Senior debt and poor performing loans	0.7
Fannie & Freddie Mac	Cover for potential losses	0.4
Other	Including loans by Citigroup and BoA	1.0

Total $-Trillions: $8.9

Source: Treasury Dept, FRB, FDIC, as quoted in the *IHT* on 24th March 2009

More Improbable Corporate Disasters

Wall Street had no monopoly on the corporate excesses that led to Global Crunch. There were plenty of other corporate shenanigans on view all over the world, but the only common theme was the Degenerate Persons corporate egos driving to create debt-ridden monopolies as a result of their pursuit of personal aggrandisement. Here are the outlines of several examples of the greed of Degenerate Persons. Remember, man's irrational nature is part of economics too.

RT Digs a Hole for Itself

Rio Tinto (RT), the giant international mining group, bid top dollar at $38.0 billion in November 2007, after the Bear Stearn's collapse and after the boom had already peaked, for Canada's Alcan aluminium business, hardly an important strategic business fit. Then in May 2008 BHP Billiton, the former Broken Hill Proprietary of Australia and the world's largest mining concern, bid $186.0 billion for RT, when RT's post-Alcan debt of $39.0 billion was added in. Both companies have dual listings in London and Sydney, but the bid was referred to the competition regulators in several countries, including the EU; China was particularly wary of such a colossal and far-reaching merger as regards its huge purchases of iron ore and took a significant defensive equity position in RT, also after the top of the market had been called. With the competition authorities working out the widespread anti-trust issues, involving a concentration of 40% of all seaborne iron ore, as well as major positions in aluminium, uranium, iron ore and coking coal.

BHP Billiton's all-share bid by Degenerate Persons intent on world domination of minerals rumbled on through 2008, attempting to seize a commanding pricing position over many vital commodities yielded by the earth's bounty. The offer for the smaller RT was now worth a still immodest $113.0 billion, including RT's Alcan debt, on 5th November 2008, but by the time the EU competition authorities had worked out which assets would have to be sold by any combined grouping, the price had fallen from its original $186.0 billion to $108.0 billion, down by some 40%. By now, post-Lehman, stock markets were collapsing worldwide and credit markets had already dried up. BHP Billiton could no longer sell off any surplus acquired assets into a falling market as would-be buyers could not raise the finance either, and it aborted its now $108.0 billion bid on 25th November, when its all-paper offer had declined to $66.0 billion and RT's debts had risen to $42.0 billion, having spent $450.0 million on fees in the bid defence.

The underlying problem was that copper, lead and zinc were now down over 60% from their peak, having risen over 100% during the boom decade, but China's 2008 orders for iron ore were off a staggering 82% over 2007, boosted as they had been by the Beijing Olympics-accompanied boom, so sudden and great had been the collapse in demand. RT found itself in a bad position: credit rating down to BBB+, $19.0 billion debt to repay over the next two years, $23.0 billion after that, as the company sacked a total of 14,000 employees and contractors, and cancelled $5.0 billion investments in 2009. The Alcan bid had been a dumb deal by Degenerate Persons, almost as dumb and degenerate as BHP Billiton's attempted subsequent takeover bid for RT. This sorry tale of corporate greed ended in RT having to raise £19.0 billion from a Rights Issue in 2009, to pay for one half of a hopelessly over-priced and non-strategic acquisition.

RBS Goes US

The sad and bad distress of RBS comes next. The Royal Bank of Scotland plc, RBS, announced profits of £10.3 billion, or £1.0 million per hour, for 2006/7. It was now the fifth biggest bank in the world, after acquiring 26 other companies in seven years, and was hailed as Scotland's economic miracle. That was the Autumn of 2007, when in March of that year its shares stood at £6.06 per share; two years later it was essentially and totally bust, and in January 2009 its shares were worth a miserable 10.9 pence each. The architect of this demonic boom to bust, Sir Fred Goodwin, aged 50, who had become CEO in 2000 in the year that RBS successfully bid for the UK's third largest bank Nat-West, was now ousted when the Government stepped in and injected £27.0 billion of taxpayers' cash for 68% of the equity. This Degenerate Person was driven by the daft notion of turning RBS from a regional bank into a world titan by Compulsive Acquisition Disorder, or CAD, as he earned the nickname 'Fred the Shred' for his ability to fire staff in the acquired entities; unfortunately this short-sighted CAD approach looks good on the bottom line for a year or two, but then the need to grow the various businesses requires a very different skill-set, requiring cautious patience, not a quality noted in Degenerate Persons.

Sir Shredded Wheat's ultimate attack of CAD manifested when Barclays bid for Holland's second biggest bank in 2007, the ABN Amro, itself a former merger between Algemene Bank Nederland and Amsterdam-Rotterdam Bank, intended as a defensive merger and not much else. Degenerate Fred's CAD hackles were raised by the prospect of a rival getting bigger than his rag-bag of acquisitions and, despite the fact that Bank of America had already moved to secure the prized asset of ABN Amro, namely the US subsidiary La Salle Bank in Chicago in October for $20.0 billion, he bullied his board of compliant directors into the biggest banking takeover ever seen with a recklessly hubristic bid of £50.0/$100.0/€72.0 billion, in a hugely messy consortium bid with Spain's Banco Santander and Belgium's Fortis Bank.

The bid succeeded, disastrously, and effectively bust both RBS and Fortis, with the Dutch buying back the native part of the target for €17.0 billion, a huge discount to the price its shareholders had previously extracted from the hapless RBS, which soon had to announce that its loss on this final and blitheringly stupid acquisition was £20.0 billion, the price of over-arching megalomania of one Degenerate Person's lust for power, while Fortis reported a loss of €28.0 billion for 2008 and its Belgian operations were sold off to the French BNP Paribas, who paid €3.7 billion for 74.9% and went on to announce increased profits up 45% at €1.3 billion for Q3 2009, while the Belgian government also had to bail-out KBC Bank with €7.0 billion. The RBS consortium's combined losses were around €50.0 billion on an outlay of €72.0 billion and it later emerged that RBS had survived only with an undisclosed rescue loan for £36.6 billion, as Banco Santander limped on with the help of a Rights Issue, and the Dutch laughed all the way back to their old bank and sailed serenely on through the downturn.

RBS's acquisition of ABN Amro Bank would have, one year later, paid for Citigroup ($22.0 billion), Goldman Sachs ($21.0 billion), Merrill Lynch ($12.0 billion), Morgan Stanley ($11.0 billion), Deutsche Bank ($13.0 billion), Barclays bank ($13.0 billion) and still had change of $8.0 billion, a quarter-of-which would have turned Edinburgh into the financial capital of the world, if only they could have handled what they already had. Aaah! The benefits of hindsight!

The collapse in banking stocks between Q2 2007, just before Bear Stearns' demise, and 20th January 2009, a period of just 18 months, was completely unprecedented:

Table 4:

Decline of Banks' Market Values, 2007-2009

Market Value in Billions:	30/06/07	20/01/09	%Decline
RBS	120.0	4.6	96.2
Citigroup	255.0	19.0	92.5
Goldman Sachs	100.0	35.0	65.0
Morgan Stanley	49.0	16.0	67.3
Deutsche Bank	76.0	10.3	86.4
Barclays Bank	91.0	7.4	91.9
UBS	116.0	35.0	69.8
HSBC	215.0	97.0	54.9
JP Morgan	165.0	85.0	48.5
Banco Santander	116.0	64.0	52.0

Source: JP Morgan

The final fistful of salt rubbed into the gaping wound that used to be RBS was that in January 2009, the troubled US chemicals company LyondellBasell, a subsidiary of Access Industries, filed for Chapter 11 in America. Access is the holding company of the 51-year old Russian Monopolygarck Leonid Blavatnik, whose fortune was quoted at £3.9 billion in *The Sunday Times Rich List*, and it turns out that RBS, as a result of its acquisition of ABN Amro, is in a consortium that lent LyondellBasell £2.5 billion. While RBS is left with another enormous write-off, Len the Russian Bear sleeps peacefully at night in his lair, as snug as a bug in a rug in his £41.0 million mansion in London's fashionable Kensington Palace Gardens, and there's nothing RBS can do about it. Meanwhile, Fred the Shred earned the unique distinction amongst Degenerate Persons of being detested by all those whom he sacked on the way up, and in the manner of the Grand Old Duke of York, only to be equally detested by all those who lost their money and were sacked on the way down. When it became known that he had escaped quite improbably from the wreckage with a £6.0 million pension pot, worth £700,000 a year on a fully-taxed basis, he went to ground somewhere with his pension as his house in Edinburgh was vandalised.

When RBS sought to join the UK government's APS, or Asset Protection Scheme, with £281.9 billion of toxic assets in 2009, the UK-taxpayer underwrote £167.4 billion of loans to overseas borrowers, including over £3.0 billion in Ireland, £4.0 billion to ship-owners, and some £3.1 billion to hedge fund managers, mainly in the Cayman Islands and US!

Table 5:

Analysis of RBS's APS Loans	£Bns
UK	114.5
US	43.6
EU	75.4
Other	48.4
Total:	**£281.9 Bn**
Loans	80.0
Consumer Finance	54.5
Commercial Real Estate	39.9
Derivatives	39.0
Leveraged Finance	27.7
Structured Finance	19.2
Residential Mortgages	15.4
Other Loans	6.2
Total:	**£281.9 Bn.**

Most of us would have problems if we had to own up to "losing" £6.2 billion on 'Other Loans', let alone £281.9 billion, of which the majority was overseas. What on earth had been going on at RBS? And the UK-taxpayer also paid bonuses to these people!

Lloyds-HBUST

The most absurd take-over in takeover in British and banking history, even more absurd than the take-over of Merrill Lynch by BoA, was that of HBOS by Lloyds-TSB, which itself was the result, as we have already seen, of the pretty stupid takeover of Hill Samuel by the TSB as recently as 1987. Lloyds had suffered bad losses from its overseas adventures by Lloyds Bank International and its acquisition of BOLSA, the Bank of London and South America, in the 1970s and early 1980s. It had since retreated back to the UK where it consolidated its position and, when Global Crunch struck, was the only British bank in a completely unassailable liquidity position. In the mid-90s its stock market value was near £50.0 billion, but its UK-based strategy had led it to make some minor acquisitions only in related financial services, like Scottish Widows, which even then didn't make much sense, being a toe-hold of sorts and not much else in yet another country, Scotland , that it had done well to avoid, before its disastrous take-over of HBOS.

So, when Northern Rock Bank became available, as they say about women of a certain age, they jumped at the chance to expand in their home base with an entirely manageable, sensible and boring acquisition, but Prime Minister Brown refused to grant the HM Treasury guarantee requested. The latter, however, noted their interest in bedding just about anything as long as it was in the UK, and when the property plague-ridden HBOS, Halifax-Bank of Scotland, was bust and bleeding billions, Brown told Lloyds-TSB that he would waive the EU Competition Policy for a take-over to proceed. Lloyds-TSB couldn't believe their luck, forgot to do their Due Diligence, or DD, forgot to tell their shareholders that HBUST's ventilator was plugged into an undisclosed rescue £25.4 billion loan from the Bank of England and jumped into bed after a fast seduction scene in a Mayfair apartment. They woke up the next day in Casualty, completely bust, with Brown administering state aid to the tune of billions, realising they had gone from No.1 in British banking to No.2 in his recovery ward, with only RBS's spectacular crash ahead of them in the next bed. At their next AGM, a Scotsman even thanked the Chairman for losing half his money, with one-half of the shareholders thinking this shareholder was like a cringing Spaniel that comes crawling back to his master after having been whipped for doing something especially stupid, while the other half knew he was being genuinely sarcastic for good reason – hilarious! – but I bet the £13.5 billion deeply-discounted rescue rights issue in November wiped the Scottish smile from his wee features.

The directors of Lloyds-TSB destroyed their shareholder's value by seeking to achieve a Degenerate Person's stranglehold on a major market, the UK's mortgage market, and within a year or two to save literally billions. In Britain the overlapping branch networks and the 70,000 headcount at Lloyds and the 72,000 headcount at HBOS should yield annual cost savings alone of around £1.5 billion. Lloyds will now control over 44.4% of the British mortgage market and be number two in Scotland, while Banco Santander's acquisitions of Alliance & Leicester and Bradford & Bingley former mutual Building Societies will give it 27.5%, meaning that 72% of the UK mortgage market is now controlled by just two players. The architect of these absurd mergers and bail-outs, Gordon Brown – who else?, was still inside No. 10 Downing Street when the EU Competition Commissioner ordered the whole thing to be broken up and told Brown that he had to pay yet another £43.0 billion of UK-taxpayer's money into rebuilding the ruins, while he, Brown, was scolding Mervyn King for his Edinburgh speech on the need to deconstruct the mega banks, which Brown said was not his government's policy at all! No wonder the signature line for the bank's daft TV adverts, in a moronic and bored tone of female voice, is "For the journey ..."

The Grave Dancer

Global Crunch was essentially a banking crisis, but it badly hit the auto industry worldwide too. Another industry already in decline, the newspaper industry, was knocked even further into oblivion as its advertising revenues declined by far more than for online advertising. *The Los Angeles Times* was the first victim of Global Crunch, but a different deal stands out for its sheer unprincipled structure: on 11th December 2008 Tribune Media Group of Chicago had to file for bankruptcy protection under Chapter 11. Sam Zell, a legendary Degenerate Person and acquirer of distressed assets and so known as 'the Grave Dancer', had organised a buy-out using the company's own Esop scheme, that's the 'Employees Stock Ownership Plan', to finance this $8.2 billion deal. The Esop borrowed money and used it to buy the host company's shares, which were then to be sold to realise expansion or acquisition capital. As the company paid more money in to the Esop, with all the tax and interest deductibility advantages of a Retirement Fund, so the bank would slowly be paid off and shares released into employees pension accounts. As I said, however, the newspaper industry is in secular decline and the loss of advertising revenue in the recession meant the loans could no longer be repaid, so the company collapsed into bankruptcy.

Saved by the Bell

In November 2008 a consortium of two US investors, Providence Equity Partners and Madison Dearborn, together with the Ontario Teachers Pension Fund, were still attempting one of the world's largest ever LBOs, of the Canadian telecoms group BCE, owner of Bell Canada. The price was C$34.8 billion (£18.5 billion), to be financed by C$32.0 billion of debt, or 92% of the price – in the middle of the biggest global credit crisis ever! Were they crazy, or what? This completely mad deal had echoes of the UAL attempted buy-out that heralded the end of the 1980s' buy-out boom, only this intended transaction was ten times bigger, but KPMG Canada, the reporting accountants, did not sign off on BCE's ability to repay the debt, which was hardly a close decision as BCE had suffered four quarters of poor sales, so the deal was mercifully pulled. The offer price of C$42.75 per share promptly sank to a value of C$25.0 on the stock market, saving the 54,000 employees a great deal of job anxiety. The share price fall was saying that the price was 41.5% too high and attempting to drag C$15.0 billion too much debt onto the balance sheet! If this deal-too-far had gone ahead, it would have been interesting to see which of these three capitalist whores would have been left in the lumberyard, when the banker came looking for his money.

Tango with a Death-watch Beetle

The idea of a hedge-fund manager being run over by a Porsche is enough to make most of us laugh our heads off. It's usually the humble hedge-hog that gets singly and ignominiously squashed on the road, but this fate happened to a whole bunch of Hedgies in a major pile-up in October 2008. This strange affair is no fairytale, even though it comes out of Germany, and it goes like this.

Wendelin Wiedeking, a suitable name perhaps for a German fairytale villainous robber-baron but actually the real name of the of CEO of Porsche, the maker of fast four-wheel toys for Hedgies, had wanted for many years to buy Volkswagen, its much, much larger German big brother. The fact is Porsche was beginning to look more like a hedge fund itself than a car manufacturer: in its accounts for the year ended 31 July 2007, it made €1.0 billion from cars and €3.6 billion from options trading, so buying VW would make it look like a car manufacturer again, and Germans just love car-makers. So Porsche began quietly buying call options, to be settled with cash eventually, for VW shares in September 2005; these options effectively locked in a price for Porsche to buy large amounts of VW shares without any requirement to disclose, as it would have had to have done with ordinary options to acquire shares, and thereby sneaked up to a 42.6% stake in VW, leaving a 57.4% float on the market. Then, when the downturn arrived, shorting car-makers' shares became a fast one-way bet for Hedgies, and over a hundred of them borrowed 13% of VW's shares to do just that, namely selling stock they didn't own so as to buy it back at a lower price and pocket the difference.

So far so good, but then Porsche decided to take a leaf out of the Hedgie's books and a lot of money out of their bank accounts, and secretly acquired a further 32.0% of VW, not by buying shares in the transparent open market, but by buying non-transparent derivatives called CFDs, or 'Contracts for Difference', as in the difference between two share prices, which no one could see or know was happening. (Under UK market rules a stake of over 1.0% acquired in this way must be disclosed, but not so in the Land of Fairytales.) The architect of this deal, who outpaced the Hedgies on the autobahn of high-speed profit, was Porsche's CFO Herr Holger Härtner, a master of derivatives and complex currency hedges.

On Sunday 26th October 2008, when the markets were closed for business and the Hedgies were safely out on the golf course, Porsche chose to announce quietly to an unsuspecting world that it now had 74.0% of VW. The word 'PANIC' is inadequate to describe what happened on Monday morning at 8.00 a.m. when the markets opened: the Hedgies charged for the exit quicker than you could drive a Porsche round Mayfair's Berkeley Square on two wheels, as they raced to close their positions by buying back stock they had previously sold. Their next problem was that the free float of VW shares available on the market was now only just over 5.0%, but they needed 13.0% to escape with their money intact, so VW's shares rocketed up to €1,000.0 each, much to Porsche's great pleasure as the value of their call options soared as well, now paid for again by desperate Hedgies, so that VW was for a short time the single most valuable company in the world, with a spike in its share price that would have made the pickle on top of a Prussian's coal-skuttle helmet stand to ramrod attention! As I said, it's enough to make you laugh your head off, the fact that a hundred Hedgies lost over £10.0 billion by crashing their favourite toys into a classic short squeeze of a pile-up, in a race with Porsche to buy the 'folk's wagon'. Herr Härtner had turned a small car company into a hugely successful hedge fund and back again into a car company fifteen times bigger than the one he had started out with.

Porsche's Press Releases were not designed to put a smile back on the Hedgie's faces either: "We vehemently deny and reject the accusation of share price manipulation." And, "We make money from hedging and building cars. The difference is that hedge funds don't make cars the last time I checked," opined a Porsche Spokesman. Ouch! When Wendelin Wiedeking announced that Porsche's results showed a profit of €8.6 billion on turnover of car sales of less than €2.0 billion, he announced solemnly, trying to keep a straight face now that he had the not quite the biggest carmaker in the world virtually in his kit-bag: "This is definitely the last year our profit will exceed our turnover". Wendelin was completely right in that prediction, but things did not quite turn out as he had fondly imagined they would.

Wendelin and Holger now formed up to the VW board, led by the evil cousin Ferdinand Karl Piêch, grandson of Ferdinand Porsche, and son of Louise Piêch, the sister of Ferry Porsche and so on – they like to keep the car company in the family, you see, in Germany – but our intrepid pair had VW under their control with their shares and CFDs, options and calls, or so they thought. Wendelin and Holger wanted a Domination Agreement, no less, so that they could get their hands on all that lovely VW cash, so that Holger could settle the tab for all his hedging, and actually win VW outright, by indirectly using VW's own cash to buy the company, something banned in the Companies Act of England and Wales since about 1066 AD. Did they put on black leather biker's kit and threaten Ferdinand with whips, I wondered. Then the great credit crisis appeared on a screen right next to the two would-be dominators, just like the Big Bad Wolf, and over-night the German banks, who were more bust than they cared to admit, were not interested in lending Wendelin and Holger the €10.0/$14.2 billion they needed to complete their evil machinations to take over a major German icon ever since the days of the Führer. So Wendelin sent Holger out to Arabia to do whatever was necessary, to stand in a bucket of sand and sing the desert song if needs be, to divert the necessary number of the towel-heads' surplus petro-dollars back into their Porsche war-chest.

The liquid-gas rich Qataris took one look at this improbable deal-structure, of a gnat straining to swallow a camel, and realised there was a smarter way to go, by investing in VW to buy Porsche and its various holdings in VW instead. This was because Porsche's market value had dropped in the global crisis from €27.0 billion to just €7.2 billion and could not support the €10.0 billion of debt that Porsche needed. So VW engaged reverse gear and gobbled up Porsche instead, in a reverse-takeover funded by the Qataris taking a 17% stake in the combined company. Wendelin and Holger's improbable dreams of empire were crushed as though they had been awakened from a fairytale, as Porsche became the tenth head on VW's corporate totem pole of world-beating brands, Audi, Bentley, Skoda and the rest, and now Porsche. In July 2009, as Porsche announced losses of €4.4 billion, mainly on its VW options, Wendelin was defenestrated from Porsche's Stuttgart HQ by the new owners VW, clutching a cheque for €50.0 million it must be said, followed rather quickly by another thump as the lifeless corporate corpse of Holger followed him out the same window, just before the German Prosecutors raided the offices. The misuse of derivatives, as you can see, can easily ruin the rest of your day.

Dead End

Another German tycoon, Adolf Merckle, a 74-year old addicted day-trader and owner-manager of a £10.6 billion drugs and cement empire, with debts of €12.0 billion largely incurred by buying the UK's Hanson aggregates business near the top of the market, had also lost heavily by buying Puts on the premise that Volkswagen shares were bound to fall, to the extent that he had lost around another €1.0 billion. He left his home on the night of 5th January 2009 and walked the 300 metres to the railway track and died under the Blaubeuren train. His was the fifth death of an international businessman from the credit crisis, alongside: 65 years-old Réné-Thierry Magon de la Villehuchet, CEO of Access International Advisors, a feeder fund for Madoff Securities, who took sleeping pills and slashed his wrists in his NYC office when the Madoff scandal broke; 52 years-old Steven Good, the well-known Chicago property broker, who shot himself in his car; Christen Schnor, head of insurance at HSBC, who hanged himself in a London hotel room; and Kirk Stephenson, 47 years-old executive at Olivant Private Equity, who had tried an earlier death-wish of sorts by trying to take over Northern Rock Bank, before he walked in front of a train in Buckinghamshire.

These were single suicides, but the bizarre tale of serial suicides at France Telecom resembled a cult mass suicide deal; this employer of over 102.000 instigated a restructuring but then the suicides started, and as I write in September 2009, the twenty-second employee to take his own life has just jumped off a high bridge in Haute-Savoie. Interesting, isn't it, how the would-be suicides choose the time, place and method of their death, in that order. France Telecom has just

114

been ordered by the government to suspend its re-organisation for six weeks, but the whole sorry tale reveals the devastating unhappiness and human cost when economic control is lost. Apparently it takes on average six weeks for the would-be suicide to plan the act, beginning with the choice of the date, then where and finally how.

The Often Dire Cost of Corporate Bullying

There was a very interesting cameo to the whole HBOS debacle. Sir James Crosby, the former CEO of HBOS, went on to become Deputy Chairman of the UK regulator the FSA, having written a report commissioned by Prime Minister Gordon Brown on the state and future direction of the UK mortgage market. Then a former employee of HBOS, Paul Moore, the bank's Head of Risk until he was fired by Sir James in 2005, disclosed on the BBC's *Money Programme* that he had sent Crosby a memo that the bank's growth was out of control and that 'the real underlying cause of all the problems was simply this – a total failure of all key aspects of governance'. If that wasn't bad enough, the memo continued with this: 'My team and I experienced threatening behaviour by executives'. Sir James had immediately called in one of the Big Four accountants who produced the usual whitewash report for the management that had control of the cheque book that paid their fees, but then Sir James himself confirmed the *prima facie* truth of the substance of Paul Moore's allegations by resigning his position from the FSA the very next day, while the FSA waived the accountant's whitewash report in the face of anyone who still believed that Sir James was the Creative Person he had portrayed himself to be.

It is interesting that Paul Moore's allegation of corporate bullying at HBOS chimes with the experience of Keysha Cooper at WaMu. In an age where a sexist remark by the office water-dispenser can cost you your job in this so-called politically correct age, it is interesting that no debate has ever been launched on this subject of corporate bullying, which is often the pre-cursor for major corporate losses, as at HBOS, AIG FP and Lehman. I know, because I have experienced it twice, once in the US and once in the UK, the former a loss sustained, the latter a loss averted. In the US, I had to report on my employer's problems with £4.0 million owed by a customer which they intended to rescue, but my visit to the customer showed it was Mission Impossible and that whatever money they committed should be written off as they wrote the cheque out.

"Who's their treasurer?"

"They don't have one."

"Why not?"

"Because they haven't got any treasure."

The President of International started ranting at me; I looked at him coolly and realised he wasn't even a Degenerate Person in the Dick Fuld Jnr category who bullied his co-directors on a regular basis, he was a besotted idiot. My employer went ahead regardless and lost £104.0 million on their doomed rescue, while the idiot, the last I heard of him, went off to California to become one of those evangelical ranters on TV, the sort who break off in midstream during their Sunday sermon, or rant, to sell you a cheap pendant or a china bird with St. Francis; just dial up 0800-I-Love-Jesus forward/slash bird and it's yours to cherish forever, until one of the kids breaks it.

My similar experience in the UK was slightly better: my boss, the late Sir Alastair Morton who was the only Creative Person on the planet who could have built the Channel Tunnel, when he wasn't being a Degenerate Person, that is, took my advice and saved the bank £20.0 million, but not without a threatening clash, as I informed the meeting that a particular deal should not proceed, and exactly why. It was the only time I had witnessed someone go white with anger, which was fascinating to behold.

"I'm going to take a leak. You work out if you want a job here."

As Sir Alastair walked the thirty feet to the door of his office, it gave me time to think about exactly that.

"What do you say to that?" He challenged, as he opened the door, to go out.

"I always let the working class take a piss when they need to".

When Alastair returned, relieved but now freshly anxious, he was in the mood to know more.

"These people told us they had exclusivity on these designs!"

"Yeah? Well here's a list of the dealers across Europe who think they have the same deal as you think you have. You see, Alastair, exclusivity to an Italian is the first seventeen customers through the door!"

And that was the end of that deal, which soon afterwards went belly up on somebody else's books. The point is this: the corporate bullying of Degenerate Persons is a sign of weakness, the *Quod dixi, dixi or Quod scripsi, scripsi* syndrome, whereas the confidence of the Creative Person encourages him or her to throw the issue to an open debate, which is often won as a result of their confidence about the issue. It was that confident response that killed this deal stone-dead. Morton and I got along fine after that incident, as he just loved to be challenged.

The Hedgies

All of which improbable tales of German *Shortenfreude* lead us to the Hedgies themselves. Hedge funds started out between the two wars with a simple business model: buying long on shares which were going to rise and selling short shares that were set to fall. In this way they hedged their bets; for example, if Ford was on the way up and General Motors was on the way down, buy Ford and sell GM at today's prices, and sell Ford and buy GM on maturity; and the short sale funded the purchase. If the initial view of the Hedgie was right on both counts in terms of the future price, then he made two profits; if he was right on one and wrong on the other, there was a wash with no overall gain or loss if he had put the right money into each; and if he lost on both counts, then he could either run the book forward, or give up and go back to bean-counting.

Hedge Funds had $375.0 billion under management in 1998 at the time of the LTCM crisis, but a decade later it was $1.7 trillion. At the end of 2008 there were about 8,000 Hedge Funds in the world, and after $43.0 billion redemptions in September 2008 alone, along with lower asset values, meant that there was still probably around $1.5 trillion invested in the sector; and if Hedgies are down an estimated 20% in 2008, because two-thirds of them lost money that year, then they collectively beat the Dow, which was off 40%. In a normal year about 500 or so hedge funds close their doors, but in 2009 it could easily be in the thousands as 'Creative Destruction' applies to the hedge fund sector like every other, such is the battering they are still taking and the concerns of their investors. The losers have to make good their losses to investors before they can restart charging for their services, so many will cease business, either by merger or closure.

The big winner was John Paulson [not Hank], the NYC hedgie who was paid $3.7 billion in 2007 for betting against the subprime market, before he made over £270.0 million in early 2009 by shorting the shares of RBS. Losers included Kenneth Griffin's Citadel Investment Group, Chicago, with $17.0 billion under management and 1,300 staff worldwide, which had dropped 30% by mid-October 2008 and closed its event-driven funds and its Tokyo office, with layoffs in London, Chicago and Hong Kong. In 2008 Griffin was down 55% having lost $10.0 billion. Griffin was both a Degenerate Person who aggressively poached key staff and landing trades on the cheap and boasting that Citadel would become as powerful as Goldman and Morgan, but also a Creative Person, giving large sums to charities while still in his thirties. His worst two bets were to switch to convertible bonds in the belief the economy was going to rise, and then bet that the gap between corporate bonds and the insurance on those bonds, or CDSs, would narrow. Citadel stopped investors in two of its funds from withdrawing their funds, which one wag said was "like telling someone at a hotel that they can't check out and then charging them for the privilege of staying".

GLG Partners, a star hedge fund run by Noam Gottesman and Emmanuel Roman, staved off collapse at the eleventh hour by buying Société Générale's $8.2 billion UK asset management business for a nominal sum on 19th December 2008, with new facilities secured from Citigroup. In November, GLG reported a 27% drop in net assets during the third quarter to $17.3 billion after $2.2 billion withdrawals. Its debt covenants for its $570.0 million borrowings stipulated a minimum of assets under management of $15.0 billion and the fund may have slipped under that watermark, putting it at the mercy of its creditors. This acquisition signifies that some hedge funds now want to morph into less volatile traditional asset managers, but not many will be able to make that difficult transition without the availability of an acquisition like this, and the ability to pay for it. The deal not only saved GLG, but also turned it into a sector consolidator: in January 2009, GLG acquired the London-based Pendragon Partners, whose assets under management had shrunk from $3.0 billion in 2007 to $400.0 million. GLG Partners UK's director, the Belgian-born Pierre Lagrange, still saw his £460.0 million fortune halve in 2009, as he put his country pile in Hampshire, Malverleys, on the market for £12.0 million. The value of your investments can indeed go down as well as up, even if you are a hedgie.

RAB Capital is a minor quoted hedge fund manager on the London Stock Exchange and specialises in hedging mining assets, but also got mixed up in the demise of Northern Rock Bank after its collapse, expecting to be bought out in the subsequent nationalisation. This and the collapse in mineral prices meant that RAB Capital's assets were down 74% in 2008, down from $7.2 billion when minerals were booming, to $1.9 billion when they weren't. The much larger MAN Group plc, the largest quoted hedge fund manager in the world and with significant diversification through the whole investment spectrum, was down some 30% at its nadir, but soon recovered with the markets on its broad spread of risk and expertise.

This is a short account of the ups and downs of just five completely diverse hedge funds representing just 0.000625% of this global community. Yes, some rich investors made money and some lost, but how on earth can anyone regulate such a diverse community in the first place, and secondly what on earth would that achieve even if you could regulate it? Absolutely nothing of any value is the opinion of many, as this community was not in any way remotely the cause of Global Crunch.

The Big Guys

The year 2008 was the worst ever experienced by Warren Buffett's Berkshire Hathaway, the largest US stock market investor, as its value tumbled 32% to $150.0 billion, but the Sage of Omaha still beat the market, where Standard & Poor's 500 Index was down 38%. His company's quoted portfolio of $76.0 billion was only off an estimated 15%, with the real damage done in the underwriting businesses, especially claims from Hurricanes Ike and Gustav. During the year, his company made substantial strategic investments at very competitive prices in Goldman Sachs ($5.0 billion), General Electric ($3.0

billion) and ConocoPhillips ($4.0 billion) and the reduced prices of these investments in the downturn will no doubt recover much more in the inevitable upturn.

Buffett predicted he would make twelve acquisitions in the opportunistic environment of 2009, compared with eight in 2008. When his biggest investment ever was announced in Q4, it was a real surprise: Berkshire Hathaway bought the 77.4% it did not already own of the Burlington Northern Santa Fe railroad for a total price of $44.0 billion. "It's an all-in wager on the economic future of the United States. I love these bets." Let's hope he does better than Dagny Taggart.

In November 2008, KKR led by Henry Kravis, founded in 1976 and the largest unquoted share manager in the world, pulled its own planned flotation, having filed its registration statement for an IPO in July before the crunch had truly re-appeared. It had taken the Amsterdam pre-IPO flotation route at $25.0 per share, which now traded at just $4.50. KKR Private Equity's portfolio valuation had fallen by $999.50 million, two-thirds of it in the third quarter of 2008. The only time Kravis ever wants his name near a round billion dollars, it seems, is when it's a profit or the amount of professional fees on an acquisition. KKR's funds performed badly as well: the 2006 fund, which was the world's biggest at the time, declined by 26% by the end of 2008; and its European Fund II, which includes the high profile Pages.Jaunes Group, NXP Semiconductor, ProSiebenSat.1 Media and the UK's Alliance Boots, was down 46%. This last transaction may point to a way forward for KKR, namely buying a major quoted company, Boots plc, with strong cash-flows, and immediately merging it with a strategic partner, Alliance in this case, so that 1+1=3, at least that's the idea and it seems to be working at the operational level. It is a different model to the RJR Nabisco buy-out, where non-core assets were quickly sold down but no strategic plan to grow the business was in place, but it's the level of debt at Alliance Boots of £10.0 billion that is the ongoing structural drawback. The RJR-Nabisco deal, remember, didn't beat the returns available on the stock market, something that Warren Buffett wouldn't count as worth the bother.

KKR's former premier position in the mega buy-out sector was threatened by Blackstone Group's rise and success. Blackstone managed its successful IPO in June 2007 with the Chinese becoming major shareholders, just before Bear Stearns' collapse. The company entered Global Crunch with near on $100.0 billion in assets, but like everyone else it has admitted to sharp drops in its portfolio valuations. These assets can revive in the upturn, provided they survive the recession.

The Buy-out Boys

During the boom years for buy-outs in the 1980s, when corporates hadn't woken up to the value of the operations they were selling, when surging stock markets provided ready exits and when the banks were shovelling out loans like no tomorrow, the buy-out funds were returning two-to-three times their investors money over three-to-five years. It's already a very different tale in Global Crunch: stock markets are closed to IPOs, the banks have no money to lend, so there are no exits and no deals, and investment portfolios are having to pump more equity into existing investments to placate the banks, but more equity into the same deals means lower valuations by at least the new amount invested. Big names like Permira, Candover and Terra Firma have all announced big write-downs: Permira Europe IV Fund is down 61%, while EMI is written down by €1.5/£1.3 billion, leaving Terra Firma III down by 75%.

The Anglo-sphere Private Equity sectors have to refinance $500.0/£303.0 billion in 2010/2011, which will force disposals and losses, and as much as $7.0 /£4.2 trillion over the next five years, according to Terra Firma, of which £530.0 billion is UK debt. At the peak in 2007, before Global Crunch, European banks issued €33.0/£29.0 billion of 'Collateralised Loan Obligations', or CLOs, but in the first half of 2009 the volume fell to €2.0 billion. The EU problem, according to Fitch's Ratings, was that more than 58% of all leveraged loans are now rated B- or below. The new, or old, reality is that the banks are engaged in 'Pray and Delay' loan renegotiations which take all the spare cash-flow from what have become 'Zombie Companies' with no equity value upside left, as they are working for the banks but no longer for their investors. In November 2009, Moody's reported that in the US four out of six of Cerberus's buy-outs were in distress or in default and that two-thirds of Apollo's were in equally dire straits, as virtually no capital had been invested in these deals. All of which calls to mind the Mullah Nasruddin, who fed his donkey less every day, until it dropped dead.

"Pity." said the Mullah, "Just one more day, and I would never have had to feed it ever again!"

Investee companies where Degenerate Person buy-out managers loaded them up with more debt in the boom in order to take out their gains by way of dividends before realising the investors' money, are also at the head of the pack of strugglers: Yell, the Yellow Pages buy-out by Apax and Hicks Muse from BT in 2004, struggled in Q4 2009 with its 300 lenders to renegotiate its £3.8 billion debt, as a pre-condition to a £665.00 million rescue rights issue, which came with a tab for £85.0 million. Nor are the institutional investors in these MBO funds in any better shape: the three biggest investors in private equity are the state pension funds of California, Oregon and Washington, which since 2000 have invested $53.8 billion and recouped $22.1 billion, a shortfall of 60.0%, representing un-realised deals and losses on declining unsold portfolios. The figures for Oregon tell their own story: it has received $18.0 billion back but still has $20.0/£12.0 billion invested, which it has written down to just $8.0 billion.

New activity is thin on the ground too: in 2008 there were just two big buy-outs, the $3.5/£2.1 billion acquisition of the Weather Channel by Bain Private Equity and Blackstone, and Carlyle's $2.5 billion takeover of consulting firm Booz Allen Hamilton. In the first half of 2009 there has been only one significant billion dollar deal, KKR's $1.8 billion buy-out of Oriental Brewery in S. Korea. This is a far cry from Blackstone's $38.0 billion purchase of Equity Office Properties Trust in 2007.

The buy-out sector is set to shrink in any number of ways and is unlikely to emerge as a highly-leveraged/wafer-thin capital model in the future. In a historical perspective, it may come to be perceived to be the final chapter of the unwinding of the conglomerate structures so favoured in the 1960s-1980s era. The reality, as we saw in the 1980s, was that most buy-outs were just methods for Degenerate Persons to transfer ownership by incurring huge debts on already existing assets, as opposed to investment by Creative Persons into new businesses for the future. The amount of institutional money thrown at the buy-out industry deprived the real venture capital industry of capital during this era, but interestingly the only new fund in 2009, up to August, was the $1.1 billion funds raised for early stage, high-risk, tech and green start-ups by Vinod Khosla, a former co-founder of Sun Microsystems. His approach harks back to the 1980s style of venture capital, when fiduciary issues were not to the fore and were seen as barriers to scientific breakthroughs. Maybe a different wind is now blowing away the old structures in Private Equity as well.

Cash and Carry

The final quarter of 2008 saw the extraordinary events begin to exercise a major realignment in currency exchange values. Friday 24th October saw the Pound Sterling fall 10% against the ailing Dollar in a single day, down by 25% on the year, the worst slide since Britain was forced off the Gold Standard in 1931, when it plunged 24% against the Dollar: bad budget figures, a bad PSBR borrowing requirement, the Governor publicly using the "R" word for the first time, that and the fact that business confidence has fallen out of bed as panic gripped the market, as insurance companies are clobbered by the crashing stock market, and so on. On 9th December 2008, the UK's collapsing pound cost twice as much to insure in the CDS market than for McDonald's and other large corporate bonds. There was clearly something else going on too, namely the end of the "Cash & Carry" game.

The Yen Carry-trade as it is, or was, called was always a risky deal that was destined to blow up and kill and injure those in the immediate vicinity, namely the highly-leveraged hedge fund and buy-out managers, but as we now see it's also injuring the rest of us who were nowhere near the scene of this particular bank raid. These managers, the Hedgies, Big Guys and the Buy-out Boys, had all borrowed the Japanese Yen to finance their highly-leveraged deal structures, no doubt supported by derivatives in the ERS, IRS and CDS categories – that's to cover exchange, interest and credit default risks.

This particular heist worked like this: Japan has been experiencing deflation for over ten years now; so interest rates are 1% or less, so you borrow Yen at, say, 1 to 2% and pay off your borrowings in Sterling which were costing you, say, 6 to 7%. The temporary profit was the cash back in their pocket. The risk, however, is that the Yen appreciates against Sterling and the debt in Yen rises by more than the interest rate saving, called the "Carry". Ouch! Quick, unwind the carry trade and dump the assets, thus knocking Sterling and the markets yet again.

The Carry-trade involved borrowing strong currencies only, especially the Yen and Swiss Franc. As they were strong currencies, the downside risk to Sterling borrowers was consequently high. This all sounds so obvious, you say, why take this risk? Answer: simple, it was just good old greed at work again. And who pays for this now? Simple, Stupid! You and me, as our key strategic imports, such as oil and food, have to rise in price along with our holidays abroad, as we try to escape all this nonsense, as the Carry-trade bubble bursts and damages the markets and all our pension funds. In fact the correlation between the S&P 500 and the Yen-€uro rate from 2005 to October 2008 was exactly in step, ranging from 1200 on the S&P to 850 over the period, with a high in Q3 2007 of 1575.

The Carry Trade leaves many unanswered questions: should deal-makers be allowed to finance deals in a soft/softish currency, by resorting to borrowing in another, but much harder, currency? Should any derivatives entered into to minimise these (and other similar) risks be transparently displayed on a global internet platform for all to see, to make the market transparent as opposed to opaque? Is there a way, if these deals go wrong, of punishing the ever-so-greedy ones who took on these dangerous risks to maximise their own returns? Or is it best left to the market which, unlike regulators, doesn't charge for its services, to inflict the punishment by way of losses to investors and managers – the Adam Smith "preferred remedy", the 'Invisible, and cost-free, Hand of the Market'?

The Bernie Madoff Celebrity Send-off Crunch-Bowl Party

Every short economic cycle ends with a giant fraud or two, but in the middle of all the mayhem of 2008/9 one Degenerate Person in

Manhattan was forced to come clean and admit that he had been running his own celebrity crunch-bowl party. As the end of 2008 approached, the biggest scandal ever inevitably became compulsive viewing on breaking news. Bernie Madoff, pronounced Made-off, aged 70, had done just that with $65.0 billion of investors money, but over 20 long years, the longest-running punch-bowl party in history, but he'll go down in the *Guinness Book of Records* under several other headings as well. Madoff, who had been chairman of the Nasdaq Exchange in his time, cut a modest figure, short, quietly normal, rather like a small town attorney from Hicksville who is respected by all as an unassuming solid citizen, but with the face of an owl on the prowl. He had operated a so-called Ponzi scheme: Charles Ponzi was a Sicilian immigrant in the 1920s who carried out a form of pyramid selling scheme, where the last money in to the investment fund goes, not into investments, but as returns to those already invested in the "fund", so they think they are collecting "income" from their investments, while the Ponzis and Madoffs take the bulk of the receipts for themselves. This is profitable work if you can get it, just so long as the income keeps rising exponentially and no one finds out what's really going on, until the economy suddenly worsens unexpectedly and there's no way back. Madoff paid investors 12% p.a., earning his funds the sobriquet of "the Jewish Bond". The list of those conned could fill several editions of both *Hello!* and *OK!* magazines and included fund managers, banks, celebrities, charities and Hedgies, who seem to turn up just about everywhere where there's a money-party in full swing.

The truly astonishing aspect of the world's biggest fraud is that none of the professionals and feeder funds or those advising investors had done the slightest Due Diligence, or DD, on Madoff's scam operations, run from the seventeenth floor of the curvaceous pink Lipstick Building on Manhattan's Third Avenue at 53rd. Madoff's two sons ran his genuine brokerage business on the two floors above and claimed to have no knowledge of their father's criminal activities on the floor below. ("They would say that, wouldn't they?"). The international and prestigious Fairfield Greenwich Group, for example, lost $60.0 million of its directors own money, but took nearly ten times that in fees from its clients whom they had put into Madoff's private vaults to the tune of $7.3 billion, for some of which they are now being sued. Many other Funds of Funds sent money Madoff's way and took their clients' fees for managing the money themselves, a questionable practice called 'Pig on Pork', which will no doubt cause more writs to fly.

If any of them had done their DD, they would have found that Madoff's Compliance Officer was his brother Peter, his Chief Attorney was his niece Shana, whose husband Eric Swanson used to have responsibility for compliance inspections at the SEC, which received a report in 1999 from rival market-maker Harry Markopolos labelling Madoff Securities as "the world's largest Ponzi scheme" and another in 2005 entitled *The World's Largest Hedge Fund is a Fraud*, which were both shelved with no action taken... one would like to know why. Or why no one knew that Friehling & Horowitz, supposed auditors to this vast pile of now non-existent money, were a two-man team complete with secretary and a dog in a 104-square foot office in Rockland County in upstate New York, and that the elder boss of this fine duo was an 80 year-old retiree sunning himself in Florida, well away from Hurricane Bernie. David Friehling was arrested a week after Madoff's guilty plea and faces 105 years in gaol, but his partner and father-in-law Jeremy Horowitz made a perfect exit, dying of cancer on the very day Madoff pleaded guilty and went to prison. Talk about timing. And Madoff had no recognised US prime broker such as Goldman Sachs or UBS, which is normally the case; and someone at the SEC, surely, should have seen that the lack of any real volumes into Puts and Calls was saying that the Madoff funds could never have generated these unheard of returns in the way he claimed.

The appalling aspect of this Degenerate Person's theft is the number of Charities caught up in his manipulations, as he knowingly took money from countless good causes and lined his own pockets. As Mr. Katzenberg said on CNBC, it was a "disgrace" that this Degenerate Person should be allowed out on bail, and that his charity had suffered "extraordinary damage" and would have to curtail many of its programmes. And the Eurocrats and their private banks, French billionairesses, Hollywood stars, institutions and pension pots would all agree.

So what set Madoff down this path to ruin for his clients and himself? Madoff set up a small brokerage in the 1960s and worked away at it and achieved actual success on a modest basis; the business kept growing nicely and he met an ever more sophisticated clientele and the brokerage developed a modest fund business before regulation arrived. This business slowly moved across into being an unregulated hedge fund; then disaster struck during the 1991 Short Cycle downturn, and Madoff reckoned he could survive by diverting incoming funds into redemptions and returns for his existing investors; to his surprise, it worked and no one spotted it; then he hasn't got enough money to revert to the proper model and it just develops into a growing Ponzi scheme. He needs an investment strategy to justify his returns, so he claims to trade only in large American companies and hedging the exposure by buying options on the S&P 500; that, and he only charges $1.0 for every option trade and just 4 cents for every share traded and the investors just love his returns at these rates, but Madoff has been chasing an increasing and losing game and he needs the new investors coming in rather than the fees. Then comes Global Crunch, investors want their money back but there's now no new money coming in, so Madoff is making ever increasingly desperate phone calls to his first major investor Carl Shapiro to chase a promised cheque for another $250.0 million which hasn't arrived, but when it does the game is up anyway!

It soon became clear how Bernie pulled the wool for all those years: the auditor PricewaterhouseCoopers, the auditor of the feeder fund Fairfield Sentry which lost $7.2 billion for its clients, is being sued for $2.0 billion for failing to verify the actual existence of billions of Short Term Treasury Notes, representing 97.3% of the assets held by Bernard Madoff Investment Securities as *Custodian* of the money, a dual role involving a clearer conflict of interests than can be imagined. The Red Flag to this set-up was doubly reinforced when Madoff purportedly liquidated the entire portfolio every year-end and equally purportedly put the proceeds into US short Term Treasuries. The key element in the scam was the lack of a prime broker, which everyone involved should have noted and questioned. If there had been a prime broker, all Bernie's puts and options on the S&P 500 would have long been spotted by their absence, let alone the absence of all the Treasury Notes at the year-end, which is why he was his own broker.

Finally, some money managers hedged their exposure to individual Hedgies via the widely followed Credit Suisse/Tremont Hedge Fund Index, which unfortunately had Madoff in its composition. On restating the Index post-Madoff, the returns of market-neutral funds went from 0.85% positive YTD, that's 'Year-to-date', to a loss of 40.0%! And KPMG is being sued by Tremont group's investors who lost $3.3 billion. Truly, the Fund of Hedge Fund management business must now be dead in the water, circled in lipstick, while Bernie the architect of this misfortune has been put away in the slammer for 125 years, which in anyone's language means he isn't coming out alive any time soon, with his chief assistant in crime set to follow.

2009: The Crunch Hangover

If 2008 had ended in a ticker-tape parade of busted business plans, as the world went to its financial hell in a fanfare of shredded spreadsheets and blasting trumpets, then 2009 opened with a truly horrid reality: all those bail-outs of banks and auto plants hadn't really worked, they had just saved the day of reckoning. They were still all bust and bleeding losses and cash and destroying capital, and in 2009 the perception of the central bankers was that far more money would have to be spent, or printed, to get the credit that makes the real economy get moving again. The issue, however, was whether the never-ending stream of cash being pumped into the economy by the central banks would begin to have any real and sustainable effect before they had run out of credible monetary capacity. So the year turned out to belong to the theories of five dead economists and a funeral, but the economy's funeral was narrowly averted, or perhaps merely postponed.

The year had opened with interest rates across the world at all time lows: US at 0.0 – 0.25%, UK at 2.0% and going down to 1.5% in early January and on to 0.5%, EU at 2.5% and going down to 2.0% in January, Switzerland at 0.5%, Sweden at 1.75%, Japan at 0.3% going down to 0.1%, South Korea at 3.0%, Taiwan at 2.0%, China after five rate cuts in three months down at 5.58%, and so on. The world was entering what promised to be a long and deep recession, with deflation implying that real interest rates were much higher than as stated above, with the banking systems in the US, UK and

EU and in several emerging markets still seized up and unable to make new loans, as the banks desperately sought repayment of existing loans, as their necessary deleveraging process of their over-geared balance sheets tried to get underway.

The fact was clear for all to see that the $2.5 trillion Anglo-sphere cash bail-outs, $10.0 trillion when guarantees and insurances are added, may have saved the banks in 2008, but not the real economy. On the day before the Inauguration Ceremony of President Barack Obama on 20th January 2009, the British banks let their bad news hit the street, so that the next day's newspapers and TV would all be focussed on Washington. RBS announced that it would be declaring the biggest corporate loss in British history, of around £28.0 billion, including a £20.0 billion write-down of its goodwill on Degenerate Person's acquisition of Holland's ABN Amro Bank; its shares fell another 67% to just 11.6 pence, from a high of a 606 pence just two years earlier, and they fell the next day too; from 8th October 2008, Barclays had fallen 68% to just 88 pence, having tapped Middle Eastern investors for £7.0 billion in October for 32% of the increased equity of £22.0 billion then, now worth just £7.4 billion three months later, while top management denied any fundamental valuation problem and that pre-tax profits for 2008 would almost equal its market valuation; Lloyds-TSB was down 33% on the day it formally acquired HBOS and restyled itself as Lloyds Banking Group, with a shattered-looking chairman Sir Victor Blank going on Skynews to assure shareholders the deal was a good one in the long term, like well into the next decade already; and the mighty HSBC with all the right ratios and seemingly having avoided the slaughter shedding 42% on the day, down to a relatively strong £60.8 billion valuation, but still needing a £12.0 billion Rights Issue within months.

The Keynesian Stimulus Cure

The first approach favoured by governments in a downturn is to engage, without proper planning it seems, in economic stimuli packages by throwing money at infrastructure projects, such as buildings, roads, bridges, pipelines and so on. A good-old dose of old-fashioned

Keynesianism is always how governments seek to replace lost economic activity, by the public sector taking up the slack, and politicians smell votes in it too, and the US elections were round the next corner. The trouble with these projects is they take ages to select, design, plan and implement and often only get going after the recovery has already started. And there is a second major problem too: when governments get involved with trying to manage anything, it costs the taxpayer 30-to-40% more than if the private sector was running it, such is the inherent inefficiency of government.

If Keynes were alive today, I would propose asking him if it might be better to boost the economy by cancelling a range of taxes for the duration and letting the private sector get on with it, the approach favoured by Friedmanite anti-government/fiscal prescriptions, with the government taking on the same amount of debt as though it was borrowing to fund its own supremely inefficient stimuli programmes. Indeed, Gordon Brown's 2.5% reduction in UK VAT until 31st December 2009 headed off in this very direction of pro-Friedmanite but reverse-Keynesianism thinking, and even more pointedly Chancellor Merkel announced that Germany would reduce taxation by €24.0 billion in 2010 and by more in 2011, as the state took on the borrowing but not the implementation of the stimulus spending.

When the newly-elected President Obama gave his inaugural speech, his transition team had already received 11,391 "shovel-ready" Keynesian-type projects for consideration for government stimulus money. These included a $1.5 million project to get prostitutes off the street in Dayton, Ohio; a few hundred thousand to heat a public swimming-pool in Hawaii – average unheated temperature 20° C; and a small matter of $80.0 million for loading docks at the Philadelphia Museum of Art. Of course there were many more sensible projects, but this is not the way the private sector would set about spending its money. I mean, how could anyone sensibly evaluate so many projects in the context of their comparative economic benefit?

A far more effective scheme was devised by the Americans and the idea was immediately taken up by the UK, France, Germany and Japan. The Yanks called it the "Cash for Clunkers" scheme and the Brits endearingly called it "Cash for Bangers", as that at least rhymed with "Fish and Chips". Under these simple but effective schemes, old cars were taken off the road by a scheme that gave substantial cash rebates of €/$2,500/£2,000 to buyers of shiny new green cars, with the UK scheme demanding a similar discount from the dealer. The US scheme consisted of $3.0 billion dollars for 700,000 cars, of which $2.8 billion was utilised to purchase 690,114 cars, with Japanese US implants accounting for 41% of the take-up, whilst Motown's Big Three, of which GM and Chrysler were already in Chapter 11, took 39%. In the UK the scheme was extended into Q4 with a further £300.0 million being made available, but as Margaret Thatcher observed: "The trouble with Socialism is that eventually you run out of other people's money". This was a useful form of economic stimuli, however, because it was immediate and sent cash down the biggest industrial food-chain in a modern economy, the automotive chain.

The Friedmanite Monetary Cure

The New Year was also set to belong to QE, Quantitative Easing, nothing to do with Her Majesty this time, but the latest acronym to help get the world's economy out of bed. The first time I heard of it, I thought it was a description of Barbra Streisand singing in the bathroom and straining on her bidet, but no, it is an infelicitous phrase that emerged from the BoJ, the Bank of Japan, as it struggled to overcome deflation in its economy in the 1990s and 2000s. 'Quantitative Easing' is the Japanese, you see, for 'Printing Press' spelt backwards. QE is a volatile compound that if taken in doses that are too big or two small, or taken too early or too late, or for the wrong prognosis altogether, might make the patient more ill, or even kill them.

Inflation, on the other hand, is a much more certain concoction; it's not rocket science that you can create as much inflation as you want by resorting to the good old printing press, so that more and more money is chasing the same amount of goods and services, and reducing real debts, but also savings at the same time. Milton Friedman's monetarist theory sought to reduce inflation by controlling the money supply, so his corollary was to expand money supply to fend off deflation. His view was that the Fed's allowing US monetary supply to contact by a third after the stock market collapse of

1929, which he described as a "normal recession" but which is referred to in this edition as a "natural recession" caused by the cycles, was the cause of the ensuing Great Depression. Friedman, needless to say, advocated active monetary policy over Keynesian fiscal policy.

So, how does a central bank put QE into practise? Simply print more money, and debit 'Cash' and credit 'Notes and Coins in Circulation' on the central bank's balance sheet. This unsubtle methodology is referred to by bankers as the 'Nuclear Option', and is not their preferred approach to QE. Other methods abound up their sleeve, however, such as buying up sovereign debt, mortgage securities, corporate debt, or any other asset, including troubled assets, or making cheap loans to banks, which all have the same effect of shovelling money into the banks, but not necessarily on and out into the economy, as we all learnt in 2009. The Bank of England has another trick up her skirt called 'Under-funding the Fiscal Deficit', which sounds like hanky-panky behind the sofa, but all it is, is that the Old Lady simply prints money for HM Treasury without issuing Gilt-edged Securities, or Gilts, to third parties for cash, by debiting HM Treasury and crediting liabilities, thereby injecting cash via HM Treasury into the banking system. In the US, the Fed has a similar ruse for picking up the banking system after the punch bowl has been removed, namely charging the banks 0.25% interest while the banks buy T-Bills with the "money" that yield 3.5% or whatever, thus automatically restoring profitability and liquidity, but devaluing the currency in the same breath. QE is essentially any action taken by a central bank which has the effect of expanding its balance sheet footings or total assets and which shovels money into the banking system, essentially an inflationary as opposed to a deflationary stance.

The risks in QE are twofold: firstly, huge volumes of QE may not revive asset prices or confidence and get bank lending and the real economy moving again, to the point where there are only two things to do: admit defeat and be a double-loser, or continue with ever greater doses of QE, and more risk, which is where Ben Bernanke and Gordon Brown find themselves in Q4 2009; secondly, the more QE applied, the greater the subsequent inflation, or possibly super-stagflation and a return to very high interest rates. Then you have only two options: devalue the currency, which the foreign exchange markets will do for you anyway, and slash government expenditure and raise taxes, which is how the US and UK dealt with the high inflation in the early 1980s. The key to the turn for central bankers is the speed at which interest rates are raised: already in Q4 2009, Norway has followed Australia in the turn to higher rates, with Norges Bank Governor Svein Gjedrem citing that "asset prices have risen sharply and probably excessively" and that "asset targeting" had begun. None of this is pain-free for anyone.

There are dangers inherent with untimely or ineffective applications of QE, as is shown graphically by the frightening example of Japan. Its bubble economy went into melt-down in 1988, when the Nikkei collapsed from 38,000 to 8,500, and deflation set in; there was a delay before the Government resorted to QE; then it ordered big Keynesian infrastructure projects that took too long to get started; then it eased off QE, hesitated and lost the initiative, before applying several more doses of QE, but it was too late. Twenty years on the Japanese economy is still stuck in deflationary mode, but the national debt now stands at 227% of GDP, the highest in the world, and rising. And with interest rates stuck at just 0.1%, with not much room left for any more QE and its exports falling fast, down 27% in November 2008 alone with Toyota reporting its first loss ever of £1.1/¥ 437.0 billion, Japan is stuck in a very awkward and dangerous position, somewhere between a damp tissue and a soft place with nothing hard to push off on. And Q3 showed the UK getting into a somewhat similar situation, as the only G7 country still reporting a negative GDP. So the Bank of England, which hesitated on its £150.0 billion initial QE programme when it had dispensed £125.0 billion, has now raised the total to £200.0 billion, which is one-sixth of GDP. The stimuli and QE packages have led to Sterling losing over 25% of its value, the biggest devaluation since Britain left the Gold Standard 1n 1931. The stakes are high indeed and, mercifully, so are the odds against Gordon Brown's re-election in 2010.

And having hosed the system down with repeated doses of QE, the central bankers have to get it back, or "find their exit". To the extent that QE failed to reach the real economy but ended up back at the central bank as deposits from commercial banks, then those deposits unwind as the economy recovers and pose little inflationary threat. The difficulty is unwinding all the other lending programmes, as each one requires recovery in the sector and then recovery in the borrowing entity, some of which will go bust or end up with recoveries out of bankruptcy and some – keep your voice down! – even found its way into the stock markets that galloped into the quickest bear market recovery in 2009 ever recorded. When Ben Bernanke, Greenspan's successor Chairman of the Fed, spoke in January 2009 in that shiny new LSE building opened by you-know-who, he went to lengths to explain his exit strategy from QE, but it seemed his greatest success in this will be because the QE didn't work in the first place, as much of it boomeranged straight back into his coffers at the Fed.

In October 2009 the Deputy-Governor of the Bank of England, Charles Bean, said that QE was working, but admitted its precise impact might never be known: "The truth is that we will probably never know exactly how effective the policy ... has been, for the simple reason that we can never know with precision what would have happened in its absence!" Try doing the maths on that one, or interviewing Charlie when inflation re-ignites and takes off like a WW2 V2 flying bomb, which used to destroy whole street-loads of housing! And it's exactly the same with Keynesian economic stimuli run by government. The conclusion is that there is no positive evidence that the Keynesians were more right than the QE monetarists in the context of economic recovery, or vice versa, or that either of them was right at all in 2009, until we see the results play out in 2010 to 2012. True, the US recorded a 0.9% increase in GDP in Q3 2009, which no sooner led to extrapolations of 3.6% growth for the next year, than economists pointed out that it had not even registered a dent in unemployment, as they called for more Keynesian stimuli.

The Minsky Moment

The late Hyman J. Minsky hypothecated that Big Government and an increasingly Big Banking and Financial Services Sector would simply self-implode on account of their interaction and size, and the number and complexity of their financial products. Today we call this 'Systemic Risk' and refer to the 'Too-Big-To-Fail' syndrome, when governments breach the "Moral Hazard Territory" and prop up busted banks, and when newfangled derivative instruments, which were meant to reduce risk, achieve the exact opposite of their purpose by spreading risk everywhere. Minsky loved maths but even he couldn't do the numbers on this one, no doubt because it was just about impossible. He was writing back in 1985, before derivatives and structured finance and new mortgage rules existed, and before bankers geared their balance sheets out of sight and governments borrowed many times their countries' GDP, but he could smell the trend towards accumulation of excessive risk. That trend reached its Minsky Moment the day Hank Paulson produced the TARP bail-out, when Big Government underwrote the Big Banks that were Bust.

His theory, nevertheless, has credence simply because he formulated it and there's nothing else in the economists' locker to describe Global Crunch and how it could still morph into Great Depression 2. The Minsky Moment is when capitalism as we once know it goes to the great undertaker in the sky, just as when the Chief Rabbi blew his great horn in olden times at the Jubilee and all debts and leases were extinguished, which blast at least allowed for a new beginning to be made. This is the day in the Judaeo-Christian tradition which is described in *Leviticus*, Chapter 25, Verses 8 to 24, the day known as The Day of Atonement, no less, which is not about to be renamed the Hyman J. Minsky Moment, but you never know, as it's not over yet.

Minsky would say that the governmental and banking reactions to Global Crunch, of not letting busted banks go but saving them instead and with Keynesian and Friedmanite Cures applied as well, is all part of the Minsky Moment, and is already setting up the next and bigger Moment. If Banking Crisis 2 does break and government's again decide to suspend the "Moral Hazard" regulation in favour of bail-outs, the public sector finances can no longer possibly hold the position, and then the printing presses will be on overtime and Great Depression 2 will be upon us, with debt-deflation and/or stagflation, as measured in real interest rates, throughout the next Short Cycle towards 2019.

The problem countries are, first, the US, with the key debt/GDP ratio way-out-of quilter, with M3 apparently in contraction, and with growing unemployment and consequent further banking losses to come; second, the UK with M4 monetary supply in contraction by

0.9% in September and by an annual 1.7%, with still declining GDP; thirdly, Germany and Austria with their failure to recognise the extent of their banking losses, and with their threatening exposure to East Europe; and third, Spain whilst she's in the €uro-zone, has no way of avoiding a lost decade.

The UK's problems are twofold: its close involvement with the US which is not about to change, and its over-blown public sector and public debt; luckily there is a general election in Q2 2010, and although the Conservatives are likely to win it and have talked about austerity to come, their plans need to address reducing public expenditure by up to 15% at least, as they will need to cut public expenditure by a figure nearer £100.0 billion than £50.0 billion to get the overall shape of the economy back into balance. Indeed, the Confederation of British Industry, the CBI, in Q4 2009 called for £50.0 billion savings by 2013 and then another £70.0 billion to balance the budget by 2015/16, which seems an optimistic target. And within days a financially-literate ex-Harvard Conservative MP, Brooks Newmark, published the actual level of the UK's National Debt, which was officially stated as £805.0 billion, but under his calculation was actually £2,200.0 billion.

Table 6:	
Official UK Govt. Debt, per the ONS – 57.5% of GDP	**£805,000,000,000**
Unfunded Pension Obligations	1,104,000,000,000
PFI/Public Finance Initiative debts	139,000,000,000
Network Rail debt	22,000,000,000
Bank Bail-out liabilities	130,000,000,000
Unofficial Govt. Debt – 157% of GDP	**£2,200,000,000,000**

I felt quite ill as I digested this economic reality, and then I reflected that Newmark had at least spared us with the omission of unfunded future healthcare costs, but his arithmetic shows just how big Minsky's Big Government has become. Governments have run their pension obligations on an unfunded basis, meaning that receipts from current taxes are used to pay retirees with no other income or fund in place, which has worked for the post-WW2 baby-boomers, but they are now becoming the new retirees: when the demographic economics of the ageing populations are factored in, then the position looks far from rosy for everyone.

The only countries that have fully-funded pensions and healthcare costs are Norway and Switzerland, while all the G7 economies have approximately the same national scale of National Debt distortion as the UK, according to a 2008 report by Berlin's Stiftung-Marktwirtschaft think-tank. And within two years the Official National Debt of the UK will be 105% of GDP, 125% for the US, 135% for Greece and 270% for Japan, according to SocGen's calculations, who reckon that worldwide sovereign debt could reach a total of $45.0 trillion by 2011, which is exactly double Moody's calculations by 2015! The sovereign debts are ballooning so fast that no one seems to know where the graph is really going, but then again it's what you count in and what governments try to keep out that's the difference.

So we end 2009 with the financial system apparently saved for the time being, by the expedient transfer of great debts and questionable assets from the private to the public sector, but with any number of financial time-bombs still ticking away around the global financial system. It seems as though 2010 will see low interest rates continue while governments and central bankers try to nurse the recovery along while private sector bankers try to deleverage at an increasingly faster rate, but at some point any recovery, especially with increased demand for commodities from the BRICs, will cause deflation to turn into inflation during 2010/11, driven by all the QE money thrown around like confetti during Global Crunch, and then the central bankers will have to move fast to raise interest rates, which if done too slowly will have to be accelerated. Then this cycle becomes harder to predict, but a caution must now be applied as to the timing of the current Short Cycle, which began in 2010: Global

Crunch itself, or rather the Keynesian and Friedmanite reactions to it, are a major man-made distortion which may shorten the cycle by one, two or more years, and a Minskey-corrugated recovery may ensue, in which the financial system finds itself walking along a precipice that has a nasty drop on either side, and a fall over the precipice could come at any time ...

This predicament for the US economy was clearly articulated on 10th November 2009 by Janet Yellen, the President of the Federal Reserve Bank of San Francisco, who said that the recovery was not secure, that unemployment would persist and that more stimuli would be required. The next day, Angela Merkel, the newly-re-elected Chancellor of Germany, told the Bundestag that her government was going to abandon fiscal rectitude and go for growth, as she stared at a 6.5% budget deficit for 2010 and beyond, and opted for €24.0 billion tax reductions for 2010 and more still in 2011. "The full force of the crisis will hit us next year. The problems will get bigger before things can get better", she said. Unemployment in Germany is officially at 8.3%, but 1.4 million workers are on the *Kurzabeit* system, which encourages employers to put employees on reduced hours rather than sacking them, a programme that Merkel intends to expand. None of the 16 €uro-zone participants will be any-where near within the maximum 3% fiscal deficit range ordained, ordured might be a better word, by the Maastricht Treaty, before 2013.

Hyman Minsky postulated in *Stabilising an Unstable Economy* that when governments work to end a recession, as with Keynesian and Friedmanite solutions, that they are distorting the Short Cycle and setting up the next phase of instability. There is no macro-economic thinking other than Minsky's that can explain the increasing severity of the post-WW2 Short Cycle downturns, and he points to the gov-ernmental and financial sectors' overall size as the cause, which is only a minor issue in the current debate, while governments and bloated banks bump and lumber around like so many Frankenstein monsters. Central bankers, the Fed, the Bank of England and the ECB are still nursing distressed banking systems and continuing low interest rates will start causing the next banking crisis: the inevitable interest rate rises will further deflate assets such as property and stock markets, while any continuance of questionably and increasingly ineffective QE and similar moves to provide excessive monetary expansion could lead to a crash in the bond markets and Great Depression 2, which would confirm the point at which the downturns in the Short and Long Cycles did indeed coincide.

The Irving Fisher Reality Check

With Keynesian and Friedmanite remedies visibly failing to perfom to expectation in Q4 2009, as the UK's GDP was slipping further backwards by 0.3% in Q3 and the US claiming just 0.9% growth, economists were dusting off the theories of Irving Fisher and his views on debt-deflation, knowledge of which, it must be pointed out, didn't prevent him from losing his fortune in the crash of 1929. His debt-deflation theory defined a sequence of events that leads to the debt-bubble bursting: debt liquidation and distress selling lead to a contraction of the money supply as bank loans are repaid, causing a fall in the level of asset prices and a greater fall in business assets, causing bankruptcies and a fall in profits, a reduction in output, trade and employment.

The debt-deflation/credit cycle in the late 2000s is strikingly similar to the 1930s, where the preferred remedies of the business cycle, such as lowering interest rates or creating ever greater amount of public debt infrastructure projects, as in the Keynesian approach, did not achieve a quick recovery. The maths on the debt-deflation collapse in The Great Depression is straightforward: in 1929 the US debt/GDP ratio was 1.95; as the GDP fell by 50% in nominal terms, the ratio rose to 3.0 before collapsing to 1.4 in 1950, which coincided with the longwave.com's K-3 downturn, after the destruction of $100.0 billion of credit in the process, just less than GDP had been in 1929.

The US debt/GDP ratio in 2009 is now approaching 4.0, at 3.73 in Q2 2009, with $52.8 trillion of US total debt against GDP at $14.2 trillion, but could rise to 4.5 times or more, or 450%+ from the current 373%, especially if events caused GDP ever to fall at a faster rate than in 1932. These figures translate into $3.73 of debt for every $1.0 of output, which sounds pretty much like being near the top of a precipice, if you ask me, as shown in Graph 3 overleaf. The

UK with lower debt had a ratio of 2.0 times at the end of 2008, but it's also rising, but that's based on the official level of Government debt, which is now under challenge, as shown in Table 5 above. As in 1932, an exponential and uninterrupted rise in debt and a fall in GDP can only end eventually in this equation with a crash, when bond markets collapse and Great Depression 2 unfolds.

So what is the reality of a crash? It is that debts incurred in fiat money cannot be repaid with that devalued fiat currency, as previously-assumed debt repayment prospects from rising asset values cannot be made in contracted currencies which have gone into an uncontrollable free-fall. In the second half of 2009 the competitive devaluation of the Dollar and Sterling against the €uro and Yen is

Graph 3

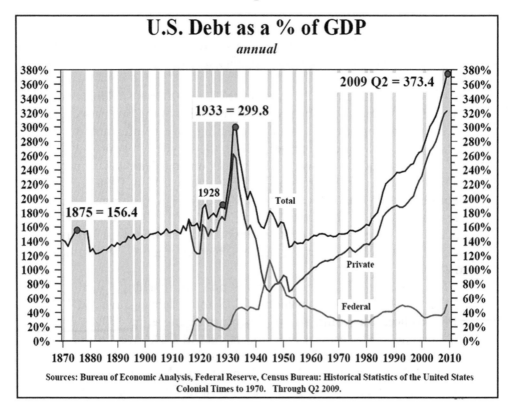

seeking to gain a trade and a debt value advantage, with the Chinese working out how to position the Renminbi: the longer the Chinese peg their currency to the Dollar they will have outsize trade surpluses and outsize foreign currency reserves of Dollars, which could over time wipe out the real value of those reserves. The uncomfortable truth of currency devaluations is that only up to one half of the world can do this against the other half.

History shows the time-period for a decline is around a quarter-to-a-third that of the previous rise, so from the lowest point of K-3 in 1950 to 2009 is 59 years, so a debt-default crash, where the bond markets go in to free-fall, could be at any time from 2010 towards 2019, as indicated by the cycles. As total debt in these conditions cannot be paid down sufficiently in the short or medium term, if at all, it can only be eliminated by hyper-inflation or by default, meaning bankruptcy, or by downward negotiation or downright negation, such non-repayments leading to currency collapses, suspensions and replacements. The latter option was successfully implemented, for example, by Germany's Currency Commissioner Hjalmar Schacht with his introduction of the Rentenmark on 20th November 1923 that ended the Great Inflation; but whichever solution "works" effectively destroys pensions, savings and house values, as bad money drives out the former values established in the now-forgotten days of better money.

The tipping point of a ship is known as 'Gladwell's Tipping Point', where recovery is no longer possible and the economic perception becomes that certain debts can never be repaid and inflation is the only realistic exit. This economic ship was rolling all over the place in 2009 but was not moving through the water faster than the headwinds and cross-currents, and so was going backwards, which reminds me of...

> Then the bowsprit got mixed with the rudder sometimes...
> But the principal failing occurred in the sailing,
> And the Bellman, perplexed and distressed,
> Said he *had* hoped, at least, when the wind blew due East,
> That the ship would *not* travel due West!

Lewis Carroll explains what is going on between Bellman Bernanke/King and Helmsman Geithner/Darling in *The Hunting of the Snark*: 'The Bellman, who was almost morbidly sensitive about appearances, used to have the bowsprit unshipped once or twice a week to be revarnished, and it more than once happened, when the time came for replacing it, that no one on board could remember which end of the ship it belonged to. They knew it was not of the slightest use to appeal to the Bellman about it – he would only refer to his Naval Code, and read out in pathetic tones Admiralty Instructions which none of them had ever been able to understand – so it generally ended up being fastened on, anyhow, across the rudder. The helmsman used to stand by with tears in his eyes: he knew it was all wrong, but alas! Rule 42 of the Code, *'No one shall speak to the Man at the Helm'*, had been completed by the Bellman himself with the words *'and the Man at the Helm shall speak to no one.'* So remonstrance was impossible, and no steering could be done till the next varnishing day. During these bewildering intervals the ship usually sailed backwards.'

The truth is no one really knows what they are doing, other than struggling through the water as best they can. Meanwhile, it was already clear over the summer of 2009 that the economy had sailed off on holiday as well, and by Q4 what little signs of recovery there were no longer indicated a V recovery in the West and were pointing to an L, U or W instead, or possibly a square root sign like the Bellman's bowsprit, but upwards it most certainly wasn't. The central bankers were tapping their QE gauges but the trouble with QE is you cannot tell anything about what is, or is not, going on, just like you cannot measure the effect of a general stimulus, unlike a targeted stimulus like Cash for Clunkers, but these clunker schemes had ended with Q3, apart from in the UK with its old bangers scheme continuing on. Then, somewhat hilariously, the Governor of the Bank of England summoned the City's economists round to explain their QE strategy, but it was already clear that both the Keynesian stimulists and the QE-reflationists were running out of road, but with not much to show for it. The only country which successfully implemented a general stimulus that clearly worked was China, but as it was part of the 5-year plan anyway, it really was shovel-ready.

The problem of course was with the banks. Much of the QE had ended up back at the Fed and the Bank of England as deposits from the banks. The money had not got out to the real economy, as the banks were deleveraging and not looking for new business. Deleveraging is like playing spillikins, where you have a help stick in order to try to remove one spillikin from the heap at a time without disturbing the other ones. This is a tricky game especially at the beginning, but it slowly speeds up with each new spillikin removed. For example, by mid-2009, $400.0 billion tied up in 29 out of 33 SIVs had been wound down, representing 95% of the total, with big losses for investors, such as Sigma Finance's $2.0 billion SIV which only returned $306.0 million, an 85% loss.

The real problems were still the toxic assets, for which Barclays came up with an apparently ingenious solution, by sending 47 investment bankers/mortgage brokers to sit on a rock in the Cayman Islands with $12.3 billion of the stuff, leaving a tidy receivable over 10 years on the supposedly newly-purged books back in London from the newly incorporated Protium Finance, while Barclays pays Protium $40.0 million a year as a management fee and hopes to receive $16.5 billion back. Some hope, but in a decade from now no one will be any the wiser, but in the 1960s such structures were known as 'playing down your own trouser-leg', and were ridiculed as such. Meanwhile the banks that got caught with loans to LBOs and MBOs and commercial property loans are engaged in debt-for-equity swaps and rescheduling loans forward as they struggle to preserve capital, as the rising unemployment in every major economy is melting plastic and other consumer debt, causing housing repossessions to rise in a reduced market and so bank losses are set to rise. And in Q4 distress in the shipping market appeared as Eastwind Maritime defaulted on its $300.0 million+ debts, but loans by European banks to this sector total $350.0 billion. But signs of new lending are there none, nor even new opportunities for lending, which is more to the point.

Moody's announced in Q3 that losses of UK banks will reach £240.0 billion over the next few years, of which they have so far written off £110.0 billion, while there is still outstanding credit card debt of £54.0 billion. It's the position in the US that is more worrying, however, as the FDIC reported that the banking industry lost $3.7 billion in Q2, with a surge in bad debts from property developers,

SMEs and consumers, with problem banks up to 416 from 305, while 45 banks failed in Q2, making 81 failures YTD. The Q3 US bank earnings reports were bizarre: Goldman Sachs profit for the quarter was $3.19 billion, after deducting the bonus pot which had already reached $16.7 billion YTD and was forecast at $23.0 billion for the year; and JP Morgan reported a $3.6 billion profit against $1.2 billion for Q3 2008, and is forecasting a bonus pot of $29.0 billion for the year. These exceptional profits were generated by fixed income, currency and commodity trading, both as principal and agent, and were fed especially by QE money that had seeped through the underground capitalist aquifers into the stock markets. Finally, Morgan Stanley was back in the black in Q3 with a profit of $757.0 million, after charging employees' remuneration of $5.2 billion.

These sensational results by the investment banks were driven by less competition post-Bear and Lehman and therefore wider margins, plus the booming stock markets around the world which were enjoying the fastest recovery ever from a bear market. It seems that no small amount of QE ended up there rather than in bank lending, from New York, to London, to Shanghai, as it appears stock markets had gotten well ahead of themselves. In sharp contrast, the commercial banks had a torrid Q3: BoA reported a $1.0 billion net loss for Q3, after $9.6 billion credit losses for the quarter, up from $4.4 in Q3 2008, and CEO Ken Lewis's retirement was announced, as well as the news that he would pay back his entire salary for the year and "receive nothing", an oxymoron of an exit for "I've had all the fun I can stand in investment banking" Ken; and Citigroup posted a paltry $102.0 million profit, after writing off $8.0 billion credit losses, but this was turned into a $3.2 billion loss for shareholders after the cost of the share conversion that gave the US Treasury 34% of the equity. Citigroup had now written down $100.0 billion during Global Crunch. As US unemployment heads past 10%, there will be many more billions of credit write-offs to come.

More worrying still, in Irving Fisher's analysis, was that US M3 contracted at 5% pa and the annual pace of bank lending fell by 14% in the Quarter to end-August, from $7,147 billion down to $6,886 billion, and at an epic annual pace of 9% in August alone. The velocity of US M2 or Money Supply has contracted by 12.7% over 2008/9. In Q3 2009 bank lending in the 16-nation €uro-zone contracted by an annual 0.3%, the first decline since the introduction of the €uro in 1999. In effect, the QE treatment isn't working as regards lending because the banks have an over-arching need to deleverage and shrink their balance sheets and thereby maintain capital ratios, while central banks must start by coping with deflation in 2010, then inflation. The outlook for German banks is poor as well, and if the currency pegs in Eastern Europe snap, especially in Rumania and Hungary, they will cause huge losses for the banks there, and also for the Swedish, German, Austrian and Italian banks that lent them the money. And don't even think about Spain, where Moody's latest prognostication was for losses of €108.0 billion over the next five years, of which the majority has not been provided for.

The mathematics of Irving Fisher's theory were attested to by the Great Depression, but Minsky offered no more than a prescient notion of an indeterminable future possibility, but increasingly the creep of government's bureaucracy and financial intrusion as evidenced in the reactions to Global Crunch, together with the incredible profusion in financial services and products, are adding credence to his theory. Indeed, if Global Crunch was the opening bar of the Minsky Moment, it may well be the beginning of the first movement of his Unfinished Symphony ... And then the world economy might fall into the category of that other US economist, the late Herbert Stein, whose even slighter rule said only: "If something cannot go on forever, it will stop". Or, as the Mullah Nasruddin said centuries ago: "Death is Nature's way of telling you to slow down".

Could the crisis that ended the Noughties Decade have been handled in any other way? Yes, by realising that debt levels were too high as a total, but saving the banks' depositors and letting the seriously-collapsed banks fail ahead of their recapitalisation under new management and ownership, (including a welcome return to mutual society status where appropriate), enduring a bad two-year recession or so, but thereby purging the system and reinforcing the "Moral Hazard Territory" for the future.

PART IV:

Where Else Was Affected

EVERYWHERE in the Northern Hemisphere was directly affected and just about everywhere in the Southern Hemisphere indirectly too, so we will start with the EU and work our way around from there, asking 'What sort of Crunch did you have?'

EU Continental

The European Economic Community has come a long way since the Treaty of Rome ushered in the so-called Common Market in 1957, so-called as the earlier Iron and Steel Act of 1953 had locked in a system of subsidies for these basic industries, including for coal. In 1986 at the Treaty of Madrid the Single European Act established the European Union and the Exchange Rate Mechanism, the ERM, the preliminary to establishing the €uro as Europe's own trans-national currency. The €uro was soon introduced by the Treaty of Maastricht in 1993: out went the Deutschemark, the Franc (including the Benelux countries francs), the Lira, the peseta and the Guilder, but the Pound, Swiss Franc, and the Scandinavian and East European countries and Greece, stayed out, leaving the inner core of six adopting the €uro. Subsequently, Greece and Slovenia joined the €uro, while Eastern Europe entered into ERM fixed currency pegs in the new millennium.

A casual observer could surmise that these developments were looking like a version of the United States of Europe, but they would be very wrong to assume anything of the kind. The Anglo-Saxon democracies of the US and UK are distinctly different politico-economic structures to the EU, built on very different philosophies, with different DNA encoded at their creation. The US constitution was "the greatest idea ever struck from the mind of man", according to the great Liberal British PM William Gladstone, as he admired the Jeffersonian principles that elected power should pervade at all levels so that even all government functionaries should be elected. The EU's style is the antithesis, as the continental Europeans, still convinced that democracy gave rise to the fascists who unleashed WW2, prefer that the *fonctionnaires* must be unelected and so invulnerable to public opinion. Not for nothing is the latest EU Treaty of Lisbon in 2009 ten times longer than the US Constitution of just 7,600 words, seeking to appoint an unelected President of the EU, chosen by the EU's 27 Heads of State *in camera* over a slap-up dinner in Brussels, as though he were of equal democratic standing as the President of the US. Even in the UK, whose constitution inspired the US, the elected representatives are constrained to toe the line or face effective de-selection by having the "party whip withdrawn", as they are treated by the main parties as so much pre-ordained lobby-fodder.

As the EU struggles, or doesn't struggle, to create a political union that is truly democratic, its efforts are hamstrung by the democratic deficit inherent in its own bureaucratic federal structure. This vulnerability shows up most in key economic issues, beginning at the European Central Bank, or ECB, and the various economic ministries, because it is not a central bank of a unified political hegemony, as was clear when Global Crunch put the €uro-zone to its first real test. The ECB is beholden to set interest rates to suit its two main constituents, at the Franco-Germanic centre, which cannot possibly be right for those on the fringes, such as Ireland and Spain, which both had unsustainable property booms on the back of their entry into the €uro-zone and the EU's largesse with its Regional Support Grants, but Ireland is now suffering 9% inflation with an interest rate, set by the ECB, stuck on 2%, the sort of highly combustible mixture an atomic scientist would die for.

And it's the same in Spain, where entry to the €uro-zone created an interest rate regime, just as in Greenspan's America and Brown's Britain, which directly fuelled a massive boom and over-build of property, which has gone horribly bust. And Ireland and Spain, whose demographic age profiles put them with the youngest populations in Europe, are facing the highest unemployment rates, approaching 20% and concentrated in the under-27s, and the same percentages pertain in France too for the under-25s. When the backlash of civil commotion gets going, expect the people of Ireland and Spain to lead the charge, with Rumania set to follow.

The second biggest global industry hobbled by Global Crunch was the auto industry. When GM went bust, its UK and EU operations were also threatened with survival. These involved SAAB in Sweden, Opel in Germany and Italy and Belgium, and Vauxhall and Bedford vans in the UK. These European countries immediately set off to save their own industries and no European approach even got off the ground, whereas Washington moved fast to restructure Motown with TARP money. The US "Cash-for-Clunkers" scheme was first adopted by Germany, quickly followed by France and then the UK (and Japan), while the Swedes worked on a domestic solution for SAAB. As Opel was the largest GM employer in Europe, with over 50,000 employees, the 25,000 majority employed in Opel were Germans who commanded first slot in negotiations over its future, while the UK was at the back of the queue to save Vauxhall and Bedford, with 16,000 employees, hardly getting a look-in, whilst reluctantly having to cut government support to the LDV van business and let it go broke. There was no EU-wide co-ordination because the EU is not in reality a functioning political union: passing treaties saying it is, does not mean anything when the chips are down.

Then at the last minute, GM really upset the €uro-cart by withdrawing from the long-protracted sale. And don't even mention the EU's policies on fish, which really stink, and allow Spanish fishing fleets to enter British waters legally for the first time since Raleigh finished his game of bowls at Plymouth Hoe, before he sank the Spanish Armada in 1588.

In May 2009 the IMF pointed out the dysfunctional €uro-zone's banking regulatory regime: €uro-zone institutions had written down less than 20% of projected losses of $900.0 billion by 2010, and €uro-zone banks had a Tier One capital ratio of 7.3% and will need to raise $375.0 billion in fresh capital, compared with US banks' need for $275.0 billion despite a capital ratio of 10.4%. There was a sense that the €uro banks and their regulators had adopted an air of complacency and even disbelief in the face of the reality of Global Crunch. The other fault-line in the EU is Eastern Europe, the former Comecon States that escaped the collapsing communist USSR when the Berlin Wall came down in that seismic year of 1989, which will be examined in some detail below under 'Eastern Europe'.

Euro Punch-Up in the Crunch-Up

The cacophonous world of the EU was thrown up for all to see when Global Crunch blew away the rhetoric and revealed the shenanigans behind the scenes. The following exercise in pure EU gobbledy-gook is taken from actual quotations at Euro-summits from EU leaders responding to the Crunch, with a touch of licence for the author to play continuo, by chucking in the odd splash of prurient sauce to make the debate have some discernible taste.

Starring GORDON "SUPERMAN" BROWN, ANGELA "PRUDENT" MERKEL and SUPER-SARKO, playing respectively the *'Saviour of the World'*, the *'Swabian Housewife'*, and the *'Bed-Hopper'*

GORDON BROWN (UK's Prime Minister):
"We saved the world!"

[Fraudian slip: he meant to say he 'saved the British banks'!]

PEER STEINBRÜCK (Germany's Finance Minister) reacts:
"Crass Keynesianism!"

THOMAS MAYER (Chief Economist, Deutsche Bank):
"I believe we are in a once-in-a-century event where you really do need drastic economic stimulus. We are facing the true Keynesian moment."

GERMANY'S POET LAUREATE:
"Mr. Steinbrück is doing a remarkable amount of damage. If Germany prevents an effective European response, this adds significantly to the severity of the global downturn."

ANGELA MERKEL (Germany's Chancellor), stealing Brown's favourite line:
"I will be Prudent!"

SARKOZY (France's President) aka 'SARKO':
"Oh, zut alors! Tu es Madame Non!"

MERKEL:
"I certainly won't get pregnant with debt just to please the siren voices!"

STEINBRÜCK:
"Rightz! No sliding down ze moral slippery slope into recession. I will give a stimulus of just 0.2% of GDP. Who's saying Germany is going down by 4% in 2009? I don't believe it. Zat's not in my plan!"

[German GDP went down by 6.9% for the year ended March 2009, as its exports fell 16%, and its fiscal deficit for 2009 was 4.2%.]

BROWN:
"It wasn't in mine either: I thought I had got rid of 'Boom and Bust', but then everything went wrong in America, for which I am not responsible!"

[Brown remains in denial for the rest of the show]

Ms ULRIKE GUÉROT (Berlin Head of EC Foreign Relations):
"Cars are emotional here. Italians like Sarko's bride do clothes. We do cars. We can't let that fall apart!"

STEINBRÜCK:
"I vill balanz my budgetz."

He fumbles for his portable calculator-cum-chess-set, on which he lost out on Move 35 to the world champion.

"I betz half a case of wine zat I will do this by 2011!"

[So he can keep the other half if he loses?]

BROWN:
"In time for my 2012 Olympics, where our gold reserves will rise at a faster rate than yours!"

MERKEL (sounding like the great she-elephant of yore, Lady Thatcher):
"We Germans must take our *Verantwortung*★ very seriously, like the good responsible Swabian housewife that I aim to be. We cannot live beyond our means in the long run."
                              ★Responsibilty

BROWN:
"In the long run we are all dead!"

[He smiles to himself, as he realizes he has just quoted JM Keynes accurately, with no spin intended.]

MERKEL, thinking ahead to those 2012 Olympics in London:
"We are not going to participate in this senseless race for billions."

STEFFEN KAMPETER (German MP quoted in *Der Spiegel*):
"After years of lecturing us how we need to share in the gains of uncontrolled financial markets, New Labour politicians can't now expect us to share in their losses."

JOHN JUNGCLAUSSEN (UK Correspondent for *Die Zeit*):
"These pompous, hyper-active, noisy people in London telling us we're not doing enough, not daring enough, not moving fast enough ..."

GUÉROT:

"You're going to have an 8% deficit in the UK, you're renationalizing the Banks, refusing to lower taxes: it's very scary for Germany."

[In 2009, this is exactly what Germany had to do, continuing into 2010.]

BROWN:

"Who's playing internal politics now? Hey, that's my game!"

JUNGCLAUSSEN, still dreaming:

"… Germany is so reticent to move, slower to change. Britain has the ability to change on the hoof. Achtung! They still have their own currency!"

[He starts slowly whimpering.]

SARKO, railing at Airbus's strategy to source components from outside Euroland:

"We didn't create the €uro so that we couldn't build the whole of an aeroplane in the EU!"

[Thinks: 'Why did we create this suffocating, job-destroying single currency, then?']

JOSÉ MANUEL BARROSO (EU President.):

"Don't worry! People in high places in Britain want to join the €uro, but I will not name them."

[As they are traitors – understood. Thinks: 'When they join we'll shut them up for good with our democratic deficit, and then strangle their economy as without the Pound they cannot do anything without our €uro say-so, and then they will be at our mercy!']

LORENZO BINI SMAGHI, the man we've all been waiting for, (ECB International Affairs):

"Great Britain does not meet the entry criteria for the €uro."

[Huge cheers all round!]

"The Public Sector Deficit will rise to around 6% of GDP in 2009 [actually 8% at least] and even higher in 2010. Sterling's exchange rate is not yet sufficiently stable."

[Huge sighs of relief all round!]

[BARROSO dreams:
'Aah! These unelected B€urocrats! Why don't we do the reshuffle thing, just like the British do?']

BROWN, a confused closet-Europhile and would-be Patriot, looks knowingly at BARROSO:
"I need some relief after that Smaghetti chap. Err... where's the €urinal?"

Those who think the UK will join the €uro any time soon are about as short-sighted as those who think the €uro will stay together indefinitely as currently constituted, as Germany strengthens and all the others, except France, weaken. The structure of the €uro was never designed to cope with a global crisis.

Germany, and Austria

One has to sympathise with the German position as, ever since reunification in 1990, they have swallowed the hard economic medicine in doses that would not be accepted in the Anglo-sphere world today, but early in 2009 reality dawned in Berlin that there really was a crisis on, and the Government announced a €50.0 billion, or 1% of GDP stimulus package, with a cash contribution of €2,500 towards the purchase of every new German car. Germany's banks were woefully slow to own up to their toxic bad debts, until the Bundesbank and the regulator BaFin investigated twenty leading banks and did the job for them and in early 2009 estimated their losses at €300.0 billion, of which only a quarter had been written off. A few months later, in May 2009, a BaFin internal memo stated that the level of toxic assets on German bank balance sheets had risen to €816.0 billion and they needed €203.0 billion of additional capital: Hypo Real's "problematic" assets were €268.0 billion, followed by HSH Nordbank at €105.0 billion and Commerzbank with €101.0 billion, the latter two also having lent heavily into the collapsing shipping sector: ships are a worse asset class than housing in a slump, as you can't foreclose on the sea, and they cost money to lay up when you shut the front door. When Deutsche Bank announced Q4 2008 losses of €3.9 billion, its boss called for the setting up of a 'bad bank'. Finance Minister Herr Peer Steinbrück, living on his own on Planet Frankfurt, exclaimed: "How could I take such a proposal to the federal parliament? The nation would think we'd gone crazy!"

Commerzbank of Frankfurt announced in November 2008 that it was drawing on €8.2 billion from the German Markets Stabilisation Fund to strengthen its capital base, raising the bank's core capital ratio to 11.2%, and the bank will pay no dividend for 2009 or 2010, as it announced losses of €4.7 billion for 2008 and 2009 was not set to be any better. In May 2009 Commerzbank drew an additional €10.0 billion from the German government, and in August agreed to buy Dresdner Bank from Allianz Insurance for €9.8 billion, but that deal proceeded at a lower price, with the Government agreeing to invest €18.0 billion for a 25% stake in Commerzbank. Hypo Real Estate was seeking €500.0 billion from the Government, while HSH Nordbank received €13.0 billion from the Länder of Hamburg and Schleswig-Holstein, BayernLB was seeking another €5.4 billion on top of the €10.0 billion it received in 2008, and WestLB wanted €4.0 billion. Deutsche Bank, however, avoided a direct Government equity bail-out by acquiring the German Post Office Bank, Deutsche Postbank, owned 30% by the Government, by issuing 8% of its own shares. Perhaps the assessment in November 2009 by the Bundesbank was nearer the mark: this venerable institution's view was that German banking losses in 2010 would be €90.0 billion.

It was the failure of the Austrian Creditanstalt Bank in May 1931 that triggered the double-dip W that led directly to The Great Depression, so it was not surprising when the ECB ordered the Austrian Government to nationalise its sixth largest bank, Hypo Bank with assets of €42.0 billion, in December 2009. Its previous owner, Bayern LB, was rewarded with a single €1.0 for their former 67%-owned subsidiary, as they wrote off €825.0 million in loans. Austria's banks, including Hypo, had exposure of €230.0 billion to

Eastern Europe, equivalent to 70% of Austria's GDP. The full extent of the debt crisis in the East is dealt with below.

France

Société Générale in Paris got January 2008 off to an inelegant start with the announcement that a junior rogue trader, Jérôme Kerviel, had lost €4.9 billion in unauthorised and unregulated trading. The French bankers handled it superbly over a week-end and by the time the announcement was made later on the Monday, all the loss-making trades had already been unwound and Société Générale had been recapitalized, all done with supreme timeliness and elegance as only the French can do and, it goes without saying, all in complete contravention of strict EU rules on competition and subsidies. Bravo! The really odd part of this strange saga was that the French public, noted for their rather outré sense of humour, found it hilarious that a major bank had been taken to the cleaners and Monsieur Kerviel, when he surfaced from hiding, must have been somewhat surprised to find himself a national hero for his lone part in nearly bringing a major institution to its knees. In 2009, the prosecutors are after Evil Kerviel for falsifying documents, abuse of trust, and computer hacking. He faces a maximum five years in jail and €375,000 in fines, for building his position of €49.0 billion at risk, equivalent to the bank's entire market capitalization, from which he never personally profited by a cent.

After this bad opening to the year, President Sarkozy was the first in Continental Europe to appreciate the scale of the global problem and announced a €26.5 stimulus programme in October 2008, and was soon working on a package to shore up a bail-out for France's successful auto industry, in a range of €5.0 to €10.0 billion. His real problem, though, was Airbus, which has no alternative but to procure increasing numbers of components from outside the €uro-zone, not to mention the new A 320 production line in China, so that its selling prices are lower, a strategy that the UK's Rolls Royce started implementing twenty years ago when it bought Allison Aero-engines in the US as its Trojan Horse into that huge market. The state-owned Renault and the stock market-listed Peugeot got the message of the job-destroying €uro in 2004 and have since set up manufacturing plants to produce 1.0 million vehicles a year in East Europe. The Single Currency saves currency exchange costs but at a huge price, as the 'One-Size-Fits-All' doesn't mean 'One-Size-Suits-All', and the side-effects are deflationary unemployment within the €uro-zone and uncompetitive export prices for anything moving beyond it. As the €uro-dollar rate moved towards $1.50 in Q4 2009, Mme Christine Lagarde, France's Finance Minister, complained that "it was intolerable that Europe should pay the price" for a dysfunctional link between the US dollar and the dollar-pegged Chinese renminbi. Those who create glass-houses should have first thought about the stones this contrived €uro-zone market would have thrown at them.

If Kerviel got Global Crunch off to a bad start for France, Sarkozy ended 2009 with a truly shocking state-corporatist borrowing plan, *Le Grand Emprunt*, to raise €35.0 billion to finance five new universities and investments in renewable energy and the digital economy, all of which are expensive and easy places to lose money. The record of politicians making a dash for the future, and this time with borrowed money, is not a good one. France's state finances were in comparatively good shape before this mega-debt was taken on, but now they're back level with the rest of the herd.

Ireland

As the downturn developed, it became clear that the soft under-belly of Europe within the €uro-zone could not possibly hold their own with the northern industrial giants of Germany, France and Northern Italy. This fact became increasingly apparent with the widening spreads in the 10-year €uro-bond markets: whereas the €uro is purportedly a pan-European currency, it is denominated right down to its coins into the respective issuing countries – just in case it ever blows apart. German citizens had already begun demanding change in shops in German-denominated €uros as early as 2007, following the markets differing €uro-bonds' pricing. The first country to see the splits in the €uro-markets was Ireland.

During the Maastricht Treaty debates in the early 1990s I had edited and contributed to a symposium book against the whole undemocratic affair called *Visions of Europe*. I telephoned that great

Irish figure Conor Cruise O'Brien and invited him to contribute, but his reaction was succinct and he wasted no time at all.

"No! Why would I want to write against an organisation that is giving Ireland a lot of money, now?" I was flabbergasted. "We Irish are not stupid, you know: if someone is determined to give us money for a 'Yes' vote, of course we'll vote 'Yes!'"

"But what if it leads to long-term problems?"

"Then, having checked first that there's no more money coming our way, we'll say 'Good-bye, nice knowing you', and vote 'No!'" And with that he put the 'phone down, with a Celtic chuckle.

Just before Christmas 2008, the Irish Government announced it was in talks to rescue its three major banks with an injection of €7.0 billion. Anglo-Irish Bank had been hit especially hard, with its shares down 98% in 2008. The problem for all three banks was, yes, the collapse of the residential and commercial property markets, which had taken off after Ireland joined the €uro and its consequent low interest rates sparked a completely unsustainable property boom in the small Irish economy, especially when inflation set in, as €uro-rates were far too low to constrain rampant inflation at nearly 10%. Anglo Irish Bank's negotiating position was undermined when it was revealed that its chairman, Sean Fitzpatrick, had enjoyed the benefit of loans for €87.0 million from the bank over eight years, which had been hidden from Anglo-Irish's accounts by moving them a day before the year-end over to rival lender Irish Nationwide, as the "golden circle" looked after its own. A condition of the bail-out was that the entire board of Degenerate Persons resigned.

Ireland had let wages spiral up during the boom, eating away at competitiveness, and as at the end of 2008 its currency denominated in €uros was up 29% while interest on its €uro-bonds cost 180 basis points above Germany's, house prices were forecast by Fitch to fall by 45%, unemployment was 4% and set to rise to 12.5% in 2009 and to 15.5% by 2011, as GDP was set to contract by 4% p.a. and the national debt is set to double to €160.0 billion by 2013, with public sector pay down by 7% and a further 6% in 2010. And when the Irish voted for the Lisbon Treaty in October 2009, having previously rejected it, how much do you think the unelected B€urocrats of Brussels had agreed to support Ireland's National Asset Management Agency's €54.0 billion fund to buy up its banks' toxic assets? In the €uro-zone, you see, the 'One-Size-Fits-All' comes with Regional Support Grants to lever you into your €uro-tunic and keep you there. And just how unwise was the late Conor Cruise O'Brien's delight at the prospect of what he grossly misperceived as a €uro-free lunch.

Iceland and a New Banking Rule

Iceland has about the same population at 300,000-plus as Citigroup had employees at the end of 2008; that, and the fact that they were both for all intents and purposes bust, is about all they had in common. And yet the coincidental story of this tiny nation and the world's biggest bank brought about a new perception in the crisis, about what banks could be saved and what could not, that was to have a positive impact on sentiment towards the Dollar, which rose by 20% between July 2008 and March 2009, before losing much of this gain as confidence returned, just as it should have done in its role as the world's reserve currency.

Iceland's bankers and businessmen went madly after overseas assets in the 2000s, especially in the UK: Kaupthing Bank acquired the old-style merchant bank Singer & Friedlander in London which had acquired a stock-broking arm in 1986's Big Bang and was also heavily engaged in property lending, as was its own UK subsidiary Heritage Bank. So Kaupthing formed the internet Icebank to attract UK deposits with high yields, which are the real sucker's punch. The depositors lured into this death-trap included the usual Degenerate Persons list of greedy idiots, such as Local Councils, Oxbridge Colleges, Government Agencies, Charities and individual investors, whose deposits funded the acquisition of retail and leisure assets by the Icelandic Baugur Group and associates from House of Fraser, Hamleys and retail food chains to West Ham United Football Club, for goodness sake! Iceland's three leading banks were insolvent and were worthless. Landbanski, the biggest, had its UK assets seized by the UK Government, and under the anti-terrorism laws would you believe, and Glitnir was nationalised, as the country sought monetary injections from the IMF, Russia and Sweden. And Baugur itself collapsed in early February 2009.

159

If you had put $100,000 into Citigroup stock on Monday 17th November 2008, however, it was only worth $50,000 a week later on Friday 21st November, and half your loss was on that Friday. If you had put your $100,000 into Citigroup stock a year earlier, it would have been worth just $9,000 on that Friday. This is definitely not what one expects when one puts one's money into a bank, that it "evaporates" quite like that, but we're talking shares here, not deposits.

These extraordinary times were throwing up a whole startling new equation, starkly expressed as follows: is the banking sector bigger than the rest of your country's economy, or GDP? Answer 'Yes', your country, like Iceland, has a problem; Answer 'No', your country, like America, may have a solution. When the banking sector outgrows the size of its domestic economy as it did in Iceland, it either goes ex-growth or goes overseas for deposits and lending opportunities, and if it then encounters problems, the domestic economy is not big enough to mount a rescue, so in comes the IMF.

Now, the collapse of Citigroup's share price was indicating that it was practically bust, but as it's so big Uncle Sam couldn't afford to let it go bust. The good news is that the rest of Uncle Sam's economy is bigger than its banking sector, much, much bigger in fact, so it can save Citigroup, but at a cost. Who pays for the bail-out? Why, Uncle Sam's captive audience, the US-taxpayer in the first instance. The ensuing bail-out package for Citigroup had an interest-ing structure, not least as it was based on US-taxpayer funds but curiously didn't need Congressional approval: $20.0 billion followed an earlier $25.0 billion from the TARP Fund, and the US Government took $7.0 billion of extra equity at 8% p.a., while the existing dividend was pegged at a penny per share; there was a pool of toxic mortgages of $300.0 billion identified, on which the bank took the first $29.0 billion of losses, plus 10% of any excess, and the bank agreed to extend better terms to these debtors all insured by the US-taxpayer.

That's a whole better deal for the taxpayer than the first proposal for the Government to buy out toxic assets from the banks lock, stock and barrel, which is why Citigroup's share price collapsed on that announcement, but the insurance aspect would have been better for US-taxpayers if they had just taken shares and, if necessary taken the whole lock, stock and barrel. Uncle Sam may suffer a lost year or two of economic growth, and a good investment opportunity, but Citigroup will probably live to grow again another day. The point not to be missed, however, is that there was no one appointed to represent the best interests of the taxpayer in these arrangements, nor in many others, including across the Atlantic.

Now, what about Gordon Brown's Britain? Well, the big problem is that the rest of the real economy is small in relation to the banks and financial sectors, which is hardly surprising as the one named after the colour brown has overseen the loss of 750,000 jobs in manufacturing and replaced them with 750,000 unproductive jobs in bureaucracy, which the Government has to pay for, year-in-year-out, which means ... so you get the point, don't you? Now, Barclays Bank has debts which are one-and-a-half times as big as the brown ones ... need we go on? So what would happen if Barclays or HBOS or RBS goes completely broke, or all three of them? HMG cannot bail out any one of them for their total liabilities. All HMG could do is guarantee their Sterling transactions – that would be an Icelandic moment for Britain for sure.

And what about Switzerland? It's a small enough economy in which its banks account for 20% of GDP and one of these, the once mighty UBS, got badly caught out by US CDOs of toxic waste to the tune of $58.0 billion and by a collapse of confidence in its private wealth management division, following US tax evasion charges over management of US clients accounts. UBS received a massive $59.2 billion bail-out from its government and central bank in October. And the combined debts of UBS and Credit Suisse equal seven times GDP. A major advantage over Gordon Brown's Britain, however, is that` Switzerland has a current account surplus of 16% of GDP and is the only country in the world, apart from Norway, which has fully-funded reserves for all its medical and pension liabilities, and so this state can afford to pay its own way out of trouble.

The EU PIGS – Portugal, Italy, Greece and Spain

Ireland wasn't the only country having a problem keeping up with Germany: the PIGS at the €uro-trough were also in trouble, namely,

Portugal, Italy, Greece and Spain. The PIGS are the soft underbelly of Europe, those countries that have no long term hope of keeping up with the inner circle juggernaut countries led by the reunited Germany.

Spain's bonds were at 122 basis points above Germany's Bunds when S&P stripped Spain of its AAA status, as it predicted that Spain's debt will rise to 18% of GDP in 2009 and as the EU predicted that unemployment will rise to 19% in 2010. On Sunday 18th January 2009, 35,000 unionists marched through Zaragoza to demand "job creation". By 22nd January 2009, Spain's bonds had slipped further to over 130 basis points above, Italy's and Portugal's to over 150 above, Ireland to over 270 over and Greece, downgraded by S&P to A-, to over 290 basis points above the benchmark bond yield, the German 10-year Bund. The elastic in the 'One-Size-Fits-All' €uro-zone was fast becoming stretched to the limit. The idea that Greece should be in the €uro-zone, with a deficit of 12% and national debt of 135% of GDP and rising through £270.0 billion, is an absurdity. It was already clear that the €uro-zone should for all practical purposes be confined to Germany and France as the economic axis of the western continent, Holland because of its gas exports to Germany, the Benelux countries because they are not economically material on their own and their geographical and cultural ties are to these countries, and Italy, or more sensibly, Northern Italy.

Why Northern Italy? Because Southern Italy's economy is so weak in relation to Northern Italy's, where all the commerce and industry is based, that the South needs its own Lira to enjoy the competitive advantage just to keep up, a point not lost on President Berlusconi nor on the architects of the Single Currency with their Regional Support Grants. Spain's and Portugal's economies were always a €uro-step too far, but an Iberian €uro with a competitive advantage could also work well for Eastern Europe and Greece, an Iberian-Baltic-Balkan or an IBB€, a practical idea that would set up the two-track inner and an outer €uro-zones so detested by those in the inner zone. Although Italy was originally designated one of the PIGS, as the 2009 downturn developed, it looked increasingly as though Ireland would replace her in this acronym of the walking-wounded, as Italy's forecast deficit for 2010 is surprisingly less then Germany's.

I remember clearly driving into San Sebastian in 2006 and being utterly dumbfounded by the amount of ugly tower-bock apartments going up all over the outskirts, none of them finished, so all of them were empty. It seemed as though every builder in the region had decided to come to this old town and start building on a massive scale and all at the same time too. And who was going to live in these endless towers, I wondered. In September 2009 we had the answer: no one. There are 1,623,000 houses and apartments on the market in Spain, with a normal annual demand of 218,000 dwellings, indicating an overhang of nearly eight years supply. The construction industry will shrink from 18% of GDP to just 5%, while GDP is contracting by 11% for the next three years, according to the Madrid-based RR de Acunya research company.

Then I was astonished to watch the giant Spanish construction company Ferrovial. S.A. bid top dollar for BAA, the British Airports Authority, which owns Heathrow, Gatwick, Stansted and four regional airports. BAA is a regulated operation, which means the government controls the prices and therefore the profits and the investment required to be made by the owner, which you thought would be enough to put most investors off, and the timing was awful, towards the end of the Short Cycle. More amazing still, the acquisition was funded almost entirely by debt, of £10.8 billion! Then, as had been widely telegraphed, the UK government moved to split up this monopoly, and Ferrovial was looking at selling off businesses affected by the downturn, where would-be buyers would also have difficulty in raising their finance. Ferrovial eventually received a bid of £1.5 billion from the US Global Infrastructure Projects for Gatwick, which will just about enable it to stay in the survival game.

Then in June 2007 HSBC sold its Canary wharf HQ in London to Spain's property developer Metrovacesa for £1.09 billion, lending the buyer £800.0 million. At December 2008 Metrovacesa had failed to refinance the loan as Global Crunch killed the credit markets, so HSBC bought its HQ back at cost plus interest for £838.0, a bigger haircut than Raleigh had given the Spanish Armada in 1588, or as he termed it in that more elegant age, his 'singeing of the King of Spain's beard', that so endeared him to the first Queen Elizabeth. What on earth were the Spanish up to? They had joined the €uro at the wrong time and at the wrong rate, just as the UK had done in October 1990, and on entry their interest rates halved and for most of the 2000s were at a real rate of minus 2%! This is what is wrong with the €uro's 'One-Size-Fits-All' deflationary side-effect.

Spain's private and corporate debt rose to 230% of GDP, funded by French and German savings. Unemployment is at 19%, with youth unemployment at 41%, figures not seen since the Great Depression that saw the Dictator Franco come to power after the Civil War. Spain is the first major western member of the EU to be entering depression, as Moody's downgraded its own subprime mortgage debts, known as Cedulas, and many state regional debts from Aaa to Aa1 in December 2009. The problem is that being in the €uro-zone Spain cannot devalue or even engage in a stimulus package. Spain is caught in a straitjacket, a place where *manyana* is here today and is not about to go away, as this bust economy hunkers down for a long *siesta*. The real question is, how long will the Spanish people endure this misery for the supposed benefits of being in the €uro-zone.

Eastern Europe

The fledgling ex-communist democracies, who were all lining up to join the €uro-zone, have had their property-led booms stopped dead in their tracks by the credit crunch, and by pegging their currencies to the €uro at fixed exchange rates. Austrian banks have been liberally lending, up to 70% of its own GDP, and the same percentage of its financial profits come from the East: their Swiss Franc and €uro-denominated mortgage loans to locals and foreign second-home buyers in the Baltic States, Hungary, Rumania, Bulgaria and elsewhere, are threatened by the collapse of local currencies and property markets, creating a nasty double-whammy for both borrowers and the banks who unwisely assumed the East European story was a safe one. In October, Austria announced a $130.0 billion bank aid package and soon announced an expansion injection of $2.7 billion into

Erste Group Bank, and December saw the state rescue of Hypo Bank.

By far the largest country to the east is the Ukraine, an original signatory to the United Nations Charter in 1945, and its problems in 2008 were manifold: inflation at 25%, stockmarket down 80% and the currency, the Hryvnia, at a seven year low against the Dollar; and having the sixth largest bank, Prominvest, experiencing a Northern Rock-style run completes this doom-laden outlook. And that's before the political vacuum is included: with Russian tanks recently making incursions into Georgia, the West has no alternative but to intervene in the Eastern democracies in the form of the IMF, with Sweden propping up the Baltic and Germany and Austria the Balkans, as there is no concerted EU move to formulate an Eastern Europe support plan.

The IMF has been fairly inactive in recent years, as leverage took over the world, and its reserves were not as high as they needed to be in this crisis. Its available funds were a modest $200.0 billion, the same as the bail-out for Fannie Mae and Freddie Mac, but they could whistle up another $50.0 billion, which did not add up to much of a war chest in 2008/9. The Ukraine, for example, needed $14.0 billion, which is just a fifth of the $55.0 billion - $66.0 billion it needs in 2009 to roll over short term loans, pay interest on other debts and finance the rest of its current account deficit. Hungary is much richer than the Ukraine, with GDP per Capita three times higher, but it is still in trouble: public debt at 60% of GDP is high for the region, the budget deficit was 9% in 2006 and the current account deficit in 2008 was 5.5%. The ECB had to lend €5.0 billion in October 2008 and the IMF $2.5 billion in November.

The youngest EU entrants are experiencing mixed conditions. Estonia and Latvia have enjoyed boom conditions in their own property markets, financed by foreign banks such as Sweden's Swedbank, which has a $32.0 billion loan book in the Baltic States alone, which turned to bust in 2008, as did Rumania's, whose economy was reasonably strong, but where the IMF has also been called in for a $2.8 billion loan. Bulgaria, however, is running a current account deficit of 24% in 2008, whereas Poland has public debt at 40%, growth at 6% and inflation at only 4.5%, and is the star of this economically lustreless but geo-politically strategic pack.

The Arabian Gulf

In the Spring of 2008 my partners and I were engaged on a fund-raising tour of the Middle East, visiting the capitals of Kuwait, Bahrain, Qatar, the UAE, comprising both Abu Dhabi and Dubai and others, Oman on the Indian Ocean and eastern Saudi Arabia. I had first visited the region after the first oil price hike in 1975 and fell in love with the purity of the desert and the manners and courtesy of the Arabs, their integrity and honesty in business, and the safety within their societies. I remember when Dubai had only one hotel, the old Carlton, and when Deira side gave way to the desert after only a few streets running parallel to the Creek. The Emirates had decided, however, to link their currency the Dirham to the US Dollar, so that the Fed's low interest rates in the 2000s had also fuelled strong liquidity growth in the UAE for over a decade.

About this time in the early-1970s, I and some others were enjoying dinner with the former MP and land econometrician Andrew MacLaren (d. 1975) at the 'Good Earth' Chinese restaurant, which is now in the Brompton Road near Harrods, but back then was in the Earls Court Road, when the man on the next table interrupted and said he could not help but over-hear our conversation about how land values were created by the expansion of a community's economy, starting out from the most central and valuable sites and progressively on towards the more economically marginal land. He joined our table and his eyes were opened by MacLaren's exposition of the process.

Our charming self-invited guest was Easa Saleh Al-Gurg, advisor and banker to Sheik Rashid Al-Maktoum, the Ruler and effectively the landlord of the Kingdom of Dubai. Easa took what he heard back to Dubai, and thus was conceived the idea of the Al-Jumeirah development plan, the idea of selling the land to developers to set them up with the value to spur and finance otherwise unimaginable and non-financeable developments. Easa later became the UAE's ambassador to the UK and his name is inscribed as one of the donors on the low wall by the gates in honour to Her Majesty the Queen Elizabeth the Queen Mother at Hyde Park Corner. Little did he or any of us foresee where the seeds sown that evening would spring up and flower, nor did Easa know that MacLaren had held exactly similar conversations in London between the wars with his fiend in exile, King Abdul-Aziz bin Saud of Saudi Arabia. They had both, however, missed MacLaren's intended point, that the value created by such expansion, in that it related to the unimproved land belonged to the Community, but not the Landlord.

I visited Easa in Dubai in 1974 at the Headquarters of the old BBME Bank on Deira side. Tea was served on a silver salver. I can remember the manager of the bank, a Mr. Mason, telling Easa not to expand any more at the present time as "the cycle was about to turn down", and the advice was immediately accepted by his chairman. Easa's businesses included furnishings, an agency for Siemens and other services, which all expanded over the following years, but in a carefully controlled way.

Just 35 years on and the transformation on view everywhere, except one city, could never have been imagined back then. And the exception? It is Al-Khobar, on the eastern coast of Saudi Arabia, just proximate to Dhahran, where the offices of the Arabian-American Oil Company, Aramco, are located. Saudi is the richest member of OPEC by far, but Al-Khobar looked run down, rather like one of those dreary British towns that never seem to advance, much like Newport in South Wales for example, where the ONS, the Office of National Statistics, juggles with the numbers every month and with belated corrections; in Al-Khobar, the mood was summed up in the listless youths hanging around the otherwise empty streets, as though they could be possible targets for future Al Qa'eda recruitment. In the bar of the Intercontinental Hotel in Dubai I met a Saudi businessman on holiday and asked him about this strange phenomenon.

"You see, Saudi is not like Dubai with its glitz and glitter. The difference is that Saudi Arabia is the spiritual home of the Prophet Mohammed and does not feel it can subscribe to western-style decadence and shows of wealth. We have the Holy cities of Mecca and Medina to think about, you see".

But, of course.

The single most astonishing fact during this visit was to see that inflation throughout the Gulf was nearing 30% on the back of oil prices that topped at $147.0 per barrel, and this was driving an unimaginable construction boom of incredible proportions, which in turn was sucking in so much in imports that the docks and supply lines were choked, causing prices to rise to the point where the immigrant workers couldn't afford the local prices and send remittances home as well, and so they were going home in droves instead. You could smell the oncoming collapse was already in the air. When it arrived a year later post-Lehman, just about all developments stopped, especially in Dubai which must have been the biggest single development site ever seen in the world, now all abruptly stopped, that is apart from the iconic kilometre-high 160-floor Burj sky-dagger that herald's the post-Global Crunch blind optimism for the future, which is being built by Emaar, whose shares fell by an initial 67%, until the further falls to come.

And the £13.5 million fireworks' display, also the biggest the world had ever seen, that announced the grandest opening possible of the £1.0 billion Atlantis Resort on The Palm Jumeirah reclaimed island by Nakheel Construction, came with a different type of announcement as well, that the grandiose million-pound houses on the same Palm, bought by celebrities such as Michael Schumacher, David Beckham, Brad Pitt and Angolina Jolie for up to £5.0 million seven years earlier, had now lost 40% of their value. Then Moody's calculated that Dubai's public debt at $47.0 billion was 103% of its GDP, while the UAE pumped $33.0 billion liquidity into the banks of this seven-states region to maintain confidence, but Dubai's total debt load alone was $80.0 billion, more than double this liquidity boost.

Inevitably, Nakheel Construction and its parent Dubai World sought a six-month moratorium on their $60.0 billion debts in November 2009, which included a Sharian Islamic *Sukuk* or "utmost good faith" Bond of $4.0 billion issued by Nakheel, a move that shook the world's credit markets, especially as Abu Dhabi had on the same day just advanced another $5.0 billion, following an earlier injection of $10.0 billion. One of the problems is that no one knows the status under Sharia law of this situation, because no one has written it yet. It became immediately apparent that the State of Dubai was not going to stand behind its 100.0%-owned company Dubai World, and equally apparent that Abu Dhabi was not going to bail-out Dubai: instead they were taking the hood off the Abu Dhabi hawk to get ready to pick the carcase clean at knocked-down prices. When they had looked at the books for a month, however, it became apparent that Abu Dhabi would have to put in another $10.0 billion working capital just to keep the "restructuring" on course and to avoid negative sentiment in the capital markets. If Easa and Mr. Mason had still been in charge in Dubai, this reckless expansion would never have occurred. My guess is that the eventual losses in Dubai will be $20.0 to $30.0 billion. Are the excesses of Dubai an indicatory prelude to the ongoing banking crisis?

The BRICs: Brazil, Russia, India, China

As late as 1 November 2008, *The Economist* was still writing that the emerging markets led by the BRICs, especially the BICs rather than Russia, 'will determine whether the world faces a mild recession or something nastier', a view expressed by many others including London's *The Times*. Within a month, such was the speed with which the banking crisis from the US and UK had turned first, into a recession in the Anglo-sphere world and then into a global recession, that this optimistic outlook was completely dashed within just a month, as the BRICS all went into severe contraction themselves. In particular, the economies of Russia and China were sustained by exports rather than a domestic-led economy and suffered the quickest and most: Russia's exports of gas and oil suffered from plunging energy prices, while demand for China's manufactures from the West simply dried up.

Brazil

Brazil is the odd one out in this review for several reasons. First, it is the only country in the Southern Hemisphere, whereas Global Crunch pervaded the Northern Hemisphere, so keenly foreseen by my news-vendor on Trocadero. Secondly, it was Latin America's uncontrolled inflation and credit expansion that was the scourge of bankers in the 1980s and 1990s, but not during the Global Crunch, as they had not fallen for Anglo-sphere style of leverage, having had enough visits from the IMF during the era of their emerging economies. Indeed, Brazil's last loan from the IMF for $30.4 billion in mid-2002 was repaid one year ahead of time in 2005.

The economy has come a long way since Old Blue Eyes sang "They've got an awful lot of coffee in Brazil". There is now the Embraer Aircraft Company, auto plants by GM, Volkswagen and the Japanese manufacturers, a burgeoning electrical goods sector, iron ore and steel, minerals, foodstuffs and textiles and footwear, all with big export potential. Brazil was facing a steadily rising GDP and an expansion of wealth creation, until the dollar's devaluation began to turn the Brazilian real into a hard currency with all the problems that are besetting the €uro, namely a job-destroying erosion of this new industrial base, after the Real's 42% rise against the dollar between Q1 and Q4 2009.

Hans Redecker is the currency chief of BNP Parisbas and so he knows what it feels like: "Brazil is not willing to take any more of the adjustment burden as long as China and other surplus countries do nothing", such as what, exactly? Answer: stop tying the Renminbi to the Dollar, I presume. Brazil is retaliating with a 2% tax on new money into bond and equity markets so as to head off an assumed dollar-imported asset bubble. Many people have forgotten, but not the Brazilians, that the biggest markets in the world are the FX markets, which Soros's Quantum Fund exploited so brilliantly against the Bank of England on "White Wednesday" in 1992.

Russia

The Communist military-command economy collapsed along with the Berlin Wall in 1989. In 1992, the acting Prime Minister Yegor Gaidar, (1956-2009), followed the path of Poland and Ludwig Erhard and abolished price and production controls overnight, firing the first shot for economic liberation, or so the people thought. In October 1992, President Boris Yeltsin began the Russian-style privatisation of all the state's assets, by issuing vouchers to the 144 million citizens as their share of the SOEs, or 'State-owned Enterprises', and real estate across the country. Millions received shares, including in their own apartments, but they had no idea of their purpose or value. They had not had the benefit of the UK's "Tell Sid" TV campaign to alert them to the opportunity in store for them, and the presence of the former Degenerate Persons of the KGB meant that the rise of the equally Degenerate Person Monopolygarcks and their ownership over the key industries of oil, gas, minerals, steel, aluminium and industry was assured, as they together bilked the Russian people of the assets held in their name by the now-collapsed communist state, which assets had a value of $1.0+ trillion, or over $1,000,000,000,000, and such seizures birthed their own Monopolygarck status. Great fortunes are always made by those who are alert and in the right position to exploit the collapse of the old regime.

The chill economic wind from the West began to hit Russia after the Lehman collapse and, Komrad, was it freezing? Russia, however, entered Global Crunch with $600.0 billion in foreign currency reserves, courtesy of its oil and gas exports and held on to over half of this horde in the downturn. The halcyon days when the Russian Monopolygarcks infested the Côte d'Azur and London's West End with suitcases filled with cash and snatched up yachts, jets, apartments and mansions without having to even think of filling in a loan or mortgage application, masked a horrid fact: back home their businesses now had massive debts, while $70.0 billion had left the country with the Roman Abramoviches and Oleg Deripaskas, the richest with a $28.6 billion aluminium fortune alone, and their ilk. Abramovich's Chelsea Football Club lead the UK Premiership and that other ship, Deripaska's Queen K, had caused political embarrassment to the UK's new Business Secretary Lord Mandelson and Shadow Chancellor George Osborne, caught on board with their political pants down in the summer, but it was soon Deripaska feeling the economic heat when he battled to refinance his 25% stake in the Norilsk Nickel business by a Russian Government bail-out in the form of a $4.5 billion loan from Vnesheconombank, or VNB, chaired as it happens by Prime Minister Putin.

Deripaska's problems began when his holding company Basic Element had to start taking cash from Subsidiary A to prop up Subsidiary B: Basic owns 60% of Ingosstrakh, Russia's number two insurer which enjoys strong cashflows, which has been required to pay €8.0 million for a 25% stake in Strabag, an Austrian company and the sixth biggest construction company in Europe and also owned by Deripaska, who now wants to become a director of the insurer. This has upset Petr Kellner, the Czech minigarck, who had bought 38.5% of Ingosstrakh with Generali as his partner, before Deripaska promoted a huge Rights Issue in October 2008 that diluted the Czech down to size and under 10%. Deripaska, you see, is a former nuclear physicist turned corporate nuclear raider and is seeking financially strong investors for all his businesses, including United Company Rusal, the world's largest aluminium producer, and it would clearly be advantageous to have a seat and a hand nearer to Ingosstrakh's cash pile.

UC Rusal itself is wallowing in an enormous amount of debt as it attempts to restructure $17.0 billion it owes, including $2.8 billion to Mikhail Prokhorov, the vendor of the 25% stake in Norilsk Nickel, $7.0 billion to Russian banks and another $7.0 billion to 72 foreign banks; it wants the Russian State to convert $6.0 billion of its Russian state bank debt, the loan which was made to prevent foreign creditors seizing its 25% stake in Norilsk Nickel in 2008, into Preference Shares. No wonder UC Rusal is seeking a standstill agreement, as Deripaska himself engages fast forward to save his empire from total collapse. What's really at stake is this: Deripaska wants to unite Norilsk Nickel with steel groups Mechel and Evraz, metals group Metalloinvest owned by Alisher Usmanov, and Uralkali, a potash producer 66%-owned by Ribolovyev since March 2008, in which grouping the state-owned Russian Technologies would take a 25.001% stake in exchange for debt write-offs. Deripaska's industrial logic is real 1960s' synergyless thinking: iron ore, coal, steel mills and nickel all make stainless steel, but the fertiliser operation is a touch untidy, no doubt thrown in to make the numbers add up to produce an exit solution for all concerned.

What Deripalska is really after, however, is to keep UC Rusal out of this proposed combination, and keep control for himself. In the other corner is Alisher Usmanov, owner of Metalloinvest, who wants to combine with Norilsk Nickel and Russian Technologies. Presiding over this industrial goulash is Prime Minister 'Vlad the Bad' Putin, of Russian Technologies and state-owned banks like VEB, now the $6.0 billion lenders to UC Rusal. What he wants is power for the state to avenge the 1995 infamous Boris Yeltsin's "loans-for-shares" privatisations, involving Norilsk Nickel and part of Mechel Steel, when the Monopolygarcks received cut-price industrial stakes after bailing out the near-bankrupt state, and Putin has a strategic plan for the Russian economy as well. Boris Boozer Yeltsin, remember, was the one who couldn't get out of Russia's equivalent of Airforce One when it landed at Shannon Airport to greet the entire Irish Cabinet waiting on the tarmac, as he couldn't even get out of his seat on account of the number of toasts in VAT, as in Vodka-and-Tonic, that had hit him in the head like a 6-inch rusty nail.

Deripaska himself emerged with control of UC Rusal at 54%, while Prokhorov upped his stake from 18% to 23% by converting debt, the banks extended their loans for four years plus an option over 5% of the equity, and a new entrant, Viktor Vekselberg of Sual, with his collection of 15 Fabergé eggs, took 18% and the Chairmanship. What concentrated minds and put the rush into Russian was UC Rusal's 2006 three-way merger with Sual and Switzerland's Glencore Trading, who had a Call on Desperate Deripaska if he failed to organise a flotation before 31st December 2009, to buy them out at a valuation between $30-35 billion, so UC Rusal is headed to the Hong Kong and Paris stock markets at a valuation in that range, with 10% being sold into the hoped for float. Hong Kong and Paris? Well, there's the small matter of another Russian, Mikhail Chernoy, who is suing Deripaska in London for $4.0 billion worth or 20% of UC Rusal's shares which he claims Deripaska was holding in trust for him, which is what you do having missed out on your supposed share of the *accumulated* peoples' former assets. And as these negotiations were brokered by Putin's Kremlin, so Vladimir 'Take it easy Greazey you've got a long way to slide' Strzhalkovsky of the Leningrad KGB's 1980 vintage, finds himself sliding into the CEO's chair of Norilsk Nickel.

Russian M&A is certainly different and it's advisable to visit Q, James Bond's gadget outfitter, and pick up your regulation self-exploding briefcase and assorted contents if you're going to get involved. In 2009, the Russian state is planning a new wave of privatisations of up to 5,500 SOEs to bolster the post-Crunch state finances over the next three years, but the pricing will not create any Monopolgarcks this time round. And don't apply for too many shares either, so that you don't end up like Mikhail Khodorkovsky, who used to own Yukos

Oil but is now languishing in gaol on taxation and fraud charges, or Boris Berezovsky, the former forestry engineer and used-car salesman, and Vladimir Gusinsky, who are both in self-imposed exile in London. All of which was not inputted into the LTCM black box that failed to project, after the 1995 Russian giveaway-sale of state assets, that the state would have no money left to pay its bonds and so go into default in 1998. "That's why I leave my teeth in the bathroom overnight," mulls the Mullah Nasruddin, "so I don't get bitten when I'm sleeping with my eyes closed!"

In 2009 the Russian banks were frozen too: the chairman of the Centmestment Banks was cutting staff fast as revenues collapsed and dried up. Savers were fearful of a run on the banks, as happened in the UK with Northern Rock, and took their rouble deposits out of the private banks and put them into the safer State banks such as Sberbank and VTB, or put them into Dollars to the tune of $3.5 billion, or simply put their cash under the mattress. On 13th October the State's Foreign Trade Bank became the Government's vehicle for a $50.0 billion bank bail-out, when Globeks, Russia's 35th-largest bank, stopped disbursing cash and was taken over: the depositors' money was safe, but their accounts were nevertheless still as frozen as the Steppes.

Already, the once overheated Moscow real estate market was now also as frozen as the Steppes themselves. Just as in the West, the Credit Crunch had spread to the Stock Market. The MICEX was down 70% in just six months, compared with 40% on the US S&P Index, and the market was closed for the fifteenth time on 27th October to enable investors to catch their breath before the next heavy pounding. And the cause of all this was? Firstly, over-leveraged hedge funds in the West got cold feet and pulled their cash, and secondly, there were no domestic investors to replace them. The hot money had left town and gone abroad. In Russia only 1% of the population are investors, compared with 50% of households in the US. The minerals and oil sectors are important exports and represent 25% of Russian GDP and the savage falls in commodities and fuel prices had also come as a shock.

The crisis had ruthlessly exposed the structural weaknesses in the economy. Alexei Rybnikov, MICEX's chief executive, explains it all like this: "I think the crisis put into focus the problems in Russia; the lack of pension reform, lack of structural reform. It's very clear that we do need pension funds for long-term money." Well, at least he's still smiling optimistically through the bloodbath, and is addressing the future structural requirements. The current collapse is potentially worse than the 1998 Russian default crisis, but it's nowhere near its end yet, as the Lada auto-plant in the one-horse town of Togliatti employing 102,000 workers went bust in October 2009. No wonder that the Russian state-owned Sberbank was in the Magna consortium hoping to buy control of GM's Opel division in Germany, with the ubiquitous Oleg Deripaska advising Sberbank. President Putin, you see, knows what he's doing and knows how to play his cards through whichever indebted Monolopygarck, no fool he.

In 2008, the 101 Russian Monopolygarck billionaires created by the botched privatisation of former state assets by the perennially-drunken Yeltsin were reduced to just 49, and the fortunes of the top 10 reduced like this:

Table 7:

Decline of Monopolygarck's Wealth: $-Billions	1/1/2008	31/12/2008
Mikhail Prokhorov – Metals	21.5	14.1
Roman Abramovich – Oil and Gas	23.0	13.9
Vladimir Lisin - Iron and Steel	22.2	7.7
Vagit Alekperov – Oil and Gas	13.5	7.6
Suleiman Kerimov- Banking and Oil	18.0	7.5
Mikhail Fridman – Alfa Banking and Oil	22.2	6.1
Vladimir Potanin – Industry	21.5	5.0
Oleg Deripaska – Aluminium, Energy, Construction	40.0	4.9
Dmitri Ribolovyev – Cell Phones and Potash	11.7	4.6
Alisher Usmanov – Iron, Steel and Lumber	13.3	4.5
Totals $-Bns:	**$206.9**	**$75.9**

As noted, this is just the top ten of the 101 billionaires whose wealth post-privatisation indicates that over $1.0 trillion of state-owned assets, that's over $1,000,000,000,000, was seized from the people, a daylight robbery that makes Britain's 1963 night-time Great Train Robbery haul of £2.6 million look like a waste of time and torch batteries. Then Global Crunch struck and as Alisher Usmanov commented ruefully: "Today's crisis is merciless for raw-materials producers. It will take back everything we *accumulated* yesterday". So there you have it, despite appearances to the contrary, this is a Democratic Global Crunch, if you're a Russian.

It's not all bad for those Russians who got their money out when they could, like Roman Abramovich, who had the good sense and timing to sell his Sibneft oil company to the state-controlled Gazprom in 2005 for $13.0 billion, and then head for London. His extraordinary life began with both his Jewish parents dying before he was just three; he was educated at School No. 232; then he came to Moscow and made money selling rubber ducks from his apartment; next he made money by trading barrels of Russian oil abroad; with this money he bought up privatisation vouchers from those Russians who didn't know what to do with them or what they might be worth; and then he teamed up with Boris Berezovsky and bought 50% of Sibneft for £50.0 million; Yeltsin invited him to take an apartment in the Kremlin, he was elected in 1999 as Governor of Russia's remote far eastern province of Chukotka from 2000-2008, where he dispensed $1.3 billion on charities.

The specification for his new 557-foot/167-metre gin-palace, Eclipse, as in eclipsing all others, is costing £310.0 million or £724.0 million depending on which newspaper you read, requires a crew of 60, and is the largest motor vessel in the world at 64 metres longer than the pitch at his Chelsea FC's ground at Stamford Bridge, beating the Ruler of Dubai's eponymous yacht by a clear 46 feet, who will now need a new one too, so as not to be eclipsed. That, and the specification which includes a mini-submarine for exploration and escape, 6-foot wide TV screens in the 24 guest cabins, two helicopters in case one's ash-trays are full or the gas is on empty, anti-missile defences and bullet-proof windows as is standard for all Russian Monopolygarcks, two swimming pools in case one is being used as a dance-floor, and wait for it, an anti-paparazzi laser shield that disrupts digital cameras, an anti-divorce defense system if ever there was one. The Eclipse will join his Boeing 767 and Airbus A340-313X jets, his two Maybach bomb and bullet-proof Limos, his Ferrari FXX, Bugatti Veyron, Maserati MC12 Corsa, Ferrari 360 and his bespoke Porsche Carrera GT. From rubber ducks to MV Eclipse via Stamford Bridge was one helluv'a strange Odyssey.

India

India's population is 1.2 billion and rising, second only to China's 1.34 billion and rising. India is the world's biggest democracy, whereas China is by far the biggest communist country ever, but the only one to embrace the market economy. China's GDP is more than twice India's, however, but why? First, the Chinese peasants are being lured away from their increasingly drought-ridden lands in the west to seek their incomes in the cities and factories that line the eastern seaboard, whereas Indian culture and tradition hefts two-thirds of the population to their native villages, dialects and farmlands. Secondly, China's unbridled, lawless, raw and bracing go-for-it manufacturing-for-export capitalism is in stark contrast to the framework of India's economy: when India achieved independence from Britain in 1947, Prime Minister Nehru clung to the old British Fabian-socialist anti-free-market bureaucratically-controlled formula, the very footprint and profile for a sclerotic economy.

In 1992 I visited Dr. Jamshed Bhabha, CEO of JRD Tata in Mumbai, India's largest conglomerate with 1.9 million employees at the time, engaged in railway manufacturing, tea plantations, nuclear energy, printing ink and chemicals, you name it and they were in it and at it. Jamshed was also Chairman of the Tata-sponsored National Performing Arts Centre, built on reclaimed land on the promontory, opened by Prime Minister Indira Gandhi in the 1980s. During our visit to this impressive Centre, Jamshed was rustled into a meeting with the Fire Brigade, who demanded a bung in exchange for ... the necessary fire licence for some extension or other. Jamshed was ashamed rather than surprised. As JK Galbraith caustically commented about India: 'The sale of indulgences did not end with church reform'.

177

The flip-side of bureaucracy is corruption. Satyam Computer Consulting Limited's massive fraud, discovered after eight years in Q4 2008, put the US Enron Inc. debacle to shame in the corporate corruption stakes: whereas Enron involved fictitious profits of $613.0.0 million in 1997-2000 with a corresponding understatement of liabilities of $628.0, giving a reduction in reported equity of $1.2 billion, the Satyam fraud involved $2.6 billion. Satyam was an out-source provider based in Hyderabad, quoted on the Mumbai and New York stock exchanges, where it raised $161.9 million in ADRs, American Depository Receipts, in May 2001, and which numbered Citigroup Inc., Caterpillar Inc., the Coca-Cola Company and Microsoft Inc. among its prestigious client list. B. Ramalinga Raju, Satyam's founder, had been siphoning money out of the company via his family and investing the ill-gotten gains in land around Hyderabad, mainly hidden in a company called Maytas Properties Limited, which owned 1,065 properties and 6,000 acres.

The fraud involved the inclusion of 13,000 non-existent "employ-ees" on the payroll of 53,000, 7,561 fraudulent invoices and seven fake customers, understatement of liabilities, forged bank statements and inflation of cash balances, fictitious accrued interest, $1.0 billion cash on the balance sheet but nowhere else, dividends paid out of false reserves, forged board resolutions, and with more pricks in the company than a second-hand dartboard, it only needed two bent partners of PricewaterhouseCoopers India to hold it up while they were being paid well over the odds to "do the audit". Tech Mahindra, a joint venture between the venerable Mahindra and Mahindra auto-motive and transmission drivelines business and the UK's BT Group, bought Satyam out of its founder-inflicted debacle, but not before India's corporate reputation had been badly tarnished, as often happens in bureaucratic regimes.

Meanwhile the emergence of a burgeoning Middle Class in India is an epoch-breaking manifestation for all lands east of the Urals, where throughout history the wealth has been concentrated in the hands of the very few, in the hands of the Sheikhs, Oligarchs, Maharajahs and Dynastic Emperors, while the mass of the popula-tion, the serfs, peasants, wayfarers and journeymen staved off starva-tion and eked out a living wherever and however they could. This newly-emerging class comprises the newly-enfranchised economic band of bankers, accountants, architects, artists, lawyers, doctors and dentists and in India alone could number around 300 to 400 million people, who want all the usual consumer goodies, from apartments to autos, from education to foreign holidays. In Global Crunch, property values in the emerging newly-built cities of India tumbled like everywhere else in the world, which was a necessary correction, as apartment prices in Mumbai had even gotten ahead of equivalent properties in London, such is the indication of future value and potential capital concentration throughout the Orient. By Q3 2009 city residential property prices had recovered their 30% falls, inflation had fallen from 12% to 1.0% and a strong recovery was already under way.

China

After the huge success of the Beijing Olympics in the summer of 2008, no one in China reckoned they would be looking at an economic melt-down before the year was out. By the end of 2008, shipping rates from Asia to Europe had sunk to an unheard of zero, with brokers asking only for the bunkering charges, as exports fell off the cliff in just two months. The dangers of building an economy principally on exports was exposed as a deeply flawed concept, as Japan's exports were down 27% in November, Taiwan was down 42% and South Korea down 30% in January. The Baltic Dry index of shipping rates had fallen by 96% during the year, and there is considerable new tonnage to be delivered in 2009. The speed of the collapse was quite extraordinary and completely unexpected, as over 62,000 factories closed in the Guandong province of China alone, causing 20.0 million unemployed and local riots.

China is deemed to need 8% growth p.a. to maintain its momentum to absorb internal migrants from the hinterland to the coastal areas, but the Forecast for 2009 was only an "unsustainable" 5% or lower, which would have signified a very hard landing for China and further potential civic unrest; five interest rate cuts in three months took the rate to 5.58%, the lowest since the Asian crisis of 1997; a $586.0/£382.0 billion, or 4.0 trillion Renminbi, infrastructure stimulus package was approved in November, but it soon became apparent that much of this was in the 2006-2010 5-year plan anyway, but growth was soon restored to that 8% rate which equals sustainability. South Korea also announced in November that it was preparing an $11.0 billion stimulus package.

Amazingly, China survived this first real test of the global market economy and after losing 20 million jobs and exports declining by 25%, the government was still looking at over 8% growth by Q3 2009. The Chinese realised, however, that their cheap exports/low wages economic model would need to be adjusted in several ways: development of its own infrastructure and direct investment in overseas resources, from food, to minerals and energy, were now the new priority, along with climbing further up the manufacturing food-chain by the application of technology, as in the West's technology.

Japan

When the Japanese 'Bubble Economy' of the 1980s eventually popped in 1988, caused by the same type of excesses as seen in the US and UK, when the Nikkei collapsed from 38,000 to 8,500, the government kept pumping Keynesian stimuli packages into infrastructure projects in attempts to stop the deflation that had taken hold. As prices were falling every month, the Japanese consumer kept saving and not spending, because anything you wanted to buy this month would be cheaper next month. This syndrome is the great menace of deflation. After the government had spent ¥100.0 trillion but to no avail in unnecessary projects, a decade had passed and the millennium came and went, marking the 'Lost Decade'; but ten years later in the new millennium it was unbelievably the case of the 'Lost Two Decades'. Keynesian infrastructure spending was clearly not the answer to Japanese deflation.

And talking of Japanese banks and property, I had to make a business trip to Tokyo in April 1993, where about the only thing left working and not pledged to the banks was the apple blossom. Arriving at the Industrial Bank of Japan on time, and having dispensed with the Japanese opening protocols and having made my presentation on UK industrial prospects to the head honcho and his corporate minder, I was treated to the most amazing, eye-opening scene. The head honcho stood up and raised his clenched fist and shook it in real anger, not at me thank goodness, but at the ceiling and at the floors above us and he then railed at his bosses that they had destroyed this so-called industrial bank with loans to, to, to-to, TO … PROPERTY DEVELOPERS! His minder was even more astonished than myself, and looked nervously at the roof as if it was about to collapse, or possibly because it was not sound-proofed.

I was then invited by the fist-shaker, on the grounds that my presentation demonstrated that I could sell a farmer a dead horse, that I should in all seriousness raise a giant fund to bail out Japanese Inc.'s property sector! And I was even given a fast-pass through to the government entity in charge of property; intrigued, I attended these offices later that day and found myself seated in front of an impassive young functionary, who was not about to break out into smiles. In our discussion on the parlous state of the Japanese property market which had sucked all the liquidity out of every bank in Tokyo, I was left speechless when the functionary informed me as a matter of absolute fact that property values in Tokyo's central district could never fall, come hell or high water.

"Why, on earth, not?"

"Because they all overlook Imperial Palace!"

That was the weirdest day on the road ever. I took the next plane home, still in a state of disbelief, about the self-delusionary Japanese state-of-mind about their property values. The Imperial Palace on its island site in the middle of Tokyo was supposedly worth more at the time than all the real estate in California. Twenty-five years on, and I bet the properties are still nowhere near their former valuations, and the same functionary is still repeating the same mantra as he bows graciously to the Imperial Palace twice a day, just to make sure that this great benchmark of Japanese delusion is still there.

The real explanation of why Japan has suffered two lost decades is not that their repeated economic stimuli failed as they did, with endless motorways and bridges going nowhere, but that their financial sector was in a totally sclerotic state on account of a single idea. Five years after the collapse of their Bubble Economy, their banks had still not written off the bad property loans. Why not? The bankers could not overcome their *Wah*. Their *What*? Their *Wah* is the collective style of Japanese group responsibility, that works for them so well in manufacturing, but in the financial sectors it means no one dare write anything off because they were all part of the original decision to lend, which cannot therefore be wrong. *Wah*, you see, is Japanese for Narcissus spelt backwards. So the bankers just sit around like zombies year after year, on into the new millennium and beyond, bowing twice daily to the Imperial Palace, refusing to admit defeat and clear out all the bad loans by liquidating the assets and move on to allow recovery, as the Americans did so promptly with their S&L crisis.

So, a whole nation's economy is gridlocked, transfixed and skewered by a single syllable! And all the while national debt is rising and is now 227% of GDP, and forecast to rise to 246% by 2014; while the CPI has fallen 4.3% since 1998 with the BoJ forecasting further deflation of 3% overall for 2010-2012, while land prices in Japan's top six cities fell 8% in 2009 alone. Then the Minister of Finance Hirohisa Fujii tells Masaaki Shirakawa of the BoJ that its upbeat comments on the recovery are just plain wrong. When the CPI fell by an astonishing 2.5% in just November 2009 alone, Shirakawa of the BoJ, stung by criticisms of 'sleeping on the switch', couldn't even wait two weeks for his regular monthly meeting, but ordered another $115.0 billion of QE lotion to head off further deflation. Japan, with its ageing demographics and endless borrowing, is doing a 'Slow, slow, quick quick, slow' in the Kabuki Theatre of Economic Hara-kiri, while in 2010 it will raise more in debt than in taxation, on the way to going completely bust.

For those who perhaps may have under-estimated the effect of human psychology in matters economic, this short trip around the G20 has revealed two countries, Japan and Saudi Arabia, whose economies are each held back by a single idea; another, Russia, whose feudal mind-set of yore, still governed the privatisation of its entire national assets in the very hour the citizens had their first whiff of freedom as opposed to grapeshot, or worse; and a whole region, East Europe, which has embraced the deflationary and employment-destroying currency of a dry EU-Nurse for fear of something worse; and don't forget that greed, one of the seven deadly sins, still pervades the bankers of the Anglo-sphere world. How can an economist worthy of the name ignore history and the element of human and national psychology, of Degenerate and Creative Persons? I can hear the Mullah Nasruddin, it's that man again, gnashing what's left of his false teeth getting ready for that forlorn love-bite, as he proclaims "You might as well try putting all that into your computer as trying to excite my wife!", as though he were directly addressing those flat-earth Nobel Laureates who designed their equally-ineffectual LTCM black box.

Some Geo-political Issues

Three out of four of the BRICs, namely the RICs, find themselves in the world headlines for a quite different reason. A month after India launched its latest nuclear submarine, named *Agni* after the Vedic God of Fire, President Hu Jintao's Peoples' Republic of China, the PRC, celebrated 60 years of communism in September 2009 with a march-past of 200,000 men and women of the People's Liberation Army, the PLA, in Tiananmen Square in Beijing. They were in 56 formations, one for each of the 56 ethnic groupings within the PRC. The implied statement was that the PRC is not in the business of ceding territory any time soon nor about to allow any civil disorder. The formations of sailors were all exactly the same height, emphasising that China is the land of the Law of Large Numbers, where the individual is blotted out by subservience to the state, always assumed to be the servant of the greater good, until it isn't.

The PLA's standing armed forces, you see, count 2,300,000 under arms, up from 1,000,000 at the time of the Ming Dynasty in the seventeenth century. And the parade showed off six new battle systems, beginning with the QBZ-95 assault rifle, the ZTZ99 battle tank replicated with Sino-enhancements but derived from the Russian T 72, and the JL-2 submarine-launched missile with an 8,000 kilometre range, which were all duly hauled before the carefully-selected audience in Tiananmen Square, while the new Jian-10 fighter, the ultra-secret KJ-series command and control jet and the Zhi-10 helicopter gunship roared overhead in a truly impressive display of becoming power. What wasn't on display, however, was the corruption in the promotion system and the low state of morale and low devotion to duty to the country, as explained by General Zhang Shutian, now a political commissar, who fears mutiny in the army, particularly amongst the officer class. Communist China had been born in 1949 when Chairman Mao, who said "All power comes from the barrel of the gun", closed the borders and the world's eyes to the murder and famine of 30 million in his Utopian Socialist State, and has come a long way since the borders were re-opened in 1979; in just 30 years the growth of China's economy and military have been astonishing. So why does China feel it needs 2.3 million under arms, to invade Taiwan? Or repel another Japanese invasion into Manchuria, or avenge the 1931 incursion and the occupation of Shanghai in 1933? More likely is an invasion of Myanmar to control the strategic waters of the huge Irrawaddy Delta and to police the border with North Korea. Or put down any internal insurrection, as occurred in the ethnic clashes between the Uighurs and Hans which left nearly 200 dead and six awaiting execution in the far north-western city of Urumqi in July 2009? This latter incident could well look like a storm in a tea-cup if the water crisis in north China continues to worsen. Even if China was forced into a situation where she had to do all of these at the same time, this would surely still only require less than 1.0 million troops. If, however, China had to fight a war to the west, then the logistics of the immense supply lines involved would be a quite different proposition. China last fought against India in 1962 over control of the Tibetan Plateau, and the long simmering dispute is fed by India's continued hosting of the Dalai Lama as ruler there, while the 30,000 Chinese internet censors do nothing about blog sites discussing the merits of a new war with India, as the secular Maoists think of the joy of kicking the religious Buddhists' backsides out of Nepal, once and for all.

When President Hu Jintao addressed the UN in September 2009, on his way to the G20 summit in Pittsburgh, he declared "all countries should strictly comply with non-proliferation obligations, refrain from double standards and tighten and improve export controls" of nuclear components and enriched Uranium. This was fine, but do not quite forget that it was China's supplying its know-how for an atomic bomb to Pakistan with a view to weakening their joint-rival India that was the key move for the onward proliferation to North Korea and Iran in the first place. The biggest collection of Intercontinental Ballistic Missiles, or ICBMs, in the world is in the Indo-Pakistan subcontinent, where these two countries enjoy constant border skirmishes over the disputed Kashmir and the life-giving waters of East Punjab, just as Israel and Palestine fight over the River Jordan, while the north-west border of Pakistan is infiltrated by the Taliban guerrillas who gave succour and protection to Osama Bin Laden and his Al Qa'eda terrorists of 9/11 infamy. Al Qa'eda and the Taleban have their eyes on destabilising Pakistan and gaining control of all those lovely ICBMs, with which they will seek to takeover Saudi Arabia and hold the world to ransom over a barrel of oil, or more exactly over the 260.0 billion barrels of proven reserves in Saudi, and that's just the ones they know about. And the gunmen who attacked Mumbai in 2008, now identified as the Lashkar-e-Taiba terrorist militants based in Pakistan, sailed from Pakistan's southern shoreline, but financed by who and at who's beck and call? Where is James Bond to fight the Manichean Evil when we need him?

Then the discovery by the French later that very month of the Iranian nuclear facility, hidden from the world in the mountains around the Holy City of Qom, puts a whole new angle on China's support for Iran in the UN, along with their support of other questionable regimes in need of a facelift, such as Kim Jong Il II's North Korea whose warships have just clashed ominously with the South Korean Navy, Mugabe's terror-state of Zimbabwe and the strife-torn Sudan, three countries whose only other common thread is starvation. While Kim Jong Il is an illusion trapped in his own space-bubble and Mugabe is a psycho-manic thug destroying the country that he is stealing from, the hot-headed Iranian President Ahmadinejad, as in 'I'm-in-bed-with-ma-Jihad', threatens to "expedite the last breath of the Zionist regime" in Israel. China's relationship with Iran is predicated around her massive investments in Iranian oil and gas that are vital to her own economy. It's just as well Dubya Bush is no longer in the White House and that neither America nor Israel have any stocks of 30,000lb Multiple Ordnance Penetrators. So, it's back to sanctions, but they cannot work without China (and Russia), but China has no interest in making itself unpopular with the hot-headed one by interfering with Iran's *Affaires d'Etat*.

In 1970, I asked the late Sir John Cecil Masterman, universally known as JC, a historian and former Vice- Chancellor of Oxford, if, when and where he thought WW3 might break out. JC had been caught on a post-graduate trip when WW1 broke and he was imprisoned in Germany, where he proceeded to perfect his knowledge of

German, and in WW2 was Chairman of the Committee of Twenty, the XX, or the double-cross system. His most brilliant achievement, Operation Fortitude South, had been when he detained the German 15th Army with its 150,000 men and its Panzer divisions, including the 116th and Erwin Rommel's own 7th, at the Pas de Calais while the Allied D-Day invasion forces landed in Normandy, achieved by planting false messages in the German mind from fake double-agents who only existed in the more fertile mind of JC himself, a complicated and witty ruse aided by the fact that by then all Germany's actual agents were paid by their Lisbon embassy, but actually funded unbeknown to them by the British embassy down the road. JC, a master of complicated plots as you can see, had obviously considered this question himself, as he answered unhesitatingly:

"Oh! It will begin in the region of the Sinkiang Pass. There will be burgeoning populations to the east on one side of the Pass, while on the other side to the north are the great granaries of Turkmenistan, Uzbekistan, Kazakhstan and especially the Ukraine beyond, and to the south are the rich oil-fields of Iran, Iraq and the Arabian Gulf. It will all start over food and oil. The Map tells it all!" And indeed it did, and it still does. It is worth studying the Map on these issues, but then turn it upside-down and view the whole oriental arena from the position of Moscow, where the Bear's gaze observes the whole play from Europe to the Pacific, from Lisbon to Vladivostock, and with Afghanistan and Pakistan at the centre of it all, but now seen from a very different vantage point, the vantage point of President Putin, no less.

Meanwhile, the armed forces of the US, UK and their allies have removed the dictator of Iraq and replaced an evil regime with a fledgling democracy; they are now in Afghanistan fighting the Taliban terrorists, but this is a very different type of war than as against a regular army. The decision to fight terrorists in the most unforgiving theatre in the world is not a politico-military decision to be taken lightly, but Bush and Brown did not really tell us why. President Obama has decided on a do-or-die surge with around 40,000 extra troops, but there is the Viet-Nam suspicion of an unwinnable war in the air. My view of what is called America's failure in Viet-Nam is that it was an essential attempt to rid the world of potentially aggressive communism and end the Cold War, and one has to admire the American courage and belief, or political naiveté perhaps, in their fight to establish freedom based on

186

democracy across the whole world, the vision of *Pax Americana* no less, where the aim is not a landed empire but one of free trade between free markets, a noble vision, to which modern Viet-Nam stands as a proud testament. Was the war there really a failure?

It was clear on the day that the 9/11 attacks were the first of a new Jihad or Holy War. These run in cycles, like trade, weather and temperature cycles, and the Jihad seems to be a seven hundred year cycle: the first Jihad, or for Christians the First Crusade, was in the seventh/eight centuries and the second was in the fourteenth century and on until the fall of Constantinople in 1453; whereas 9/11 was at the beginning of the twenty-first century. The first two Holy Wars, fought over the Holy Lands of the Near East, each lasted about a century, with the theatre of the Second covering southern Spain, eastern Europe, north Africa right through to south-east Asia. So, there is the birth of Christ – 700 years – the First Crusade – another 700 years – the Second Crusade – another 700 years – then the Third Crusade began in 2001 in America, and within just ten years the Christians have conquered Iraq, are fighting in Afghanistan and are now threatened by Iran. It is a sobering thought that the first century of the Third Millennium will probably be dominated by terrorism.

The Natural Causes of Conflicts

Wars are caused by the natural and minute oscillations of temperature, of less than 1° Centigrade as shown in Graph 4 below, around the Equator that affects the Tropics; this determines rainfall, and water is the source of life and food. Without water there is famine and migration in search of land with water to grow food on; and any ensuing war is often fought in the name of religion, as the ultimate justification for the ensuing slaughter.

The Greens, politicians and the media spread the myth that man-made CO_2 emissions are the cause of Global Warming, but the *Inconvenient Truth* for them is that such emissions are responsible for only 0.3% of the carbon dioxides in the atmosphere, which consists for 94.5% of H_2O, but you are called a maverick by the Global Warming Lobby for stating these facts. Climatic history, however, shows that the earth in the early Medieval Ages was much hotter than at present, when human impact on CO_2 was minimal. A rate of change in the long-term tidal element, caused by movements within the solar system known as the De Vriess Suess Cycle of 200 years, or some say 178.2 years to be exact, apply additional pressures to sensitive margins around certain coastal regions, which in turn cause volcanic action. This phenomenon is as old as the Ancient Greeks' attribution to the powers of Poseidon, who was the God of the Sea, for whom Homer's epithet of the 'earth-shaker' was based on their knowledge that earthquakes were linked to massive movements of water below sea-level, which we now know as the shifting of the earth's tectonic plates, that also sets off volcanoes and tsunamis. We now also know that a large volcanic eruption causes dust and sulphuric acid which form lattices in the stratosphere that shields the sun, thereby making the earth cooler.

The solar shifts also trigger a reduction in the sun's output as measured by sunspots, dark blemishes on the solar surface which form where magnetism reaches out from the sun into space, which themselves have an 11.2 year cycle; these prolong the cool periods that are known as Minima. History shows that these have been periods of exceptional social and political unrest, mass-migrations and conflict, whereas the Medieval Warming early in the 13th Century fostered exceptional crops which allowed the land-workers to be available for building cathedrals and for arming the second crusade. The latest tidal peak was on 20th April 1990, and there is a delay of around nineteen years before high volcanic activity kicks in, when unusually low sunspots may usher in a new Minimum. And indeed, it was reported in 2009 that high volcanic activity, mainly in the northern hemisphere in the Russian Kamchatka Peninsula and Kuril Islands, and in the Aleutians, but also in the southern hemisphere, is cooling the poles that have forced the storm tracks unusually far south during the 2009 summer, giving both sides of the North Atlantic a cool summer.

During 2009 solar activity has also fallen to levels unseen since the 1920s, and sunspots have been so rare that for three-quarters of the year the sun has been spot-free. If this trend continues, the sun will lose its ability to produce sunspots by 2015, as occurred during what is known as the Wolf Minimum in the early-14th Century, the Sporer Minimum in the 15th Century, the Maunder Minimum in the mid-16th and early-17th Centuries, from 1640-1710, and the Dalton Minimum in the 19th Century, from 1790-1820. The trend of unusually low sunspots may usher in a new Minimum and a new 'Little Ice Age' in Northern Europe, Northern America and the Russian Steppes, which lasted for 70 years in the 17th Century, and was immortalised by artists such as Brueghel with his paintings of frosted fairs and hunting scenes, as in his 'The Hunters in the Snow'.

The next five years will tell us if the Greens or the Mavericks are right: my money is on the so-called Mavericks and their view that the sun is primarily responsible for climate change as the agent of Nature's Cycles. It will be required viewing if a Ruination of Greens are left shivering and stammering about Global Warming through chattering teeth in the next Minimum, just as they were in a snow-bound Copenhagen in December 2009 while they tried to hammer out a global warming agreement, enough to warm the cockles of a Maverick's heart, in fact. In which case, the new cooling should be known as the Acker Minimum, after the Michigan Farmer Larry Acker, who has his own weather station, and claims that the new Minimum started in 2008 and will run to 2050.

The Pacific and Atlantic ocean oscillations are also in a dangerous relational configuration, for the Atlantic is unusually warm while the Pacific is in a cool phase. These factors are bringing some rainfall relief to some but not all American farmers but drought to northern China, Pakistan and the west coast of India, where the 2009 monsoon was both weak and late, while the Yellow River and the Indus were barely a trickle when they reached the sea, whilst the tropics were unusually warm and were forcing the rain-belts some three hundred miles away from both tropics and towards the poles, so squeezing the rain belts between the tropics and the cooler polar air masses. For example, these combining factors are pushing the rains that fall on populous Indonesia onto the arid and unpopulated north-west of Australia. Indeed, the temperature cycles suggest that a period of cooling is in prospect, giving reduced rain in critical areas of certain high populations and leading to a reduction in arable land through soil erosion caused by lack of rainfall. This will create higher food prices, social unrest, famine, mass-migrations and raises the possibility of future migrations and therefore conflicts. *The Times* of London carried a report in November 2009 on the shaded drought

Graph 4:

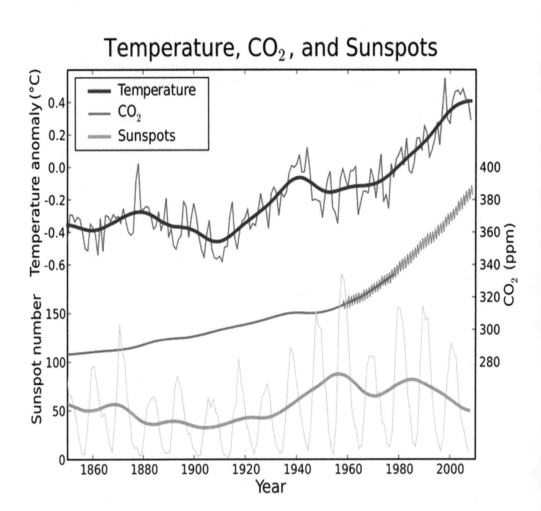

Source: Leland McInnes   PPM on RHS scale = Parts per Million

area of East Africa shown in Map 1 below, where 23.0 million people are facing starvation and soil erosion, and the dead cattle are so numerous that the vultures are not even bothering to pick the carcases clean.

Map 1:

Map of World Drought 2009

(Note: X marks the Sinkiang Pass at Kashgar/Kashi)

I refer here again to the answer given above by the venerable Sir John C. Masterman. And I question the advisability of fighting terrorism in Afghanistan, at huge expense and danger, particularly in the geo-political and nuclear environment of the Middle East (Israel/Iran and India/Pakistan) and the Far East (China/Japan). Every army sent to Afghanistan has found that the ground is impossible; there is no cover, it's unbearably hot, troops can only move down the valleys, the defenders are in the hills and can see every movement, as they pick you off with Improvised Explosive Devices and sniper-fire, and when helicopter-gunships go into the mountains the Taliban fighters simply vanish. Afghanistan is beginning to feel like an intractable problem, Viet-Nam Style, but whereas that campaign was confined to a relatively small country with few great natural assets other than its charming people, the issues blowing in the wind out of Afghanistan are perceived as an immediate danger to Pakistan, which could well spread to regional conflicts, that may then be hard to contain.

When you look at the map of Pakistan, it is worth remembering that Pakistanis do not see what the map shows to be their country is in fact not how they see their country, because the North-West is referred to on the map as the 'Frontier Territories' or 'Northern Territories', which have their own indigenous population, including Taleban elements, and are not part of Pakistan proper. The idea that the Taleban in Pakistan, who number just 10,000 to 20,000, can overturn a nation of 160,000,000 with an excellent, well-trained, well-supplied and disciplined army and somehow get their finger on the button of Pakistan's nuclear arsenal seems far-fetched. When the Taleban morphed into the Swat Valley in 2009, it was only a matter of weeks for the Pakistani army, who know how to operate in those mountainous regions, to drive them out. The Taleban are effectively restricted to being terrorists, and their attacks on marketplaces, hospitals and girls' schools are very unpleasant and horrifying, but do not lead to the overthrow of the nation, any more than the IRA's terror attacks in the UK threatened its national survival. The idea that a regional conflict may develop into something horrendous is not so fanciful, however, especially if harvests fail as a result of drought and cause migration, which is a far more serious issue.

PART V:

What To Do About It

The Issue of Effective Regulation

THE Global Crunch was aided by the failure of regulation at every successive level. Table 8 on page 194 lists these levels of the Anglo-sphere regulatory hierarchy in descending order, (with US and UK institutions listed in that order).

Looking at this impressive line-up, it seems inconceivable that they all failed to see, let alone forestall, the crisis which had been building for six years, or longer. What is immediately clear from this hierarchy of failure is that the higher up the list the failure lies the greater consequences further down, to the point where the failure at the top makes the subsequent regulators lower down the scale are incapable of doing anything effective overall. If governments and their laws and central banks fail in their roles to control the economy as a whole, it's impossible for the SEC, CFPA and the LSE, FSA, which do not

Table 8:

First Tier: the Whole Economy

The Law

Government

Central Banks:

The Federal Reserve
The Bank of England

Second Tier: the Individual Components

Regulatory Institutions:

SEC, CFTC and CFPA⋆
LSE and FSA

The Rating Agencies:

S&P, Moody's, Fitch
and their European offices

External Auditors
Internal Auditors

Investors

Executive Directors
Non-Executive Directors

Compliance Officers

Bankruptcy: "The Moral Hazard Territory"

⋆The US Consumer Financial Protection Agency,
forming in October 2009.

regulate the economy as a whole but regulate individual companies, to prevent an economic crisis. If the dam bursts, a Ruination of Regulators armed with pens, rule books and photo-copiers is not about to stop it. The politicians in 2009 are seeking to bolster regulation at this Second Tier of Regulation, when they should be focused on the First Tier, which is their territory, and which requires wise judgement. It is the regulation at the top three levels which are the most important to fix for the future, and that is why the Fed and the Bank of England must regulate the banks as they have the power as bankers to control credit and lending, and to revoke banking licences.

The reaction of the politicians, being the legislators, however, has been to call for more regulation lower down the hierarchy, and for "heavy" regulation as opposed to the "light" regulation that they blame for Global Crunch. Their idea of more skyscrapers with acres and tons of concrete propping up endless coffee conas (US) and pots of tea (UK) and water-dispensers, manned by regulators not smart enough to get a job at Goldman, will somehow prevent a future crisis, is a completely daft notion. PM Gordon Brown, the IMF and the Germans and French have even called for a Global Regulator to sit atop the whole pile, no doubt perched on the 164th floor of the absurd Burj Dubai sky-dagger, armed with night-vision binoculars that can see and hear round the curvature of the planet: "Stop, everyone, stop! There's a world financial crisis coming!"

The inherent absurdity of the idea of regulation was exposed for all to see when the regulators "failed" over the undisclosed emergency advances of £61.6 billion by The Bank of England to the two Scottish banks, as the crisis broke. Three days after Lehman went belly-up, Lloyds-TSB announced its proposed acquisition of HBOS on 18th September 2008, but within two weeks HBOS was seeking its emergency loan from the BoE, followed within a week by RBS, as both banks were totally and hopelessly bust. The BoE naturally insisted on secrecy as it did not want a run on the banks generally, and on these two specifically. So the regulators had to watch both RBS and Lloyds-TSB issue Information Memoranda to their shareholders with very material omissions, as known to the regulators themselves, namely that these banks had run out of money. The point is this: when and how to regulate is fraught with many types of issue,

195

issues which a central bank can deal with under bankers' confidence, but which could easily cause a regulator accountable to investors and the market to blow the whole system to smithereens, with the taxpayer ending up with the losses. As it was, the regulators didn't, but by not doing their proper job.

Gordon Brown *et al.* are also determined to micro-manage and regulate the whole financial system to the point where it is a sclerotic structure that cannot reinvent itself or even function, turning it, like Lot's wife, into a pillar of salt. He wants to regulate all offshore tax havens. Why? He believes they aided and abetted the shadow banking system, the system whereby banks tried to own assets, and their consequent liabilities, offshore but not on their onshore balance sheets, with their SIVs and Conduit funds; but if you regulate Guernsey, for example, or the Bahamas, you will destroy their economy and all the business will move anyway to some independent and welcoming island in the Indian Ocean, or wherever. Why not regulate the onshore banks instead and impede their ability to create offshore structures?

Politicians also view hedge funds as undesirable citizens requiring heavy new regulation, especially the Germans who view them as a zero-sum game that contributes nothing to the real economy, and whose extinction through regulation would be to no one's great loss. Whereas in actual fact hedge funds played no destructive part in Global Crunch at all, and the banks incurred no major losses on their margin loans to hedge funds, any more than they did on loans to the US Community Banks and Credit Unions. The collapse of LTCM and the $6.0 billion internet hedge fund Amaranth ten years previously had been a wake-up call for both hedgies and banks. True, some hedge funds, such as Och-Ziff Capital Management and Ody Asset Management made money by shorting bank shares in the crisis, but so what? They perceived that these shares were overvalued, which they were, so they shorted them, which is what hedge funds do and which brings about a more realistic price in the market. The authorities acted like ostriches and buried their heads in the sand, by banning the shorting of stocks as the markets crashed, but all that was clear from that suspension was that the hedge funds knew more about what was going on than the regulators.

The idea that the gallimaufry of hedge funds need heavy or even any regulation is a case that simply makes no sense, especially as all hedge funds do completely different things involving widely different strategies. As hedge funds are invested by private money, any losses they made, and they weren't significant in 2008/9, fell to their investors, with no recourse to the tax-payers, please note. Those that would regulate these funds are like someone who wants to drink coffee and then trace it all the way through their innards, a completely pointless exercise, proving nothing. Already, the first EU Directive on Alternative Investment Fund Managers (AIFM) seeks to prevent EU investors investing in non-EU managers' funds, which smacks of blatant protectionism. Citadel reported that this move could bar EU investors from 91% of funds, while HSBC's custodial bank said this limitation could cost EU pension funds £21.0 billion in lost returns. A far more sensible move would be to ban proprietary trading from regulated banks and force this activity into an unregulated hedge fund industry, where it belongs.

Within days, however, it was announced that a Paris-based super-regulator, the European Securities and Markets Authority, ESMA, would be granted powers by the EU over the hedge funds in London as their use of derivatives posed a systemic risk. Then up-popped Jean Paul Gauzes, the European Parliament *Rapporteur* who opened the hearing of the Committee on EU Economic and Monetary Affairs on the AIFM Directive – you note all the jargon and bureaucracy – with these less than immortal words: "Nothing can be left out of the regulations now, even if hedge funds did not cause the crisis". WHAT? Even the Archbishop of Canterbury, as he surveyed the dreadful returns of the Church Commissioners, concluded that "Hedge Funds are needed to maintain the temple".

Gordon Brown should know that the more government regulation that is introduced, the more it places the government, or rather the taxpayer, exactly where they do not want to be, namely making good the losses. Brown should know this: the collapse of the UK's venerable Equitable Life Assurance Society, founded in 1762, has been deemed to have been as a result of regulatory failure and the tab for £3.0 billion has been sent to No.11 Downing Street, where it remains sizzling, unpaid and angry, in the background. Over-regulation will create a situation where any financial corporation that goes bust, and its shareholders, have a claim on government funds, by potential Put-Options written by their government on the taxpayer, who did not pay their taxes to incur this type of liability by default. Nor did anyone independent of governments separately represent the taxpayers of many countries' best interests during Global Crunch, an omission which must be protected by statute law for the future.

And yet in this short volume the evidence required to inform effective regulation has been revealed. One starts with the Law, beginning with the Rudderless Decade of the 1970s and the Greed Decade of the 1980s, when barriers to the perceived availability of credit were torn down, beginning with Nixon's unilateral abolition of the Gold Standard, Heath and Barber's credit loosening, then President Carter's deregulation act that unpicked a single provision of the 1933 Glass-Steagall Act, which in turn unleashed the S&L fiasco, the forerunner of the credit crisis. The same thing happened in the UK, when Thatcher deregulated the building societies, and turned these essentially S&L structures into would-be banks, which went bust in droves during the credit crisis, while the big one which stayed as an "old-fashioned" mutual society, in which all profits are paid back into the society with no shareholders requiring dividends, namely the Nationwide Building Society, is still going strong.

The UK politicians also replaced the Money Lenders Acts of 1900/1927 over time with the new, as in *modernising*, Consumer Credit Act of 1974. The Money Lenders Act which it replaced, however, contained a very intelligent provision: if a lender made a loan on highly punitive terms as regards security taken, repayment terms or interest, the making of that loan could be deemed to be "unconscionable" and repudiated, or dissolved, by the courts. Once one or two banks had lost a few cases and loans, their credit terms improved out of all recognition, as the deliberate uncertainty created by this Act gently pushed lenders to err on the side of caution. To lose a loan in this way then became a career-stopping event for a banker, but the Consumer Credit Act removed this infra-red protective barrier and did not replace it.

And now the FSA, completely missing the subtle point of the Money Lenders Act, has now insisted that mortgage-lenders must ensure in their Due Diligence that the borrower can repay any mortgage granted, virtually eliminating any discretion or forward thinking by the lender, which will restrict the availability of mortgages generally. How clever is that? And then Clinton made the same error when he set aside the Anti-Predatory Lending Acts, as the Treasurers of many States descended on Washington and petitioned him not to do away with the legislation, but at the heart of Global Crunch was the widespread inability of subprime borrowers to repay the onerous terms of their mortgages, particularly re-set mortgages where the cost jumped upwards after an easy regime for the first few years. Thanks to the emphasis on loan origination to feed the grinders dicing and slicing on Wall Street, these toxic assets pervaded the global financial system.

It was the repeal of the 1933 Glass-Steagall Act by Clinton in 1999, again in the name of *modernization*, that removed a major safety-net to the US and global banking system. The Gramm-Leach-Bliley Act disposed of the Glass-Steagall Act, which had been passed after the Great Depression when hundreds of commercial banks failed, by investing in the stock market before the crash of 1929. The Glass-Steagall Act forbad a commercial bank from investing in an investment bank or an insurance company, and passed the setting of interest rates payable on savings deposits to the Fed. As those Degenerate Person investment bankers who cast their avaricious eyes over the large deposit bases of the commercial banks in the 2000s, deposits which are usually very stable in quantum, they found their way to leveraging off all that lovely cash previously barred to them by Glass-Steagall.

Commercial banks are low-risk businesses by design, which should basically grow with the annual rise of an economy's GDP, as Petty had formulated over 300 years ago. Investment banks are high-risk/high-growth businesses that often go out of business, as with Barings, Bear Stearns, Lehman Bros, while Merrill Lynch was rescued by take-over, by a commercial bank that now regrets this acquisition, as it happens. The combination of the two types clearly has dangers. The Gramm-Leach-Bliley Act that disposed of Glass-Steagall was described by Alan Greenspan as restoring sorely-needed *flexibility* to the financial sector and was no aberration.

No aberration? It was passed to enable Citigroup to merge with Travellers Group, largely an insurance group, to produce an all-singing, all-dancing financial supermarket selling everything from monkey nuts to alphabet soup. Travellers was the result of

Degenerate Person Sandy Weill's giant corporate ego, which had started out with the purchase of a boring little secondary lender, Commercial Credit in Baltimore, which had lost its focus whilst owned by an ailing computer company. From this improbable base, Weill hit the take-over trail, to the point where Citicorp, carefully built up by Creative Person Walter Wriston over many years into the biggest and most successful global bank, became a must-have trophy bride for Weill. The trouble was Glass-Steagall stood in the way of Weill's overarching ambition, and so would have to go. The Clinton presidency was drawing to a close, so Weill decided to telephone the Secretary of the Treasury, Robert Rubin, and make him an offer he wouldn't refuse: help abolish Glass-Steagall and come on board the Sandy Weill Layered Wedding-cake of Bolt-on Dysfunctional Financial Acquisitions Inc., now plus Citicorp. Weill's acquisitive reputation preceded him: when Rubin took the call, he wondered with some jocularity if Weill wanted to buy the US government! No such call to the Fed was needed as Alan Greenspan, as we have seen, was already pre-sold and packaged to go, in favour of abolishing any legislation which blocked financial *flexibility*.

The combination proved disastrous: the Travellers insurance business was soon sold off, the Salomon Bros investment banking business was crushed to death by internal politics and bureaucracy, Smith Barney was eventually demerged out, the old Schroders brand was buried under the heap somewhere. When Global Crunch came along the directors thought they needed, or told the first Arab investors who did invest, ADIA, or the Abu Dhabi Investment Authority, that they needed just $7.5 billion in new capital. The reality was that they soon needed over ten times that money just to stagger along their unprofitable path, all focus lost. As Citigroup sought to raise another $17.0 billion in Q4 2009, ADIA claimed that it was tricked into making the investment by Citicorp's Robert Rubin and Michael Klein, citing "fraudulent misrepresentations", in a deal which requires conversion of ADIA's 11% Convertible Notes at $31.83-$37.24 per share, which was ten times the Citigroup share price of $3.50 at end-2009!

This was clear proof that the directors no longer had a handle on the numbers of this amorphous mess of a so-called global bank, now run, if that is the right word, by a CEO called Pandit, which surname is at least better than Bandit, an epithet that surely applied to the Degenerate Persons whose acquisitions created this monstrous and unmanageable pile of disparate corporates, rustled together as it was from all corners of the globe. So Vikram Pandit with a P started the inevitable dismantling process, one month after he had made a presentation to senior management that sought to endorse the supermarket Citigroup business model, just as it was visibly collapsing. Call me a sucker, but please give me a break! All this nonsense was in the name of *modernization* and *flexibility*?

The abolition of the good law of Creative Persons from 1970 to 2006, and its replacement by bad law and lacunas by Degenerate Persons, lay at the heart of Global Crunch, right alongside subprime CMOs, CDOs and CDSs, false ratings and fraud. Democratic governments, however, want their economies to do well and for people to own their own house, as in the "ownership society", but not for any altruistic considerations, but for one reason only: votes. When Dubya Bush was calling for more mortgages for the 5.5 million US subprimes still blessedly without a mortgage, he wasn't talking about home ownership, Stupid! He was talking about votes! That's what Thatcher had been looking for when she sold off the UK's council houses in the 1980s to their tenants at knocked-down prices.

Government's principal function is to create the right conditions for the economy to function efficiently, mainly by preserving the value of the currency. When Degenerate Persons changed the law to suit their own intentions, as with allowing a mad merger in the private sector, they well and truly let the baby out with the dirty bath water. Government needs to readdress the issues of the bad economic legislation of the past thirty years that it has so idly implemented, without due thought for the consequences. Much of the old and robust law had the Colgate Ring of Confidence about it, curbing the "animal spirits" of Degenerate Persons, whilst not impeding the good ideas of Creative Persons. Table 9 chronicles the drift towards ever-looser credit with the growth of regulation that was meant to control it.

Table 9:

Enactment/Repeal of the Anglo-sphere's Relevant Financial Laws and Regulations, 1971-2006:

1971, US: Unilateral Cessation of 1944 Bretton Woods Agreement ends the the post-WW2 Gold Standard

1972, UK: Barber's Budget for 'Competition and Credit Control' lifts credit restrictions and causes post-WW2's first banking crisis

1974, UK: Consumer Credit Act replaces the Money Lender Acts,1900/1927

1977, US: Community Reinvestment Act, which made it illegal to refuse mortgages to lower income groups and minorities, starting the trend towards subprimes

1980, US: Depository Institutions Deregulation and Monetary Control Act, repealing Regulation Q of the Glass-Steagall Act, 1933, and causes the subsequent S&L Crisis

1981, US: Gramm-Rudman-Hollings Act approves the first $1.0 trillion Budget Deficit

1982, US: Tax Reform Act, which kept tax relief for mortgage interest, but removed it for auto and consumer loans

1982, US: The Alternative Mortgage Transaction Parity Act, which loosened restrictions on lenders

1986, UK: First Building Societies Act, replacing the 1874 Act and introducing regulation to deposit-taking and lending Societies

1987, UK: UK Banking Supervision Act, which allowed authorised EU banks to accept UK deposits

1991, US: Home Mortgage Disclosure Act, which demanded racial equality by lenders, a contributory step towards the subprime debacle

1997, UK: Second Building Societies Act, setting a permissive rather than a prescriptive regime, with new "nature limits" on lending which become a contributory factor in Global Crunch

1999, US: Gramm-Leach-Bliley Act repeals rest of the Glass-Steagall Act, 1933, which separated commercial banks from investment banks and insurance companies, which repeal was a major contributory cause to Global Crunch

2000, UK: Financial Services and Markets Act, establishing the FSA as UK regulator, which failed at its first hurdle in 2007 over the Northern Rock Bank collapse

2002, US: Sarbanes-Oxley Act, which sought to strengthen accounting issues post-Enron etc., but which proved inconsequential in the face of Global Crunch

2003, US: The American Dream Downpayment Act, which gave up to $10,000.00 to low-income families towards a downpayment on a house, spurring subprime borrowers

2006, US: Financial Services Regulation Relief Act, which reduced the capital banks had to maintain.

President Barack Obama and other leaders should take a leaf out of the life of President Calvin Coolidge: a man of unimpeachable integrity, hostile to new ways, the terms *modernization* and *flexibility* and *deregulation* would have been beneath his contempt, and he believed in as little government as possible. In the face of idealism or zeal for reform, he adopted a stance of masterly inactivity, to the point that when Dorothy Parker heard he had died, she remarked: "How could they tell?" Coolidge was a political shrewdie whose silence spoke volumes, a quality that is now at a premium amongst the mad-cap schemes for regulation being bandied about daily by today's politicians and regulators.

"People should be very frightened of the FSA", said it's chief Hector Sants. The only thing that's global and which I am frightened of in this debate is the confusion of tongues. The legislators and regulators of this modern-day Tower of Babel are missing a fundamental point: one dollar spent wisely just *once* at the level of The Law is worth much more in effective regulation than one hundred dollars spent vainly every year attempting daily regulation at every lower level. This principle was evinced by the Glass-Steagall Act, and others, that operated successfully for 66 years and at minimal cost.

I would like to propose a new law formulated by a Creative Person of my acquaintance, which would apply to the officers and agents, or the regulatory functionaries, in the Second Tier of the Regulatory Hierarchy in Table 8 above, at the level of individual execution of their respective duties. The Proportionality Act would impose on these functionaries a duty not to enforce a solution which would produce a greater mischief than the mischief which the functionary was seeking to remedy by following a particular provision in the first place. This principle would grant discretion to the regulatory functionaries over whether to enforce or not enforce an order from the Regulator, and embraces the *manner* of how these functionaries go about their duty. In effect, this law would cut those minor public servants running around like petty-Hitlers off at the knees, to counter the fact that such tribal behaviour is indicative of a lack of leadership in the first place. The idea seems so sensible that the passing of a Proportionality Act in the field of regulation might over time reinforce one of those unwritten principles of society that pervade the operation of the Law, such as 'to act in good faith', or the idea of 'breach of fiduciary duty', and now 'it's out-of-proportion'. The British sense of fairness and compromise is lurking somewhere behind this issue.

One law that needs changing immediately is the charter governing the Fed, which is to ensure "maximum sustainable employment and price sustainability", to which must be added "with overall financial and markets stability as a priority". That the Fed must share a large part of the blame for Global Crunch goes without saying, as it left interest rates far too low for far too long after 9/11, stoking up the housing bubble until it burst disastrously for the global economy. Alan Greenspan had looked at the earlier dot.com bubble and decided it was not the Fed's function to prick a stock market bubble by raising interest rates when the real economy was doing nicely, thank you. That was Greenspan at his best, because when the dot.com bubble did explode it didn't affect the real economy at all. One giant bonfire of failed business plans and worthless share certificates was all it took to clear away the wreckage.

A housing bubble, however, is a completely different phenomenon and does very serious damage to the real economy and people's lives when it crashes and burns. It was the failure to distinguish between these two distinctly different bubbles that led to the failure to raise interest rates in time and contain the boom. Greenspan wrote: "The Fed has no explicit mandate under the law to try to contain a stock market bubble. Indirectly we had the authority to do so, if we believed stock prices were creating inflationary pressures". It is very difficult to discern a trail between booming stock prices and inflation in the economy as a whole; and it is extremely difficult to justify raising interest rates when inflation is subdued in the wider economy but property prices are soaring. As Bernanke said in 2008: "I and others were mistaken early on in saying that the subprime crisis could be contained. The causal relationship between the housing problem and the broad financial system was very complex and difficult to predict".

There are a number of structural deficiencies here that clearly need addressing. On 22nd December 2008 Sir John Gieve, the retiring Deputy Governor of the Bank of England, a touch de-mob happy and with the prospect of Christmas beckoning, candidly admitted "Why didn't we see that it was so serious? I think that's because we, perhaps, hadn't kept pace with the extent of globalisation... We need to develop some new instruments between interest rates, which affect the whole economy... and regulation of specific institutions", and he might have added "and specific markets".

Precisely. So, why not separate the interest rate for property loans and mortgages out from the interest rate for the economy as a whole? If overall inflation is low but property prices are rising and creating a bubble, then the property interest rate will be higher than the Fed or base rate. Banks deal with many different interest rates and exchange rates every day, so adding another one won't make the slightest difference. The Bank of England has the MPC, the 'Monetary Policy Committee', which, like the Fed, democratically votes on interest rate changes; so why not have MPC 2 to vote on mortgage rate changes? And, why not have two rates, one for commercial and one for residential, just as MBSs, or Mortgage-Backed Securities, are divided between CMBSs (Commercial) and RMBSs (Residential)?

Professor Shiller at Yale has been compiling the S&P Case-Shiller US housing index for several years now, and in the UK the Nationwide and the Halifax maintain their own residential indices, and likewise the big realtors do the same for the commercial markets, separately covering offices, leisure, retail, factories and warehouses, so there would be no shortage of data for MPC 2 to consider. The US commercial real estate sector had $3.0-3.5 trillion total debt and values had fallen from $6.0 to $3.6 trillion, (that's CRE loans plus CMB securities held by banks), representing an average LTV, or Loan-to-Value, of 85%, against the Fed's assessment of US bank equity at $1.316 trillion, which are big and scary numbers.

And the UK commercial property loan sector in mid-2009 owed the banks £225.0 billion, up 450%+ over the decade with an average LTV ratio of 80%, and with £43.0 billion due for repayment in 2009, it seems like big enough numbers to receive a separate interest rate to micro-manage the sector that lies closer to the boom-bust cycle than any other, especially as UK commercial property was off by 45%, and by 40% in the US, during Global Crunch, a far higher dip than in the residential sector. The old rule of 'Too much borrowing on an asset kills its value' also applies to any sector as a whole, and to the economy as a whole, and LTVs need to be reduced to 66.6% at most.

The Bank of England, meanwhile, made the same error as the Fed, that of leaving interest rates too low for far too long, but it wasn't the Old Lady's mistake, however, it was Prime Minister Gordon Brown's. When Brown became Chancellor of the Exchequer on Tony Blair's and New Labour's election victory in May 1997, the first thing Brown did, amidst much fanfare, was allegedly to set the Bank of England free from his control. Previously, the UK Chancellor controlled the two main levers of economic power, taxation and interest rates, but now the Bank was free to set interest rates, or so we all thought. Having taken the handcuffs off the Old Lady, however, the self-defeating Brown proceeded to hobble her around the ankles instead: she would now set interest rates purely to control inflation by reference to the CPI, the EU's Consumer Prices Index, which excludes the cost of housing and reflects EU inflation but not the UK's higher actual rate of inflation, until mid-2008.

So, by different routes, the Fed and the Bank of England allowed the 800-pound Gorilla of Global Crunch to stalk up on them unseen. The absurdity of trying to manage an economy by reference to just one index, like a submarine with just one gauge, was shown up in mid-2008, one year after the collapse of Bear Stearns and Northern Rock which were both heavily involved in the over-blown housing sectors, meant that the UK's RPI which included housing, plunged below the CPI which did not, so that the Bank of England, seeking to get to zero interest rates as it positioned itself to fend off deflation, was following the RPI down to the bottom, but in defiance of Captain Brown's orders to follow the CPI! Brown's new controls for inflation also made arrangement for the Governor of the Bank of England to write a silly letter to the Chancellor if the inflation target of 3% was exceeded:

Dear Prime Minister,

We were going along quite nicely, watching the CPI gauge just like you said, when a nasty storm blew up which was completely unforeseeable and unfortunately we bought some experience we were unable to pay for: following the CPI in the periscope and ignoring all other gauges, I happened to spot the RPI crashing down and so there was nothing we could do but follow it down instead.

Please authorise another £25.0 billion of QE so that we can blow our tanks and try and get back to the surface!

Yours Below the Waves,
Mervyn King – (Your Governor of the "Independent" Bank of England).

The regulatory institutions in the US and the UK, the SEC in the US and the LSE and the FSA in the UK, unlike the central bankers, were powerless to prevent the economy sliding into the abyss. Their brief is to regulate quoted companies, not the whole economy. The SEC had a long run-in with AIG in the early 2000s, arguably the ground zero of the subprime crisis, concerning its accounts and reported profits, which were shown to be over-stated, and the then-Chairman, Hank Greenberg, was unceremoniously booted out, which is about as much as regulators of the marketplace can hope to achieve. Unfortunately, with the removal of the savvy Greenberg, his successors lost control of the business, took on far too much risk around the world and effectively went bust. The plain fact about regulation is that there is very little a regulator can actually do without becoming a "wretched, rash, intruding fool!"

When Gordon Brown "freed" the Bank of England, he also made another catastrophic mistake: he passed prime responsibility from the Bank which knew what it was doing with over 300 years' experience, to the decade-old FSA that had no experience at all of banking supervision, with the Bank and HM Treasury on a tripartite dotted line of this regulatory trio. Why? Inevitably three organizations were bound to prove less effective than a single regulator that was keenly aware of its sole responsibilities. The FSA was soon caught with its pants down when Northern Rock Bank in Newcastle went bust for that most basic of banking errors, borrowing short in the intermediary financial markets and lending long in the 30-year mortgage market, and at up to 125% of valuations, so when the credit markets seized up so did Northern Rock. But what were the regulators meant to do? Stop a public company from making money by exploiting a seemingly robust credit market? This would have been an extremely difficult call, until the market collapsed, which was then too late. The cause of this crash was higher up the Regulatory Hierarchy, at Tier One's central bankers, who under-priced the cost of money.

Later in the crisis, Gordon Brown persuaded the Chairman of the profitable and liquid Lloyds-TSB Bank, Sir Victor Blank, on a plane returning from a trade trip to Israel, to ride to the rescue of HBOS, a doomed merger of the Halifax Building Society and the venerable Bank of Scotland, but HBOS was HBUST and Lloyds-TSB was soon writing off £21.3 billion over the next eighteen months to June 2009. HBOS had a mismatch of £200.0 billion between its loans and deposits that left it completely vulnerable to the now paralysed credit markets, which Lloyds imported unwisely onto its own balance sheet. According to Lloyds-TSB's CEO, the American Eric Daniels, his bank did just one-fifth of the necessary DD, or Due Diligence, an incredible omission from a senior banker. What could regulators have done about that? When HM Treasury launched its Asset-backed insurance scheme, Lloyds was first in the queue with a £260.0 billion begging-bowl; a few months later Lloyds tried to get out of this expensive arrangement, which it had not yet formally signed up for, but soon learnt that HM Treasury was looking for a £1.0 billion exit fee for the pleasure.

Wherever Brown's Big Bother Boots went in this crisis, disaster inevitably followed, as the ousted Sir Victor Blank can testify to, but no doubt a peerage from the departing Brown after the next election will conveniently seal his lips over the precise details. Otherwise Sir Victor Blank Cheque owes all Lloyds' shareholders the explanation that he hasn't given yet, as to what he thought he was up to – running a bank? Or ruining it? And what were the regulators meant to do about all these shenanigans, short of telling Brown to stop running across the cricket pitch with his football boots on? Regulation is inherently flawed by its own constrictions. Banking supervision, in the meantime, should be with the Fed and the Bank of England and no one else.

The next on the tariff of the regulatory hierarchy come the Rating Agencies and the Auditors. I bracket them together for a simple reason: they are both paid by those that they are rating or auditing, which is an inherent conflict of interest that has gone on for far too long. The Rating Agencies rated BB- subprimes as AAA-rated, as we have seen, and must be blamed for their central role in Global Crunch. As the Rating Agencies' fees are Issuer-driven, the investment banks had a great time playing off one agency against another to get a better rating, and not least as an agency's fee for rating a $100.0 million CDO/CMO was typically $40,000.00, or four times greater than a normal fee. So the agencies engaged in their own turf wars to win the business, as their executives had a focus on their own incentives and stock options in their agency.

As regards the big corporate collapses of the past thirty years, they all had had their accounts signed off by their Auditors in the year or two before they collapsed. The demise of Enron even brought down Arthur Andersen, one of the Big Five Auditors. Section 404 of the Sarbanes-Oxley Act 2002 requires certain accounting principles to be enforced by Auditors, who in turn are reviewed by the Public Company Accounting Oversight Board, or PCAOB, an acronym that drew derision when its epithet of Peek-A-Boo stuck. None of this was of any use when Global Crunch appeared, however, nor did it deal with the central conflict of interest issue, which is often exacerbated by the auditing firm also providing extensive advisory services to the same client, as Andersen Consulting had done with its audit client Enron. No one gets to see the inside workings and key personnel in a company quite like the Auditor, other than the Compliance Officer, but all the outside world sees is a bland report expressing the view that the accounts are "true and fair".

The idea that the Rating Agencies and Auditors of publicly-traded companies should have their own independent regulators opens up many possibilities. When the UK government-owned water companies were privatised by Thatcher in the mid-1980s, meaning they were turned into publicly-traded companies on the stock market, which was a politically sensitive issue in many ways, a regulator was appointed, termed Ofwat for the Office of Water, which controlled charges, investment, profits and the quality of pipelines, rivers and beaches and the quality of the water itself. Many sceptics couldn't see this structure working at all, but over the last 25 years Ofwat has worked reasonably well. With the Rating Agencies and Auditors, with Ofrat and Ofaud – if you will pardon the acronyms for a moment – in place, it then becomes feasible for the regulators to receive all rating and auditing fees direct from their client companies and then pay out monthly to the actual providers of these services, now subject to their over-sight.

To complete the dissolution of the inherent conflict of interests issue as regards Auditors, there should be a provision that Auditors are automatically replaced every few years, so that an outgoing Auditor knows that the next Auditor will be reviewing their work and reporting to the Regulator, Ofaud. And no Auditor should be allowed to provide consultancy services whilst appointed as Auditor, but should be free to provide such services to any other companies. All of this proposed structural shake-up is actually much easier in the high-tech age: a change of auditors is now just one click-on-a-mouse away. And it will remove the stifling presence of the 'Big Four' and open up the profession to the 'Best Twenty'; and remove the profession's potentially-corrupt self-regulating disciplinary functions from the grasp of the 'Big Four' as well, as the independent PCAOB/Ofaud regulator takes on this function too.

And audit firms should be required to write an actual report on the Company and its results and prospects, and provide additional salient data as appropriate, such as the number, type, average spend, and churn rate of subscribers to a subscription operator, like a telecoms company, for instance. An Internal Audit function for companies of a certain size should be mandatory and should report to the External Auditor and not to the directors in the first instance, and the External Auditor should be required to report to both the directors and the regulator, namely the central bank or stock market sponsor. The days of cosy relationships of rating and auditing would be over, the audit function would become much more creative and valuable, and everyone would know a lot more about the strengths and weaknesses of public companies. Come to think about it, why not have Offeff as a regulator for non-executive directors, of financial companies at least, on the same sort of lines? If they challenged the executive directors and were told to "Effoff", as a certain Jim Leng at RT the miner was, it would encourage them if they knew Offeff could award them redundancy, payable by levies on the institutions themselves, which leads to the obvious issue that these levies should cover the remuneration of Non-execs in the first place.

The next level of regulatory oversight are the investors themselves, namely the large institutions, pension funds, insurance companies and private investors with their US 401(k)s and UK SIPPs and ISAs and private portfolios. One of the more surprising aspects of capitalism is investors' supine attitude to their investments, regulation and corporate governance. They explain their *laissez-faire* hands-off approach by saying that if the management are not doing a good job, the 'invisible hand of the market' will operate and they will sell their shares and buy better prospects elsewhere. It is hardly surprising that the most successful stock market investor is Warren Buffett and

Charlie Mungo's Berkshire Hathaway, who are very active in the management of their investments.

Things are slowly changing and today's chairmen and CEOs are increasingly subject to stringent enquiries from analysts, active investors and professional corporate second-guessers, whose aim is to put executive directors on their mettle and keep them there. Knight Vinke for example, the activist investor, has been giving the HSBC Chairman Stephen Green the bird over the ill-fated $13.4 billion acquisition of the US Household Finance Corporation for nearly three years already, and their points are sound, so irrefutable in fact that they make Green look like the proverbial ostrich as he continues to ignore their message. This deal that has now cost HSBC some $40.0 billion, with very little to show for it. Then the £50.0 billion Hermes pension fund, following the lead of Soros, called for banker's bonuses as financed by public funds to be cancelled, which was more like it. Such challenges are a lot more bracing than the US Sarbanes-Oxley Act of 2002's post-Enron requirement that the CEO and CFO sign off the company's financial statements.

This constant challenging review is also what the non-executive directors are meant to do. I met an acquaintance who was sporting a rather luxurious sun-tan in the middle of a London Winter and on enquiry it transpired he had been on a corporate bonanza in the Caribbean, at the behest of one of London's big banks.

"Hundreds of graphs and figures", he complained, "couldn't understand any of it! Nice cheque in a brown envelope, though. You see, I'm a non-effective director!"

Well, that frankness about says it all, about the non-effective directors at Barings, Enron, World.Com, Lehman, Bear Stearns, Merrill Lynch, RBS, WaMu, Citigroup, Lloyds-TSB, BoA, HBOS, Northern Rock, I could go on. The problem is that non-execs are generally chosen by the CEO and are considered by most CEOs to be rubber-stampers, so there's not a lot of regulatory value there.

A rare exception caught the eye recently: a new Chairman came into RT, the miner, where the CEO was trying to sell 19.6% of the capital to the main customer, China, for $20.0 billion cash which RT desperately needed. This was a clear value-destroying deal both for prices and therefore profits, but also would lessen the bid premium if the Chinese launched a full bid for RT. The new Chairman, Jim

Leng, advised a Rights Issue instead, but the CEO and most of the rest of the board insisted on the Chinalco deal, so the Chairman resigned after just 26 days and the CEO was forced into the Rights Issue. Was it a set-up, I wondered, but the outcome was the right one. The potential power of the non-exec is great and is hugely under-utilised in practice.

The Compliance Officer is potentially in a much stronger position than the external Regulator, and Non-Executive Director, because he or she is internal to the organisation itself. The weakness of exter-nally-applied regulation is that it doesn't grab the 'hearts and minds' of the 'animal spirits' on the inside, whereas internally-produced pressures are the best way to ensuring compliance. The role of the Compliance Officer needs to be further defined and reinforced by legislation, linked into the legislative proposals for Auditors, so that the Compliance Officer is invested with greater actual powers than the illusory powers currently exercised, or not exercised, by the exter-nal regulators. The thrust of these proposals is to harness the private sector functions already in place and costed into the system, to the point where ineffective external regulation becomes redundant at the level of external regulators below central banks and stock market reg-ulators. And the idea of a Financial Stability Board that emerged from Pittsburgh G20 is just another sticking plaster over an essential-ly flawed concept of external regulation.

Finally, the infra-red fear of bankruptcy is meant to keep all direc-tors, especially of banks and financial institutions, on the straight and narrow. It is a fact that banks go bust at 5.30 pm if they run out of liquidity, whereas an industrial company can stagger on for a quar-ter-century or more slowly going bust, just like GM and Chrysler and British Leyland, ever since the first oil crisis in 1974. The incredible fact of the crisis of 2008/9 was the vast number and sheer scale of actual and virtual bankruptcies and bail-outs of banks and insurance companies across the world. To the list in the US and UK cited above, we can add Germany's Hypobank and Commerzbank, Austria's Hypo Bank, UBS, Dexia, Uni-Credit, Fortis, all the banks in Ireland and Iceland, many of the UK's former building societies, the list is endless. The Degenerate Person directors of all these failed banks were guilty of not heeding the doctrine of not entering the "Moral Hazard Territory".

The horrendous fact is that they very nearly bankrupted the whole global capitalist system and right under the noses of the so-called regulators. Something has to be done about it, which raises the question of the proper function of the US CFPA and the UK FSA: these regulators should be nothing to do with bank regulation, but should be entirely concerned with consumer finance, in which there are still miss-selling and deceptions aplenty, concentrating on authorising new products ahead of launch and with a view to reducing such offerings. There is no other effective purpose for this type of bureaucratic external regulator.

The problem for bank regulators now is that The "Too-Big-To-Fail" mentality has set in to the extent that the basic banking structure has got to be deconstructed: small private banks and Lehman can go to the wall, but even Lehman's collapse triggered the wider collapse, so even a relatively small bank in today's over-leveraged and risk-correlated world can cause major systemic damage. This general review of the regulatory hierarchy leaves three main questions for the future that will now be addressed.

Glass-Steagall Issues

Back to *that* Bloomberg interview of 12 September 2008: the Greenspan solution was for investment banks to be owned by the much larger commercial banks with their huge retail deposit bases, because in a crisis these banks have access to the Fed's lending window. This would mean that the high-risk, high-reward investment banking subsidiaries would *automatically* qualify in a crisis for what is in effect taxpayer support, which brings us right back to the current conflict of interests, where the self-styled 'masters of the universe' privatise the profits and let the taxpayer nationalise the losses. This is a road to ruin in more ways than one: it points to yet more nationalisations à la Northern Rock and to more costly and ineffectual regulation – did any of these regulators see what was happening, and if they did, was there anything they could do to avert the *unforeseeable* crisis?

In other words the Greenspan solution is a recipe for long-term, over-regulated, sclerotic capital, the worst of all worlds, as he seeks to argue that the taxpayer should shoulder the risk as depositor and not as taxpayer, neatly letting Uncle Sam off the hook but putting the taxpayer firmly back on it, which amounts to the same thing. Then events took control and put the US government firmly back on the hook anyway, as it was forced to conjure up a $700.0 billion TARP bail-out fund to buy the toxic mortgage waste from the banks. And then Greenspan's idea of commercial banks owning investment banks was shown to be "nonsense on stilts", as Goldman and Morgan simply signed some scrappy bits of paper to become deposit-taking holding companies that brought them access to the Fed's support if the need should ever arise. And it arose all right, within a month. And when were you last stomping through the snow in northern Minnesota to buy gas for your auto stalled on empty, credit card in hand and chased by a grizzly, when your heart warmed as you saw the gleaming lights of a Goldman Sachs retail outlet 50 miles south of Duluth?

Greenspan's view of the future is totally asymmetric to a simple structure that worked well for 66 years: the Glass-Steagall Act of 1933 separated the ownership of investment and commercial banking, separating high-risk/high-reward from low-risk/low-reward, and deposits from investments. Greenspan wrote in May 2008: "Given the fading distinction between commercial banking and investment banking...", which is hardly surprising nine years after the repeal of the Glass-Steagall Act itself, which was successful in its time and required no regulation, as it was simply on the statute and was The Law. There was a rationale to this: commercial banking is really a utility, like a water company: you turn on a tap and, provided you have paid your last bill, water comes out; you put your card in the ATM and, as long as you are in credit, out comes liquid readies. You want a mortgage or car loan or overdraft, it can be arranged at a cost that wouldn't interest an investment banker even to get out of bed, let alone pick the phone up.

Society and the economy need liquid and sound commercial banks that don't go bust, and those who want to adopt higher-risk/reward strategies can try their luck, or expertise, as hedge-funds do, but don't call us taxpayers if you go broke. There is room for both models, but let them be separate businesses, please. President Clinton did away with Glass-Steagall in 1999 and allowed the laws against predatory lending to lapse in the name of banking freedom and available credit, just as Thatcher had done away with staid old Building Societies in the 1980s, which then became "banks", before they went bust or were bailed out – Northern Rock, Alliance & Leicester, the Cheshire, the Derbyshire, Bradford & Bingley, Dunfermline and now the biggest of them all, the Halifax. The idea was that banking and regulation and technology had moved on and Glass-Steagall was an anachronism, The US investment banks' balance sheets went from 20% of US GDP in 1999 to over 100% by 2007. Hedge funds, however, have come along since 1999 but are not part of any commercial banking or regulated structure, and their mortgage assets, quite rightly, were not covered by the US TARP bail-out.

And yet perversely, the hum-drum commercial bankers hanker after the glamour, excitement and the greater profits of investment banking, but do they know the greater risks? Barclays Bank owns the so-far successful Barclays Capital, but what does the main board do when John Varley running the commercial bank wants to buy ABN Amro, while Bob Diamond running the investment bank wants to buy Lehman? The risks and rewards are simply miles apart, so where does the capital best get allocated, as Barclays sells Barclays Global Investors for $13.2 billion to BlackRock and their high growth exchange traded funds business, Barclays' iShares, to raise cash? These asset sales, together with a $7.0 billion placing in Abu Dhabi, raised Barclays Tier One Capital Ratio from an underwhelming 5.6% at December 2008 to a more respectable 8.8% at June 2009. This dilemma of capital allocation caused Sir C.K. Chow, CEO of the UK/US manufacturer GKN plc, to split the group into an automotive/aerospace component manufacturer and a separate Brambles/Chep pallets business, which was just as well when it was later discovered that 20 million pallets had gone walk-about and were missing. Imagine such an asset loss in a hybrid banking conglomerate with an underwhelming Tier One Capital Ratio, which was the very position that too many banks found themselves in during Global Crunch.

Fortunately, Varley missed out on ABN Amro, pipped by RBS's higher price, or was rescued might be more accurate, while Diamond, equally luckily, could not get the FSA's approval to buy Lehman, but as a result managed on the first day of its bankruptcy

216

to buy valuable Lehman assets, namely its investment banking, fixed income and equities sales, trading and research desks employing 10,000 executives, along with the Seventh Avenue headquarters, for just $1.75 billion. All of which was fortuitous for Barclays on three big counts, but it highlights the dilemma of the inherent problematical structure of this new banking combination. Incidentally, $1.25 billion in that price was for bonuses for the Lehman bankers of the bust US bank.

Bank of America, BoA, soon discovered all this for themselves with their new herd of bulls, who won't fit naturally into the twice-daily milking-parlour routine of the commercial bank, and that's before the vexed and thorny issue of vastly differing rewards for the two very different types of bankers under the same corporate banner. In fact, it was reported that BoA's Ken Lewis had sought to back out of this deal which he had described at the press launch, with Thain sitting beside him in matching red tie for the losses already coming over the horizon, as "the deal of a lifetime" as early as December 2008, but before its finalisation on 1 January 2009 when he had realised the extent of Merrill's losses, but government officials told him that not to complete the deal could create 'serious systemic risk'. One can but guess at the whispered advice: "Listen pal, you rushed out with the broad, and now you've got the clap, so could you do the decent thing and not spread it around the street!" Merrill Lynch's last quarter's loss as an independent company was a staggering $15.31 billion. Good old Ken was handed a shut-yer-marff government bail-out cheque for $20.0 billion, with an 8% stinger of a coupon, and loan-loss guarantees from the Fed and the FDIC on Merrill's remaining toxic assets of $118.0 billion, on condition he kept the broad off the street, and despite a drop in market value from $176.0 billion at the merger announcement to just $39.0 billion only six weeks after completion.

John Thain, Merrill's CEO, put in a back-of-envelope demand for a $10.0 million bonus for himself for pulling off the deal, but was told to take a long walk out of his NYC $1.22 million refurbished office. It soon came to haunt Lewis that the Merrill herd had taken the right to up to $5.8 billion in bonuses right after the takeover, but also after the BoA board had become aware of the large-scale losses at investment banks. At its annual meeting in April 2009, America's largest pension fund, Calpers, voted to remove the entire board of BoA over this issue, all eighteen of them. Calpers, however, only held 0.35% of the stock and the motion failed, although Lewis was forced aside from the Chairmanship, but the point was made that these bonuses were unconscionable as regards those that took them, and completely incompetent as regards those that paid them. The US-taxpayers paid for these bonuses for failure, and were outraged. The shotgun rescue-takeovers by JPMorgan Chase of Washington Mutual and Wells Fargo of Wachovia, which deals involved four out of America's top five banks, on the other hand make better but not perfect sense as combinations of two commercial banks which have similar products and services, with duplicated costs that can now be slashed. In America alone, JPMorgan is looking for $1.5 billion annual savings from its acquisition of WaMu.

The Dangers of the 'Too-Big-To-Fail' Syndrome

Global Crunch revealed the major problem of unbridled Capitalism going forward: the collapse of Lehman, the fourth largest investment bank, triggered a global recession. It would not be possible to let any bank bigger than Lehman go to the wall in the future under the current structures. The bankers have got the taxpayer pinned to the wall, as in Wall Street, a position that needs to be reversed. The potential for Systemic Risk now pervades the global banking system and a failure of a bigger bank could bring on Great Depression 2. (That The Great Depression led indirectly to WW2 should never be lost sight of.) We need to create a world, not where a bank does not fail, but a world where we can afford to let a bank fail, to reinforce "Moral Hazard" with Bankruptcy, the ultimate link in the Regulatory Hierarchy above. This issue is called the 'Too-Big-To-Fail' Syndrome, but the reality exposed by Global Crunch is that the B side is the 'Too-Big-To-Manage' Syndrome.

I paint the stakes this high as the challenge is immense and requires solutions at a commensurate level. It was Hyman Minsky's 'Financial Instability Hypothesis' which predicated that a large global financial system's excessive emphasis on the conception and production of new investment structures leads to inherent macro-structural instability in both output and prices. Minsky was writing in 1986 when the MBO, LBO and HLT structures were getting going, before hedge funds became a major force and before structured finance and derivatives and CDOs, MBOs, ABSs, IRSs, ERSs, CFDs and CDSs and new-style mortgages were even invented. Minsky presciently advised: 'The Federal Reserve must broaden its scope and take initiatives to prevent the development of practices conducive to financial instability. The Federal Reserve needs to guide the evolution of financial institutions by favouring stability-enhancing and discourage instability-augmenting institutions and practices'.

So the first thing to do is to stop any bank getting bigger by hostile acquisition: one only has to look at the example of RBS's mad attempt at self-aggrandisement to see the sense in this. In the case of an agreed banking merger, the regulators, or central banks should need to be involved and persuaded that the logic and benefits clearly out-weigh any systemic risk: if they do not, there should be no merger, as when the UK's FSA stopped Barclay's buying Lehman before the latter's bankruptcy. Remember the UK's Midland Bank's absurd takeover of Crocker National Bank in San Francisco in the early 1980s, just as the Californian real estate market took a bath and ended up taking Midland with it, when HSBC bought it in 1992? And don't forget HSBC's disastrous acquisition of Household Financial Corporation. All cross-border financial services transactions should be looked at by both regulators and the same rules should apply, including that the acquirer's balance sheet's assets do not exceed a certain percentage of the host country's GDP.

This would be a good rule for governments to impose on any bank anywhere, that its assets cannot exceed a percentage of GDP, which should be called the 'Petty Rule' as in Sir William, a rule that would have prevented, for example, the mad foreign excursions of the Irish and Icelandic banks that busted the lot of them; and further expansion by, for example, HSBC and Barclays Bank, whose total assets easily exceed the UK's GDP. And before they think of upping-sticks and off to the US or anywhere else, no bank should be allowed to remove itself from its country of origin. Why not? Because banks were formed where they were to serve their local economies first and foremost, which is why they got their banking licence in the first place, and where their depositors are. The national and local and emerging economies don't need bigger global banks at the expense of local safer banks; HSBC's advertising seeks to make a virtue of its global presence by describing itself as the local bank, while its CEO decamps from London to Hong Kong which is its true base, and about the opposite side of the globe to its disaster-prone US Household Financial subsidiary, as if he was turning his back on this monumental corporate cock-up.

If this approach, of trying to curb over-extended expansion in the banking sector, is beginning to sound like Glass-Steagall, you are "on-message". The legislators must wield the axe at the existing behemoths, many of whom have outgrown their skins, such as Citigroup and RBS, all of which are engaged in their own downsizing agendas anyway. Where to start? Let's begin with something obvious: the *bancassurance* business model is dead and serves no purpose, so demerge and split banking and insurance, as predicated in Glass-Steagall. This is more important now that derivatives pervade the system and spread risk throughout banking and insurance – just ask AIG. And while we are about it, fund management, stock-broking and pension fund management operations inside commercial banks should all be hived off as they serve no useful purpose and absorb capital, before even taking account of the Conflicts of Interest issues. Indeed, as I write the private clients fund management business of Lloyds Banking Group's acquisition of HBOS has been sold to the independent Rathbone's, and 221 estate agency outlets have been sold to, guess who?, an independent estate agency.

The notion of the cross-selling opportunities for financial products has been conclusively shown to be starry-eyed wishful-thinking on every occasion – just take a look at Citicorp, did they sell any more monkey nuts or alphabet soup when they became Citigroup? The reason for this is quite simple: say I bank with Lloyds and want a pension plan; I may be very happy with Lloyds as my banker, but I want the best pension fund manager and unless Lloyds' own Scottish Widows is top of the heap I will not be interested, and even if it was, I might prefer to be elsewhere as I don't want all my eggs in one basket, and certainly not after Global Crunch. A shareholder told the board of the hapless Lloyds Banking Group at its last AGM in Glasgow that there was no logic to owning the Scottish Widows pensions operation and why wasn't it being sold, but answer got he none.

As a taxpayer I would ask why my tax dollars are being used to prop up the bank while they hold on to a valuable asset they don't need, and which should be sold off to repay the taxpayer.

Now for the trickier issue raised by Glass-Steagall, the combination of commercial banks with their shiny eggs in the form of deposits and the rapacious eyes and "animal spirits" of the investment banks that want to fertilise them. Global Crunch was triggered by an investment bank collapse, was spread by CMOs/CDOs in CDS wrappers by other investment banks to institutional investors around the world, including commercial banks which, as usual, had made their own unforced errors in other areas, which is hardly new news. The combination of commercial and investment banks rightly concern legislators who need to protect depositors' money. It's not as simple as re-instating Glass-Steagall, however, as the financial system is unrecognisable to the 1933s' much simpler structure. One of the developments since Glass-Steagall was abolished ten years ago has been the natural organic growth of investment banking operations within commercial banks, as they respond to their corporate customers growing needs, such as with HSBC, Citigroup and JP Morgan. Then you have the distinctly different approach of Barclays buying Lehman's US investment banking business out of bankruptcy to grow a stand-alone global investment banking business, but which sits inside a mainly UK commercial bank with all those deposits that sit there like a homogenous jelly, shaking but not moving. And that's a collateral risk the taxpayer does not want to, and should not be expected to, underwrite.

In order to "modernise" Glass-Steagall, a new approach is clearly required. Two options present themselves. First, with the organic approach, the regulators must set clear limits in relation to the entity as a whole as to how large the risk from the investment bank can grow to, before option two kicks in. Let us assume that Barclays investment banking, comprising Barclays Capital and the resuscitated US Lehman, already falls into the second option, in that it is already too big and in certain circumstances, which may even be *unforeseeable* even to experienced central bankers, could pose a threat to the whole group and lead to the inevitable bail-out by the taxpayer in order to save depositors' money and the system as a whole, thus breaching the "Moral Hazard Territory", the final regulator of all.

When a commercial bank's investment activities are deemed by the regulator to exceed option one, then control of the investment bank must pass from the commercial bank in order to cut the Gordian knot between the investment bank's business and the deposits in the commercial bank, on the legal stance that the commercial bank cannot by law thereafter bail out the disinvested investment bank.

How could this be achieved in practise? The regulator issues an injunction to cease control: the vendor commercial bank must dispose of not less than 75.1% of the investment bank, either by distributing this equity to the existing shareholders or selling the stake to a private buyer(s) or admitting the shares to a stock market and selling the required equity into the float, or a combination of two or all three routes. The vendor commercial bank may retain non-voting Preference Shares as part of the disposal which will have a prior claim on the investment bank's profits, which will reduce the value of the equity for sale, a structure that would lend itself to a distribution to existing shareholders, perhaps. The key point of this disposal is that everyone in the market then knows that the vendor does not and cannot legally stand behind the investment bank in any circumstance, and the directors of the investment bank also know that they are staring the "Moral Hazard Territory" deterrent and Bankruptcy and personal loss in the face.

And the former parent/vendor bank can decide at disinvestment on the level of its minority equity exposure, its earnings retention (through the preference share structure) and its lending risk, but on the basis that its equity position is deducted from its Tier One Capital Ratio and any lending to the investment bank from its liquidity buffer. The remaining issue is whether legislation should be passed making it illegal for government to use taxpayers' money to save any bank, unless it is to save the system as a whole in a *force majeure* situation, and for the recoverability of the money with interest, with a stipulation that the equity of any rescued bank is valued at One Dollar, the ultimate hair-cut, to reinforce the "Moral Hazard Territory". In any event, expect Kenneth Lewis to be the first in Court with his divorce petition from that bitch Merrill Lynch in his hands, 'marry in haste ...' and all that.

The regulatory-enforcers for this process would need a legal framework that gives them space to exercise their judgement, as each case must be assessed in the context of each bank's unique circumstances. Take RBS, for example, with its investment banking division GBM, Global Banking & Markets, which contributed 60% to first half profits in 2009, but which are set to decline to 30% as margins return to normal and the increased costs of regulation kick-in. RBS's future is as a UK commercial bank with its large Nat-West franchise. A sale of the distracting GBM would unlock £20.0+ billion, which would replace the £20.0 billion loss on the ABN Amro acquisition and enable the bank, together with a sale of its Direct Line insurance business, to repay the UK government's bail-out money. In fact the EU Competition Commissioner Neelie Kroes has ordered Gordon Brown's New Labour to put up another £43.0 billion capital in Q4 2009 into RBS and Lloyds and ordered substantial disinvestments by both banks. This is the positive deconstruction that was resisted by Gordon Brown, which greatly reduces risk and restores focus after the headlong expansions of the last decade. And the EU showed itself to be ahead of the UK government and to be the real wielder of power in UK financial services, administering a real slap in the face to RBS for daring to launch a hostile bid for an EU bank. And Kroes handled the news carefully, ordering the Dutch Ing Bank to divest its insurance interests on the same day.

A welcome development in UK banking is worth noting, namely the rise of new 'Narrow' banks, as opposed to 'Casino' banks. 'Narrow' banks have to keep liquid assets generally in line with their deposits, known as '100% reserve banking', or the less narrow 'fractional reserve banking'. Tesco Bank and Virgin Bank are expanding fast to offer no-frills straightforward banking. Tesco is growing organically from its supermarket stores and capturing dissatisfied customers, while Virgin is looking at acquisitions, including the sell-off of Northern Rock and the 300 branches of RBS and 300 HBOS branches that are all due to be sold. This is a healthy development, both as regards competition and minimising Systemic Risk. It will be interesting to see when the US gets the point and grasps the nettles of Citigroup, BoA and JP Morgan.

Glass-Steagall Mark II must be designed to have teeth, designed to have teeth that bite better than the Mullah Nasruddin's Teeth with their failing love-bites. Any director of a failed bank must suffer personal loss as well, and the Swedish model from 1991 was a good one that "worked": fines and confiscation of assets and reduction of salary, and if gross negligence or fraud is involved, withdrawal of the right to be a director or employed by a financial services company for life and/or imprisonment should be the order of the day. It is necessary to restore the priesthood. This tough approach would be well appreciated by the eighteenth century British legislators: in 1720, when the 'South Sea Bubble' burst, a parliamentary resolution called for bankers to be tied up in sacks with snakes and thrown into the River Thames, a colourful approach that today would be stopped by the Greens on the grounds of water pollution, and by the animal rights activists over the proper treatment of snakes, which these days would include many politicians and bankers themselves! Far more effective and to the point is the wholesale deconstruction of the global banking system by the lawmakers working with the regulators, just like electricians who put fuses and circuit-breakers into systems that are too large and pose Systemic Risk.

Bonus, Capital Adequacy and Liquidity Issues

Bonuses drove bankers to do deals that pushed the liquidity of their bank's balance sheets to the edge of the cliff and over in many cases, in their chase to augment their own bonus to the detriment of the banks' shareholders and to the banks' liquidity and survival. In the case of Lehman, RBS and HBOS it drove these banks clean over the edge. That's why bonuses are a big corporate governance issue, as in the end the taxpayer is left paying the losses. Bank Capital Adequacy ratios, introduced by the Basel II Committee in 1974, are essentially only as useful as a bank's assets are good, as the Japanese banks discovered in their 1988 asset-bubble collapse, and are not nearly as important as liquidity ratios, where cash and cash-equivalents can be easily valued. If a bank runs out of cash, having the right capital ratio to questionable assets counts for nothing. It's the liquidity that counts.

In the early 1970s I had to visit the former Midland Bank, now part of HSBC, in Bristol to negotiate a loan for a client. The bank manager was interested, but then made a very interesting statement along these lines: 'We bankers must have regard not just to our bank's liquidity but also to our responsibility to the liquidity of the system as a whole. We are a priesthood, you see: whereas you go to your priest and to church to seek the salvation of your soul, depositors come to us to preserve their money. Our lesser priesthood has an implied responsibility to the integrity of our church, which is the liquidity of the system as a whole'.

A friend of mine joined Morgan Stanley in New York in 1974, where the legendary John Young would host a lunch for the new recruits, to impress upon them the natural order of their new universe: the clients come first, the bank that serves them comes second, and you new boys are a distant third, or somewhere else. That was in the days when the business was in equities, or shares listed on a quoted market. Then as the 1970s progressed into the 1980s, the bond market volumes grew ever more important, but they were traded on an unquoted OTC basis, or Over-the-Counter, which enabled the bankers to exploit the inefficiencies of this opaque market and fatten their margins at the clients' expense, to the point where the old order was reversed, and the banker and his or her bonus came first, the bank itself stayed second so they could pay the bonuses to No. 1, while the clients were third, or somewhere else. The money-changers had taken over the Temple.

There is also the basic issue of the relativity of these outsize rewards. A debate has raged in America for thirty years ever since 1980, the beginning of the Greed Decade, about the justice of an economic system which delivers a greater percentage of new wealth to the very rich. As Sir Winston Churchill observed in the House of Commons on 22nd October 1945, "The inherent vice of Capitalism is the unequal sharing of blessings; the inherent virtue of Socialism is the equal sharing of miseries". The economist Paul Krugman writes in *The Right, the Rich and the Facts* of the position in the 1980s: '70% of the rise in average family income went to the top 1% of families ... The 1% of families with the highest incomes received about 12% of overall pre-tax income, whilst the wealthiest 1% of families had some 39% of net worth.' And the evidence shows that the top ten percent of the US population's taxable income increased from 34% to 46% during the next thirty years, up a third; it also shows that most of this uplift went to the 1.0% on top of the whole pile, whose income has doubled during this time. Taking these two statements together, the trend over the last thirty years is for the richer to get exponentially richer still, which doesn't surprise at all, until unchecked this trend will set off revolt and civil unrest. There is no sign of this in America yet, other than the current rationing of ammunition by many gun-smiths across the country, but there were signs a few years before the French Revolution, until a succession of bad harvests ushered in revolt and Mme Guillotine.

At the end of the Tech Decade downturn, the price of failure and pay from 1999 to 2001 of the CEOs of the three biggest fraudulent corporations was as follows:

Table 10:

The Price of US CEO Unseen Failure, 1999-2001

Corporation	CEO	Pay 1999-2001
Global Crossing	Gary Winnick	$512.4 million
Enron	Kevin Lay	$246.7 million
WorldCom	Scott Sullivan	$39.4 million

Paul Volcker's comment was most interesting: "Corporate greed exploded beyond anything that could have been imagined in 1990. Traditional norms didn't exist. You had this whole culture where the only sign of worth was how much money you made." How about that for the style of the times, the *zeitgeist* of success of Degenerate Persons? And it was about to get much worse: the top 1.0% of US-taxpayers, numbering 15,000, shared $385.0 billion in 2005, or $26.0 million each on average. The table below shows the detail behind this phenomenon of bankers' gold.

Bankers are paid obscene amounts when times are good, but they also get equally obscene amounts when they fail; heads they win, and tails they win again. This doesn't sound right to anyone in the Creative Person category, and it didn't look right at all either, as the price of failure of the severance packages hit the news in 2008 for those whose companies failed, mercilessly exposed by the gathering Global Crunch:

Table 11:

The Price of US CEO Visible Failure, 2007–2008

Bank	CEO	Years	Pay	Exit Deal*
Lehman Brothers	Dick Fuld, Jnr.	1993-2008	$466,000,000	$62,000,000
Citigroup	Chuck Prince III	2003-2007	$53,000,000	$40,000,000
Merrill Lynch	E. Stan O'Neal	2001-2007	$70,000,000	$161,000,000
Bear Stearns	James Cayne	1993-2007	$232,000,000	$61,000,000

*includes stock sales
Source: various, as quoted by *The IHT* on 25/09/08

[Goldman Sachs	Lloyd Blankfein	2004-2008	$176,300,000	$500,000,000 Stock]

The real difference between Tables 10 and 11 is that Table 10 shows pay for what were believed to be successful companies at the time, before it was known their accounts were fraudulent, but in Table 11 the 'Exit Deal' column shows the huge sums received before and after known failure. Not only is there a huge disparity between the Pay Levels in Table 11, but also between the Exit Deals; and also between the size of the four operations and their profitability and losses prior to exit: in 2006, the last year before the credit crunch bit, the average levels of quarterly profits were approximately as follows:

Lehman Bros.	$1.0 billion-
Citigroup	$5.0 billion+
Merrill Lynch	$1.0 billion-
Bear Stearns	$0.5 billion-

On these figures, Chuck Prince of Citigroup should have received most, not the least. The average quarterly losses when these banks started to post losses were approximately as follows:

Lehman	$.03 billion+	for 2 quarters
Citigroup	$6.0 billion-	for 3 quarters
Merrill Lynch	$5.0 billion-	for 4 quarters
Bear Stearns	$1.0 billion-	for 1 quarter

On these figures, Chuck Prince of Citigroup's Exit Pay should have been much less, not more than, his normal Pay Level; and Stan O'Neal of Merrill Lynch's Exit Pay should have been the smallest of all, not the largest.

What these figures show is that there is no such thing that even resembles a market for CEO's pay and severance pay on Wall Street, which was underlined when both Vikram Pandit and Kenneth Lewis got paid just $1.0 for the whole of 2009, as Wall Street at last admitted the 'Principle of CEO Failure Goes Unrewarded'. CEO pay appears to be governed by the law of the jungle, with he who wields the biggest club, or boa-constrictor of a lawyer, coming off best. What they said on the way out the door revealed a new style of syntax of Degenerate Persons, 'Now I see it, but you don't'.

Stan O'Neal of Merrill Lynch said: "I received no bonus for 2007, no severance pay, no golden parachute", he blubbed on, as he trousered $161.0 million of past benefits, including stock and stock options.

Angelo Mozilo of Countywide: "The goal was to reduce my holdings because of my retirement...almost all my net worth was in Countrywide", as he sold stock worth $141.0 million, before this largest private mortgage lender went bust, as in "I saw the collapse coming but got to the exit ahead of the other shareholders".

Chuck Prince of Citigroup: "His bonus was less than half the bonus he got in his previous year", said his Chairman, as good old Chuck pocketed a mere $10.0 million bonus in November 2007, but along with nearly $100.0 million in other perks and shares.

Any sign of contrition was clearly not the order of the day, but was deliberately excluded out by a self-justificatory unapologetic gesture of the Degenerate Person, as if two fingers in the face of the rest of society was all that they felt obliged to offer anyone questioning their legalised greed. Here, we have been looking at those at the very top of the corporate totem pole. Oh! The insolence of office, indeed!

According to *The Economist*, Lehman paid out $55.0 billion in the decade to 2008 to employees; its shareholders, meanwhile, after deducting the loss of their originally subscribed capital on Lehman's failure, earned zero. In 2008, 5,000 Wall Street bankers and traders, at bailed-out institutions only, received more than $1,000,000 bonus each, according to the New York State Attorney.

The rewards of the failed British bankers were much lower, although their losses were commensurate: Sir Fred Goodwin, CEO of RBS, received a package of £4.2 million and a pension pot of £8.37 million, while his chairman received a £750,000 pay-off; and the CEO of the failed Northern Rock Bank received a salary and bonus of £1.7 million, £2.6 million from share sales and a £750,000 pay-off and a £2.5 million pension pot, while his chairman received a salary of £315,000. Why any of these Degenerate Persons received a penny is far from obvious. Then the Chancellor of the Exchequer, no less, approved a package for Fred the Shred's successor at RBS, Stephen Hester, worth potentially £9.6 million. The British public found these rewards for failure and unproven future success deeply offensive, and anger pervaded society.

And it isn't just bank CEOs who have no sensibility to how the rest of society see them: when the three CEOs of Motown's Big Three went with their begging bowls in November 2008 to Washington to bail out their gas-guzzler car-making plants, they each travelled in their own executive jet – how about that for a PR blunder! Congress sent them packing back to do their homework, and then they underlined their error by each driving the 500 miles back to Washington in ten hours in their main rival's energy-efficient Toyota Prius's! They obviously hadn't heard about their fellow-struggler American Airline's special offer of $69.0 round trip in coach, in under an hour.

Finally, the extraordinary story of the oil trader and his $100,000,000 bonus, that's his one hundred million dollar bonus, came to light in mid-2009 and embarrassed Citigroup in any number of ways. Andrew J. Hall, the head oil trader at Phibro, a Citigroup subsidiary that uses tons of the bank's money to make them $2.0 billion profits over the past five years, cornered enough oil supplies in the summer of 2008 to force other traders to have to buy from them, as the price at the pumps hit $4.00 per barrel. Hall had achieved with perfect timing and positioning in this $2.0 trillion annual oil market what the Degenerate Person Nelson Bunker Hunt had failed to do in the relatively tiny silver market in the mid-1980s, but in Hall's case the Degenerate Persons were the bosses at Citigroup who allowed their customers' deposits in the commercial bank to be used to make money in this way, a legacy no doubt of the supermarket-style merger ten years previously.

Then it got worse, as the US Treasury Pay Czar, Kenneth R. Feinberg, was appointed to review bonuses of those institutions which had been bailed out by the taxpayer, the list of which was headed by the hapless Citigroup. When Hall's bosses realised that they had allowed their customers' deposits to drive up the price of oil at their own customers' expense but for the bank's profits, and that these same customers as taxpayers had then had to rescue the bank, it dawned on them for the first time that they had created a huge moral dilemma for themselves, as they hastened to shovel off Phibro to Occidental Petroleum, who no doubt knocked $100.0 million off the price to pay Hall his legal but ill-gotten bonus. As a leader in the *International Herald Tribune* on 3rd September 2009 opined: 'The case of Mr. Hall highlights the hazard of mixing public interest with capitalism at its most unbridled, and it raises basic questions of fairness'. The issue it really raises is not one of 'fairness', but whether banks and hedge funds should own, or hoard, commodities in their own name, as the purist view is that Creative Persons should only trade in the futures market as an economic function of the proper working of markets. Instead of introducing bans on short trading in bank stocks, the regulators, in the form of the Law, should ban Degenerate Persons from hoarding what the world needs.

The debate on executive pay and bonuses came alive within three weeks of President Obama's inauguration, when he roundly declared that no executive of a bank bailed-out by taxpayer dollars should receive more than $500,000: "It's a matter of common sense"; and he wanted restrictions on severance packages as well. Common sense? If bankers compensation is to be limited, what about bus drivers or professional sportsmen too? If you cap any reward, you are headed down the old Fabian road of the 'rent of ability' where everyone pays tax, or 'rent', to reduce all ability to a norm of non-excellence. The Land of the Free is not about to enter Ayn Rand's world of the senseless Board of Unification of Degenerate Persons, one trusts. The French regulator AMF and the Banking Commission and the Treasury there formulated a voluntary code of conduct that had more merit, linking bonuses to profits rewarded by options rather than cash.

Lloyd Blankfein, CEO of Goldman Sachs, whose remuneration including basic salary of $600,000 p.a. is shown in the table above for comparison purposes, spoke out in Frankfurt against current practices in the investment bankers approach to bonuses, picking up on the French idea. His ideas were for all banks to work together to eliminate guaranteed multi-year bonuses; and for claw-backs of bonuses if losses emerge; and in a side-swipe at Citigroup and Merrill Lynch, no bonuses to be paid by loss-making banks. Well, that gets us further down the line, for sure, and he spoke out because the G20 were about to meet in Pittsburgh at the end of September 2009 to discuss these issues.

The Head of the FSA Hector Sant was reported as saying, on Friday 13th March 2009, that the entire principles-based philosophy which underpinned financial regulation over the past decade is to be abandoned: "A principles-based approach does not work with participants who have no principles," he surmised, thereby confusing structure with morals. There is a basic issue of morality underlying this debate and Blankfein's approach is right: as Aristotle, who made better insights concerning ethics and logic than philosophy, said "Morality is the application of common values", to which the conclusion is that the common values applicable to the issue of bankers' bonus's must be defined or there can be no morality. It is amazing that the minds of the most seriously-paid community on the planet, it seems, even after all that has been revealed by Global Crunch, cannot get their collective mind into gear and formulate the applicable criteria for their own regulation, and reputation, before government does it for them. Is that because they *are* over-paid?

In one sense, the banking crisis reflected the collective failure of a sufficiently held Aristotelian-style belief in the moral values of society, and perhaps a mercantilist set of values must be developed. Everyone thinks of *The Wealth of Nations* when the name of Adam Smith is mentioned, but his earlier work *The Theory of Moral Sentiments* is now a best-seller, in China! In the exclusive interview with the author, I intend to ask him his view on the morality of bankers' bonuses in the light of his earlier work and current practices.

All these comments and suggestions, however helpful or otherwise, are missing the point of the debate: these bankers' bonuses reduced the individual capital of the paying banks and the liquidity of the system as a whole. They undermined both the priesthood and the church itself. The debate in 2009 is now centred on capital ratios but not so much on the liquidity issue. The regulators rightly determine the capital ratios banks must maintain; the politicians must pass the legislation that makes sure that all their off-shore and off-balance sheet SIVs and conduits and subsidiaries and affiliates and trusts are all stuck firmly back on their regulated balance sheets where they belong; and now the structure of bonuses and the resultant liquidity issues must be addressed.

There can be no earnings caps in a free market economy, as all those price and earnings controls in post-war Germany, the eastern bloc, Russia and the 1970s' controls of Nixon and Wilson clearly demonstrated. The determination, timing and form of payment of bonuses is, however, the Big Issue. The payment of a bonus before the paying bank has received the cash from the transaction underlying the bonus is clearly bad practice and must be prevented; part of the solution is to have trail bonuses, where the payments out are matched by the receipts in. Multi-year guaranteed bonuses are clearly a major market distortion that must be curtailed. The form of payment of any bonus should not all be in cash, but in cash retentions and future options as well, aligning bankers' interests with those of the bank itself. And the idea of claw-backs is absurd: once the money has been paid it's as good as gone, and all the lawyers and all the whistle in Dixie is not about to get it back; it's far better to leave the cash in the bank in a temporary credit account until paid out, being subject to the "Moral Hazard" risk in the meantime, and if the bank fails there must be no value left in the options, shares or bonus reserves: when Bear Stearns failed, JP Morgan should have paid $1.0 for the whole bank, not $2.0 per share, and as for being argued up to $10.0 per share, well, that cave-in weakened the whole system. All these points would be best dealt with by a voluntary code of conduct drawn up by the bankers and agreed with their regulators, as being in their own best interests. If they have lost sight of their own best collective interest, if they have lost sight of their church, then they must be subjected to legislation.

Bankers were beginning to feel the post-Pittsburgh heat and the backlash from an angry public. John Varley, CEO of Barclays which owns Barcap the investment bank, which bought the remains of US Lehman by luring these busted bankers with $1.25 billion bonuses for bankrupting their own employer, felt the need to hit back for these and all the other bonus-earners who nearly busted the world's financial system: "Profit is not Satanic!" He thundered at his lunchtime congregation at St. Martin-in-the-Fields Church in London's Trafalgar Square, carefully enunciating profit ahead of bonuses. Banks were the "backbone of the economy", shrieked Varley. As far as I can detect, these investment bankers are just a bunch of geared broker-dealers or stock-jobbers and are not the backbone of anything other than their own questionable riches. And bonuses, Varley asserted, were necessary because "talent is highly mobile". Did he mean they are all prepared to jump ship together, or that they are all determined to hang together like flies in the meantime?

When Hank Paulson was put under the cosh on Capitol Hill by a seething congress-woman from Ohio complaining about her constituents losing their homes and jobs, he was forced into this statement: "The people paying the price did not create the problem, but if the banks had failed they would have had a bigger problem." Is that it Hank? Bail-outs, business and bonuses as usual for the bankers, while the rest of us are required to pay the price, as we hang onto our jobs and homes at the same time? It's easy to see why people are so angry. It is interesting that in this exchange Paulson never had a second's thought about the "Moral Hazard Territory" that the bankers had transgressed over time and en masse, whilst being paid massive bonuses.

Next in the defence of "bankers" bonuses was Lord Griffiths, as in the life of Brian, who was a key adviser to Thatcher and is now an international adviser to Goldman Sachs, which has a bonus pot for 2009 heading for $22.0 billion, the exact amount Goldman received from the TARP as it happens: "We have to *tolerate* the inequality as a way to achieve greater prosperity and opportunity for all," he volunteered in the first Cathedral of the Church of England, St. Paul's. Don't you just love it: "*We have to tolerate the inequality…!*" Who's *We*? Or will the Church propose a second Toleration Act, like the one that followed on the twenty years of Civil War?

How about this, Brian: in case you lot cock it up again, why not use this money to create a special reserve – Got it? A Special Reserve! A Special Contingency Reserve! – which would then be tax allowable, a reserve against the over-weaning greed and hubristic folly of your co-bankers, and I am sure the tax inspector would readily accept that as an allowable *specific* provision given all the money he has doled out to you fellows – equal to the amount that the taxpayers handed you when you smugly signed up to get their money by becoming a deposit-taking bank over-night, so that you can now lend ten times this amount to people and businesses, that's $220,000,000,000 through your shiny new imaginary branch network, to those who really need it as a result of your colleagues collective inhuman greed and human folly, and in this way "achieve greater prosperity and opportunity for all". The next day his boss Lloyd Blankfein had the gall to claim, with an impish smile it must be said, that he was doing "God's work"! Well, quite a number of us could be converted, or bribed, by such riches.

When the G20 met in Pittsburgh in September 2009, bankers' bonuses were at the top of the agenda, and we waited expectantly for a master-stroke. All that came out of this expensive jamboree, however, was a string of the usual sound-bites: 'deferral of bonuses', 'clawbacks in the event of losses', 'avoidance of multi-year guaranteed bonuses', 'tougher disclosure requirements' and 'the imposition of a limit on the size of the bonus pool in relation to an institution's total income'. This unjoined-up-blather is going to be monitored by a new institution to be called the FSB, the 'Financial Stability Board'. Will they ask Her Majesty Queen Elizabeth II to open its glitzy new building, I wondered, accompanied by Sir Alan Greenspan perhaps? The bad news from Pittsburgh for Her Majesty, however, was her Prime Minister's announcement that he, Gordon Brown, would be regaling her in his Queen's Speech in the Autumn with his new Banking and Finance Bill, but the only announcements on the day were that the Regulators would be given powers to tear up bankers' contracts that contained risky bonus provisions. That, and a new Bill that was a memo to himself saying that it would be illegal for him not to repay half the National Debt within four years. God Save the Queen!

The current debate on bonuses has omitted the key issue, that of the affect on liquidity, as it has only addressed the affect on capital requirements. Of course the two are inextricably linked, but are asymmetric in their application, because whereas capital ratios are not less than 8% of total assets, liquidity should be, and used to be when the banker's church was still standing and had not been vandalised by the barbarians, at around 30% of total assets, or more. As the chase for bonuses is based on getting more business, so the banks' liquidity is put to work to the point where leverage goes higher and actual real liquidity is exhausted, and when the crunch comes the money needed has all long gone, paid away in bonuses.

Lloyd Blankfein's compensation figures shown above reveal that over four years he received $2.4 million in salary, but $173.9 million in bonuses, and as investment banks pay out up to 50% of their *revenues* in compensation – Goldman only paid 46.7% in the 2000s – of which over 90% is in bonuses, it is easy to appreciate that the quantum of bonuses in the context of liquidity is a massive issue. And to curb the bonus culture which has gotten out of control, the answer is to institute tighter liquidity-assessment controls alongside capital controls, and the retention of bonuses at risk in the business but not as assets forming any part of the mandated capital pool and liquidity buffer, so that they are still at risk until paid out.

In November 2009, the Bank of England's head of financial stability, Paul Tucker, said in Brussels that banks should pre-fund a deposit insurance scheme as "governments have a legal right to make recoveries from the residual banking industry over the succeeding years ... and that banks should raise Contingency Capital which would convert into equity and help absorb losses, the so-called CoCos, before `full-scale insolvency or nationalisation". Now that sounds more like rebuilding the Church, and it spells out the probability that banking costs are set to rise and profits, and therefore bonuses, are set to fall. As the Bank of England calculated, if the UK's big banks had retained 20% of their payrolls and dividends from 2000-2008, there would have been no need for taxpayer bail-outs.

Defining 'Liquidity' and the assets involved is the real issue of the regulation of bonuses as well, and is much harder than defining 'Capital', and will cost more than capital, as capital offers reward whereas liquidity offers safety. The UK's FSA reckoned in Q3 2009, based on 210 UK bank's balance sheets at end-2007 which had a combined total of £280.0 billion of qualifying liquid assets, (and the new rules would also apply to nearly 200 subsidiaries and branches of overseas groups), for extra liquidity buffers of £110.0 billion to be required. The annual "cost" of which, or the difference between holding low-yielding/high-liquidity assets such as Gilts/Treasuries which banks would have to hold in place of higher yielding lending to customers, would be around £2.2 billion pa. This "cost" would have been more of a "saving" in the case of HSBC, however, which invested its liquidity buffer in profitable but illiquid US subprime mortgages, as if its acquisition of Household Financial was not already a subprime too far. The extra "cost" of the additional buffer would on average cost each bank £10.5 million pa each, which raises the question of whether £2.2 billion additional liquidity assets is high enough, as it would be better to overshoot than undershoot, for the FSA report stated a maximum worst-case figure of £900.0 billion of additional liquidity assets, at a "cost" of a whopping £9.2 billion pa. That wouldn't just be over-kill, it would be a waste of ammunition.

The sanctity of the church requires early detection of Systemic Risk, by spotting risk concentration and the regulator having the power to order a range of solutions to maintain liquidity at all costs, from raising capital to liquidating assets. FASB 157, the accounting rule that requires 'Mark-to-Market' valuations is a basic rule that was unfortunately introduced at the height of Global Crunch, but it is the basic first test in determining liquidity. Innovation was one cause of Global Crunch, but innovation can be used to safeguard the system too: it is not beyond the wit of man to devise an encrypted suite of generic software so that the regulator of Systemic Risk can track each banker's financial situation in terms of all liabilities and assets, so that counter-party and systemic risk can be reviewed on a daily basis. Goldman Sachs, for example, and other investment banks calculate their 'Value at Risk', or VaR, every day, which is a forward-looking calculation which shows in a worst-case scenario the next day's risks. Indeed VaR is a disclosure requirement for banks under Pillar 3 of Basel II, and central bankers/regulators could then monitor a build-up of counter-party exposure and concentration of systemic risk. They could make comparative assessments across different banks of the worth of their liquidity buffers, where rules are being bent and where concentrations are occurring, and which punters are long on one-way bets that are often the cause of collapse, as at Bear Stearns, Barings and HBOS. The rule must be that open, realistic and real-time disclosure, as posed by the 'Theory of Information Flows', is the best safeguard. VaR, however, as with all computer-based analyses, cannot predict when risks will correlate in a crisis or the effects of leverage. VaR works only under normal conditions and cannot *see* a crash coming, so when it is needed most, it performs worst. Only human judgement, allied with real time information, can foresee the possibility of sudden dislocation.

The implementation of these new structures must be put in place in time in the current Short Cycle, as we are uncertain if this Short Cycle is the eighth or the ninth in the current Long Cycle. If these most important issues are not addressed by effective Law and subsidiary regulation in time, then the system as it is today could lead to global collapse and Great Depression 2, when we will know that the Long Cycle really has hit bottom. There is no need to rush the fences and botch the job, as that will lead to ineffective regulation, the path the politicians are already embarked on, as the balance will only be got right by incremental steps and observing their effects. Let's say, and hope, there are three-four years left to get the new structures in place and working effectively. Bankruptcy is the ultimate regulator, which allows 'Creative Destruction' of bankrupt structures to proceed.

Derivative Issues

As 2009 began the total derivatives market was reckoned to be $600.0 trillion, of which $325.0 trillion were plain vanilla IRSs, and ERSs also accounted for a significant part of the total, but that still leaves trillions of others where the vanilla may have been tarnished with less pure colours of questionable hew. The concern centres mainly on the $62.0 trillion of CDSs, but there is no concern for the CDSs in the corporate bond market involving blue chip companies like Big Blue itself, but on those linked to financial instruments like CMOs/CDOs and MBOs and other more exotic risk instruments. And as the market is opaque and non-transparent, no one knows which counter parties have the greater risk, and some unseeable concentration in the market may just be waiting to explode. When Lehman imploded, it was a pleasant surprise that the settlement auction netted out at a loss of just $5.0 billion, spread around scores of institutions and hedge funds, but if there's a Nick Leeson or an Evil Kerviel in the heap chasing a losing position, who knows?

The outcome of the auction liquidation of part of Lehman's CDS portfolio showed that it was relatively well managed, but the same cannot begin to be said of AIG's, which showed just how dangerous CDSs are in the wrong hands, but how do you prevent this? It begs the question of what is the purpose of CDSs in well-ordered markets: why would an investor want to spend the extra reward on a riskier bond by buying CDS cover, when he or she can just as well buy a relatively risk-free bond to achieve the same net income? The problem arises from the artificial rules of risk diversification, including diversification of credit names, geographical spread and different market price segments for investment portfolios, and the rules meant the assessment of credit risk was based on backward-looking performance of each bond but not on any perception of future macro-economic threats. These rules obliged Wall Street to use their Grinders to manufacture low-risk bonds out of high-risk ones by insuring and wrapping them in CDSs. CDSs certainly spread risk across the markets to sophisticated investors who thought they knew the risks, but the AIG debacle has put that assumption under a big question mark. The corporate CDSs on bonds issued by the likes of IBM and GE perform a sensible function and caused no problems in the crisis, and it seems reasonable on a 25-year bond for the investor to insure the principal and interest, in effect insuring that IBM and GE or their successors will be around in 2035 and can repay in full. As Americans love to say: "Hey! Stick around!" The legendary investor Warren Buffett refers to derivatives as "Weapons of Mass Destruction", whereas George Soros, speaking at the IIF conference in Beijing in June 2009 called for the outlawing of CDSs: "It's like buying life insurance on someone else's life and owning a licence to kill him", he said, as he observed that some bondholders in the General Motors collapse stood to gain more from GM's collapse as a result of their cover from CDSs, than from a reconstruction.

No one knows where the risks posed by CDSs lie or what the losses could be, other than in the AIG debacle, which is why the US is moving fast in Q4 2009 to create an open screen-based and regulated market, hoping the horse has not already bolted. The volume of derivative contracts in Q2 2009 was $200.0 billion, but with an open market everyone will be in a better position to assess their counter-party risk position and the Regulators, hopefully the central banks, can call for more collateral or margin calls, or even more permanent capital, and ultimately stop the market growing and containing risk, at least that's the idea, which is a lot better than at present. And the fact that in a clearing house any losses are paid for by the members is itself a salutary regulator on its own. There should be no problem putting the low-hanging fruit into the new system, the IRSs, ERSs, CFDs and so on, but the problem will be in the riskier areas, so the rule should be that if it's not on the market screen the contract is illegal and voided: "If you can't show it, you can't trade it" should be the rule. When the market becomes visible, no doubt many other rules will be promulgated.

Those investment banks that continue to trade undisclosed exotic "customised" derivatives should do so entirely at their own risk, in the certain knowledge that no taxpayer is going to pay for this type of loss. That should take care in the future of the issue of all those CDSs much loved by hedge funds which have no insurable risk in the original transaction: disclose, or it's illegal and worthless. In the CDS market today of $62.0 trillion, the danger is no one knows who owes how much to whom for what, as no one knows the extent of corre-lated risk. The big structural risk is that CDSs may already have cor-related risks throughout the whole financial system: on one side of the contract are the insurance terms, but the other side is coated with an invisible glue that sticks to other CDSs to spread the risk, like the legs of bees that attract and carry the pollen, but CDSs carry DEAD-LY RISK. Let's all hope and pray that there are no 800lb gorillas already lurking in this still smouldering heap of cryptic derivatives.

Finally, it's time for our Court Jester again. It so happened that Mervyn King was off on holiday for three weeks in the US to learn how to fly Ben Bernanke's helicopter and how to liberally strew bil-lions of Dollars all over unsuspecting country folk, to get them spending again. So he summoned The Incomparable Mullah Nasruddin to address the Regulators at their weekly meetings while he was away, so as to protect his turf in the battle over which institution would hold the main brief for future regulation. At the first weekly meeting, the Mullah Nasruddin strode to the podium and addressed the assembled Regulators.

"O, Regulators! Do you, or do you not know, what you are doing?"

"No, we don't know what we are doing!" they all replied in unison.

"Then," replied the Mullah, "you are too stupid to make a start on!"

At the second week's seminar, the Mullah strode to the podium and asked:

"O, Regulators! Do you, or do you not know, what you are doing?"

"Yes, we know what we are doing!" they all replied in unison.

"Then", replied the Mullah, "there is no need for me to tell you".

At the third week's seminar, the Mullah strode to the podium and asked:

"O, Regulators! Do you, or do you not know, what you are doing?"

The Head Regulator stood up and there was a hushed and expectant silence

"Well, Mullah, some of us know what we are doing and some of us don't".

"Perfect!" exclaimed the Mullah. "Then let those who know tell those who don't!"

Mervyn King was not surprised on his return to realise that nothing in the meantime had changed.

PART VI:

What Happens Next

Gold versus Fiat Currencies

I N medieval times a nation's wealth was considered to be the gold
(or silver) in the vaults of its central bank. This meant promoting
and subsidising exports while at the same time preventing
imports by protectionist measures, so as to pile up and keep the stock
of gold at home. This psychologically-driven 'beggar-my-neighbour'
constriction of world trade `enabled the "richer" nations to wage
war, as gold paid for everything an army needed when fighting
abroad. Then along came Adam Smith and pointed out that a
nation's wealth was actually all the goods and services it produced,
its GDP, and that the mercantilist view of gold lay at the heart of the
poverty of nations. And that was the end of mercantilism and the
notion that gold was a nation's wealth, as free trade prospered and
led to the wealth of nations.

The superstition that gold holds an intrinsic value, however, still had roots in mankind's perception. As we have seen, the gold standard was used to stand behind the Dollar in 1944, and the consequences when that was ended in 1971. In the Great Inflation of the Weimar Republic, when you couldn't buy a loaf of bread without barrow-loads of millions of Marks, you could buy the whole bakery if you had a gold coin. Gold would have appeared to the hard-pressed and willing-seller as an apparition from Heaven.

When the Rentenmark was ushered in as the new currency in 1923 at a time when Germany had no gold, the new superstition peddled was that it was backed by all the land of Germany, an absurd notion, but the myth worked. From superstition to apparition, gold has a definite value against fiat currencies, especially in a crisis driven by inflation or deflation: that is why gold rose through $1,000.00 and on to over $1,200.00 per Troy Ounce in 2009, as the fall of the Dollar and the prospect of future inflation and higher interest rates, driven by all the QE and stimuli packages and bail-outs, and burgeoning national debts as a percentage of declining GDPs, fuelled fears for the future. And at that level, gold had returned to its mid-13th Century level, when it was handy to have an ounce of the stuff around if war was blowing in the wind, as it could buy you a light suit of chainmail and save your life.

The story of the new Short Cycle and the unravelling of debts will inevitably be shadowed by the value of gold, which is simply a measure of the decline of over-blown fiat currencies. How wise of the US Senate to resist the IMF's requests over the years to sell its gold, and how short-sighted of Gordon Brown to sell 58% of the UK's reserves at the bottom of the market in 1999. In November 2009, the IMF did execute its long approved decision, however, to sell off an eighth of its gold stock of 3,200 tons, or 403.3 tons, as it sold 200 tons to India at $1,045.00 an ounce, with the IMF receiving $6.7 billion in hard currency. What was behind this transaction? For India, it rebalanced its gold content of its $285.5 billion foreign exchange reserves from 4% to 6%, but India's hidden agenda may be to have a greater say in the IMF's deployment of the funds, as the IMF's sale was designed to release funding available for concessionary lending to poor countries. China is widely expected to be the eventual buyer of the other 203.3 tons: since 2003, its holdings of gold have increased from 400 tons to 1,054 tons, worth $35.0 billion.

The story of gold as the superstition asset continues as a perception in men's eyes. If Great Depression 2 comes to pass and fiat currencies lose much of their value, then the way forward will be to issue new currencies backed by gold. A return to the gold standard would see the price of gold shoot through $5,000.00 or to some other seemingly impossible barrier, as a measurement only of the devaluation of paper currencies. If this does happen, a Ruination of Macro-economists will no doubt be left wondering in hindsight why they failed to spot the obvious.

An *Exclusive* Interview with Mr. Adam Smith, GPLS

Q: It is very good of you to join us today, Mr. Smith Sir, and "As we are all your scholars now", as William Pitt the Younger once introduced you, may we stand while you are seated?

A.S: How kind of you, Sir. And thank you for the special arrangements you made to bring me here today. Yes, the hearse came to Canongate Cemetery early in the morning before anyone was up and the drive to London from Edinburgh only took a day. I was very surprised when the hearse slowed down in the Royal Mile as we passed the statue recently erected in my memory. I was deeply touched and never thought my memory would outlive my passing.

Q: And how, Sir, did you find your journey south?

A.S: Incredible! I was amazed to be able to look out through the blacked-out one-way windows and see the world, while they couldn't see me! The last time I came down the A61, through God's country, it took me five whole days with horse and carriage, nearly 250 years ago, since when there has been steam, the internal combustion engine, diesel-electric, then the jet engine, and atomic and then nuclear power. Marvellous! All of it! We stopped to refresh at East Midlands airport for a break in our journey and I saw aeroplanes, taking off and landing and flying, incredible! But I reflected that when their fuel garnered from the earth runs out, they have nowhere to go but back to the *Land!* The technical changes are simply unbelievable in every direction, and now the world is wired for digital wherever you look, and news on television covers events from the far side of the world. Unbelievable!

Q: Well, we're very happy to have you here today, another miracle as one might say ...

A.S: Not as amazing as the intended final act of the Sage of Omaha, Mr. Warren Buffett. I hear he has plans to write his last letter to his investors from Heaven when he finally passes his sell-by date! I suspect some trickery, whereas all I have done is come back from the dead, Lazarus-like, to grant this my first quarter-millennium interview. And so to business.

Q: Did you foresee these huge technical advantages when you published *The Wealth of Nations* in 1776?

A.S: Good heavens, No! Call me a moral philosopher or a social psychologist, or even an economist, but I am not a scientist, and scientists have completely changed the world. The recent history of Communism and its demise shows indisputably that Free Trade is the only way to global wealth, to be shared among the nations, and that is as true today as in 1776.

Q: You have read *Countdown to Catastrophe*, which will end with this interview and I trust I have your permission to do that? [Nods agreement]. So you know that in 2008 the global financial markets seized up and nearly collapsed and many people now question the "Invisible Hand of the Market" and its efficiencies.

A.S: I think they are confusing the principle of the free market with the man-made distortions that came into these markets in recent years, or more specifically the financial markets, with their new debt-packaged instruments, and a general excess driven by greed, aided by the new computer technologies, which enabled the so-called bankers to cream off money from the system without being observed and no questions asked. So you have the new phenomenon of opaque earnings where no one can question the methodology or the result, and that is not a market, it's a stealth system: it's a mathematically-based digital scam for those in the right position. Suitable checks need to be devised to counter this artificial and unnatural environment, to restore the market's invincibility.

Q: So the "Invisible Hand of the Market" still reigns over all?

A.S: Of course, although I only mentioned that phrase three times in my works, but I am amazed that this little/big idea has assumed such proportions today. I am pleased that it has, because the free market and its efficiencies and deficiencies cost nothing and govern all production and distribution in a free market system. Unfortunately, however, an assumption or rider has crept into today's thinking that I meant that the 'Invisible Hand' would *control* markets in a "regulated manner" *at all times,* as in the failed EMH notion: of course over time it will, but not without hiatuses, especially when the market itself is invisible too, as with these new financial objects with their three-letter acronyms, UFOs and so on!

Q: The open quoted markets, like the stock markets, have generally kept their integrity, but you are talking about those hidden markets where no one, not even the regulators or proprietors or their representatives know, it seems, what is going on?

A.S: Exactly! You cannot hide a crop of grain from the market, and all these hidden financial products should be public knowledge. You see, in my day, everyone went to market and you could all see the produce, the price and what the market was saying about values and prices. You cannot do that in all today's financial markets, and the main problems seem to be in the invisible markets of bonds and derivatives, which must be made transparent. I argued that banks, in view of the first Scottish banking collapse of my era, need especial regulations and the way forward is regular Information Disclosure to the market, and with today's digital technologies that should not be difficult to devise.

Q: So a true market is where all the goods are on display for all to see and everyone can see who is buying what and at what price?

A.S: Exactly, otherwise you haven't got a market at all, you just have a closed shop for private deals and clandestine profits and huge bonuses, not for bankers as such, but for *smugglers!* If you made the markets totally transparent, you would have a real market with all its cost-free advantages, and buffers and controls, just as you have with a stock market. I saw in your text what Mr. Friedman said about free lunches, but you can have free markets as long as you can see what they're doing! The only way forward for so-called regulation is to have informational transparency, which then automatically becomes the regulator, and cost-free as well.

Q: And what about bankers' bonuses in 2009, immediately following on the bail-outs?

A.S: This is neither *prudence* nor *justice* nor *beneficence* as I used these terms. And yet after Global Crunch there are any number of future crises lying in wait, so let's just say that they are not wise to pay out this money at this time, for several reasons. They are taking *self-interest* too far, at the expense of *empathy*. Would the *Impartial Spectator* deem this behaviour to be *virtuous*, the actions of men in *self-command?* The announcement that the top thirty at Goldman Sachs are taking their 2009 bonuses not in cash but in 5-year options is an improvement as it keeps a buffer of cash in the bank, but it occurs to me that an accumulation of options will have exactly the same effect as bonuses in driving leverage and risk-taking.

Q: Hmn. It seems that financial innovation of new products was in the build-up to Global Crunch...

A.S: Yes, that is very clear from the account here, which was an idea that persuaded Alan Greenspan's economic liberality more than it should have done. I am reminded of that surprising passage in Plato, (*Phaedrus*, 274e-275b), when the God Theuth came to King Thamus of Thebes and tried to sell him the idea of his latest invention, namely that of letters, which he claimed would encourage learning, which seemed a reasonable proposition at first sight. King Thamus dismissed the invention, however, on the basis that it was harmful idea, as it would not only encourage forgetfulness but actually encourage the conceit of wisdom!

It's the same with those who prophesied that CDSs, or Credit Default Swaps, would reduce risk in the debt markets, whereas they have spread risk like a contagion and correlated the global debt mar-ket into one giant risk that could threaten the global economy! And now they have developed Sovereign CDSs too! As you showed in the text, there's no fundamental reason to have CDSs in an efficient bond market in the first place. They should be outlawed!

Q: What about the worldwide boom in the housing markets, then?

A.S: I was struck by your account of the post-war period and how practically every downturn, and especially those of 1974, 1990 and 2008, resulted in or was driven by excesses in the real estate markets, both as regards valuations and prices paid and the level of debt incurred. These debts then in the 2008 downturn entered the inter-mediary financial markets in the form of CMOs and CDOs and spread the toxic contagion to the financial markets, but in essence it was a real estate bubble caused by too much debt carrying too low an interest charge.

Q: It's as simple as that?

A.S: Yes, and No. There is a potential fault-line in the Capitalist sys-tem, when it operates in a system of total land enclosure. I must take you back to the first econometrician of the modern world, Sir William Petty, who lived from 1623 to 1687, who was the author of the Down Survey of Ireland. Over the ten years he surveyed and valued the land of Ireland, he soon realised that different parcels of land had marked-ly different values depending on their fertility, but also depending on their location and access to amenities such as roads, harbours, peat, rivers and so on. These days, as I saw on the way down here, we would have to add railways and airports and many other facilities to the list, like shopping centres and sports venues. He coined, as you mention, the memorable phrase "Hands and Lands", which also implied the economic conditions under which the two meet.

Q: And I believe you taught his descendant the Second Earl Shelburne, later Prime Minister and First Marquis of Lansdowne?

A.S: Absolutely, a great man, who had an Idea and a Plan that we discussed and considered at length from the standpoint of Natural

Law, of liberty and freedom. He formed a political club in London to push through great measures, the Independence of America, the Emancipation of the Catholics and the Abolition of Slavery. The great David Hume and my humble self were the supporters of Lansdowne, the original founders of the club in Pall Mall next to Almacks, for which Lansdowne appointed a butler from his country seat, Bowood House in Wiltshire, to be the first proprietor-manager. It was a political club and for us Scotsmen to have a home in London was a God-send. It enabled us to formulate and spread our ideas to envision the political debates of London in that important period.

Q: And what were these ideas?

A.S: Well, that's a big question! [Becomes misty-eyed]. Let me see now, I suppose the foundation of it all was the philosophic enquiries of David Hume, in his *Enquiry into Human Understanding*. He was a most sweet and excellent man and close friend from Edinburgh. He dispelled the medieval superstitions concerning the nature of the Deity, by destroying the false notion that the mind of man is made in the image of God, an utterly false notion! As if the Deity thought like a man, why, the earth would have tumbled from the heavens on the First Day! His work was the turning point that led to the enlightenment in Britain and across Europe. The only other man of the same distinction was perhaps Voltaire.

Q: Did you ever meet him?

A.S: Voltaire? Oh, yes, everyone knew Voltaire! I spent some time, two months or so, with him at Ferney, in the year that I commenced writing my *magnum opus* in 1765. We discussed economics at length, as Voltaire was an economic disciple of Turgot, the man Voltaire hoped would save France, but Turgot was dismissed by those whom you rightly term Degenerate Persons. You have to remember that in my lifetime the French Physiocrats, Condorcet, de Quesnay, Mirabeau and Dupont were the great economic thinkers of the age. Indeed, I intended to dedicate my *magnum opus* to Francois de Quesnay, but his untimely death precluded that. David Hume, who was educated by the Jesuits at La Flèche in Anjou, like Sir William

Petty a hundred years previously, was stationed in our Paris embassy for several years: he was much loved by the French, and he was a major catch for Les Madames Les Salonnières, believe me, so he could open all doors in France. It was amazing that he managed to remain, like me, a bachelor!

Q: So who were the other influential men in your time?

A.S: Well, my name has sometimes been linked to the study of economics. [Smiles quietly to himself]. I suppose my attacks on the Stamp Act were the lever that opened the debate over the future of America, the very idea of George III taxing an independent nation three thousand miles away was an absurdity and an affront to the dignity and liberty of man, and Lansdowne, who was a formidable and utterly fearless debater, put my thinking to very effective use in the House of Lords.

Then there was Edward Gibbon's great work *The Decline and Fall of the Roman Empire*, which was the weapon that destroyed the idea of empire utterly, and was I think the intellectual and moral cause that decisively shifted the debate over the Independence of America, which Lansdowne negotiated when he was Prime Minister in 1782-1783. For Lansdowne knew that his Plan could unfold, only if the battle over the Ideas had already been won, in the intellectual realm.

Q: And were there any other initiatives of importance?

A.S: Oh, yes. I don't think I should overlook my friend from Edinburgh, Adam Ferguson, who pioneered new thinking concerning man's natural relationships in society, a subject of special interest to me and essential for economists. It was a principle that he announced that so inspired William Wilberforce, the independent MP for Hull, to fight the evil of slavery: "No one is born a slave, because everyone is born with all his rights, so no one can become a slave, because no one, from being a person, can become a thing or the subject of property". I think that's the gist of what he wrote. Incidentally, did William succeed with his campaign? He was having a difficult time of it the last I knew.

Q: Why, yes, he did succeed in abolishing slavery. He died in 1833, just three days after the Abolition Act was passed into law. He is buried next to his friend William Pitt the Younger in Westminster Abbey. Why, did you know him?

A.S: Well done William. God bless him, he was a true Christian brother, you know. Of course I knew him, he was a member of the club! And what about that other great cause, the emancipation of the Catholics, another example of men denying full liberty to their fellow-men? That cause was started by Sir William Petty when he was in Ireland, and it was another cause identified by Lansdowne in his Plan, which was simply to create the modern world that you all inhabit to this day, which he fought for all his life. What happened?

Q: The Catholic Act was finally passed in 1833.

A.S: 1833? Hmm. Lansdowne was probably deceased before then. So, who was Prime Minister at the time?

Q: The Duke of Wellington.

A.S: I've never heard of him. What did he do?

Q: Well, he achieved much in the name of England's and Europe's freedom. And he was a member of your club, did you know?

A.S: Well, this Duke must have joined the club after I retired to Kirkcaldy, or after I died, but I am pleased that later members of Lansdowne's club still managed some success in life. Anyway, where were we? Oh, yes, we were going to discuss the fault-line in the capitalist system. Would you mind awfully if I refer to my own work here, two particular passages from *The Wealth of Nations*, from Book V, Chapter II, Part II, from *Articles I* and *III,* for your reference? I wrote as follows:

'Both ground-rents and the ordinary rent of land are a species of revenue which the owner, in many cases, enjoys without any care or attention of his own. Though a part of this revenue should be taken from him to defray the expenses of the state, no discourage-

250

ment will thereby be given to any sort of industry. The annual produce of the land and labour of the society, the real wealth and revenue of the great body of the people, might be the same after such
a tax as before. Ground rents, and the ordinary rent of land are,
therefore, perhaps the species of revenue which can best bear to
have a peculiar tax imposed upon them'.

Having dealt with taxation on Sir William Petty's first original factor
of production, Land, I now turned my attention to his second factor,
Labour. I argued that a tax on Labour was actually a tax on the
employer, which must surely be right because in your arrangements
today I understand that the employee only has regards to his net
salary in today's system, whereas the employer must pay this net
salary and then the tax on it, which total is his actual cost of hiring
the employee, and he is actually obliged to pay the tax over to the
central exchequer. I had no doubts about taxing 'luxuries' such as
tobacco and alcohol because they were voluntary and therefore
avoidable taxes. I concluded as follows:

'In all cases, a direct tax upon the wages of Labour must, in the
long run, occasion both a greater reduction in the rent of land, and
a greater rise in the price of manufactured goods, than would have
followed from a proper assessment of a sum equal to the produce
of the tax, partly upon the rent of land, and partly upon consum-
able commodities',

by which term I meant luxuries as opposed to necessities.

Q: Did you know that the ideas you expressed in *Book V*, encapsulat-
ed to an extent in these two short extracts which made the case for
no tax on Labour but taxes on unimproved land values and goods
other than necessities, became the central economic debate of the
Nineteenth Century, not only in Britain but also in America and
Australia and elsewhere? So, I think you are saying that if this value
created by the community is not paid into the community's tax coffers, then it must reflect back into increased land values, that then
attract debt and more debt from the bankers, until the whole soufflé
of indebted real property boils over, so to speak?

A.S: Precisely! It is axiomatic. As I wrote in Article 1:

'Nothing can be more reasonable than that a fund which owes its
existence to the good government of the state – and having travelled from Edinburgh yesterday, I would today add 'and to the
expansion of the economy through the exertions of the brain and
brawn of the population that have indubitably added to the unimproved value of the land of that community' – should be taxed
peculiarly, or should contribute something more than the greater
part of other funds, towards the support of that government – and
today I would add 'and to the people of that community's local
government' ".

You see, all this incredible growth across the world all helps to drive
up the value of land, and I mean the unimproved values of that land
which, remaining insufficiently taxed allows the market to drive up
land values, as land is a finite resource, that then become the subject
of bankers' mortgages, which extra money drives the values even
higher, creating more value in bankable assets, which as you said
finally causes the whole soufflé to boil over, which is the real underlying cause of this crisis. The freeholder has been replaced by the
banker, and the whole world is drowning in an ocean of debt!

And that's the hidden real cause of your Global Crunch, because
it was happening everywhere, America, Britain, Moscow and Eastern
Europe, Sweden, Spain and Ireland, and even Iceland! And it is
accentuated by governments, even free-thinking one's like Thatcher's
that you mention in your section on the 1980s, who aim to central-
ize all power at the expense of local democracy, which has been
deprived of just about all tax-raising powers, other than local taxes
that are meant to be based on property values, but are only a fraction
of the actual value and so raise only a fraction of the costs of local
governments, of councils and parishes, so the central or federal government sends them huge sums from the central exchequer and
holds them in economic control, and keeping control of the bulk of
the taxes, thereby reinforcing their control of the whole population.
There are several forms of economic slavery entailed in this top-
down structure.

There is a big choice for the future here: stay with the existing tax structure and "enjoy" the continuing boom and bust in property values and indebtedness, or switch to a sustainable percentage of taxation on unimproved land values and dampen land values to the point that mortgages only fund the constructions on them, whilst taxes on production are correspondingly reduced, especially on payrolls.

Q: So you mean to tax away the whole increase in land values?

A.S: Allow, allow, you must ...

Q: 'Let the dog ...

A.S: ... see the carrot!' No, no, it's 'Let the donkey ...

Q: ...see the rabbit!'

A.S: Ah! ..., no, 'see the carrot!' [Laughs]. The donkey can have a carrot, but he doesn't need a whole sackful! David Hume was the first economist who taught that a modest inflation actually encourages production, and we can all see the dangers of deflation.

Q: So Dr. Adam Posen's idea of a "Bubble Tax" on housing is a sound idea?

A.S: It's a clumsy idea. You cannot tax a bubble, but you can tax unimproved land values, or if you like the value of a house less either its original cost or the current replacement cost, but if you tax a house as such you only achieve what the old rating system achieved, which was effectively a tax on any improvements you made to the property, which is an absurd outcome. Furthermore, you cannot tax the people more overall, so there has to be relief on their tax burden elsewhere, by reducing their income taxes, particularly payroll taxes. The two alignments must go together, so that Labour and Land come back into a sustainable balance.

Q: So, Dr. Adam Posen is addressing, somewhat clumsily, just one side of a simultaneous equation?

A.S: Exactly! There is a fundamental imbalance between Petty's "Hands *and* Lands". It's like this: the *and* in the economists' equation is akin to the $=$ in the physicists' $E = mc^2$! Without the *and* or the $=$, they don't work! And now that the wealth pendulum has swung back to the East, where taxes on production are much, much lower, this fundamental imbalance in the Western economies will become acute.

Q: In March 2009 Mr. Tim Geithner, the US Treasury Secretary, said: "Our system failed in basic fundamental ways. To address this will require comprehensive reforms, not modest repairs at the margin, but new rules of the game". That's a clear admission that major changes in the capitalist system are now needed ...

A.S: Yes, but, what did he go on to say? Anything?

Q: We're still waiting ...

A.S: Sir William Petty was a man who understood number and proportion as it affected the economy, as a result of his studies over many years. His conclusion was that 'three-eighths of taxation should come from the land and houses and the value of stock-in-trade, and five-eighths from consumption'. And no one has ever conducted such a study since! At a rough guess, taxation on land values today is next to nothing and taxes on production and on the output of production are nearly 100%! We have to recast taxation between more tax on unimproved land values and consumption of luxuries, and less taxes on production. I used my 'Overcoat Argument' to show that a tax on luxuries is just, as all overcoats work the same in keeping out the cold, but if you want a designer coat with all the bells and whistles you must pay more tax. And these increased taxes on land values, excluding the improvements, will lower the costs of production including for overcoats, which in turn will re-enhance the reduced land values. It requires an iterative approach over one Short Cycle.

Q: Do you really think that voters in the western democracies are going to vote for a tax that reduces the value of their houses, their most valuable asset in most cases?

A.S: Now, you're the one omitting the other side of the argument! The increase of taxation on the land value of their houses is off-set by the reduction of taxes on their earnings at work, making the cost of what is produced lower, and reducing much of the so-called equity that causes the insane lending on property, which is nothing to do with the production of anything. It's not that difficult to work this out at a national level: even the computers at HM Treasury could be programmed to do it, along with the usual exceptions for retirees, the unemployed and others.

Q: Do you think that the electors in a democracy based on land ownership will change their mind towards this view?

A.S: That's the practical issue. You might as well ask homeowners if they would like to pay less interest on a smaller mortgage or much more interest on a much bigger mortgage; or, if they would like to pay less tax on their earnings and contribute more to democratically-accountable local services; or, even more directly, do you want to be enslaved to Big Government and pay for Big Bankers' Bonuses or be free of both of them? Let me just say this: when the current boom-and-bust cycles eventually reduce their pensions, savings and house values, as in an Irving Fisher deflation downturn, the argument for not adjusting this great imbalance would surely be compelling? You see, economic calamities are also the work of the 'Invisible Hand of the Market'. Or as one might say, 'God moves in mysterious ways!'

Q: Are you saying that economic collapse could be the moment to change the system, almost as a matter of necessity?

A.S: When all seems lost, that is the moment of greatest opportunity for Creative Person to act! In a crisis caused by a failure to find the balance between land and labour over a whole K-long wave, and with the loss of savings, pensions and house values, all the things the middle classes strive for, then it would be possible to make the necessary shift with the people's understanding. And if such a crisis of sufficient severity occurred, such that the currency collapsed, any new currency could really be launched, by Britain's post-gold sell off by a certain Mr. Brown, on the basis of Britain's land value! That really would steal a march on Herr Hjalmar Schacht's 1923 fig-leaf that launched the new Rentenmark, it would be the real thing!

Q: Have you anything specific to say on the overall level of taxation? Our current Prime Minister, Gordon Brown has instituted over 70 stealth taxes in the last decade alone. Did you know he comes from your native Kirkcaldy?

A.S: Does he? I saw him being interviewed on the in-hearse system. I know the type. In my book, I wrote: "There is no art which one government sooner learns of another than that of draining money from the pockets of the people". You say he's from Kirkcaldy? I'm shocked! And this is the man who has presided over the loss, as I read in your draft of this book on the way down from Edinburgh, of 750,000 jobs in manufacturing and "replaced" them with 750,000 so-called jobs in bureaucracy, while he let the property markets soar on the back of a borrowing binge! Just think of the effect of that on the imbalance of the incidence of taxation on production that I have been talking about!

In my day, the only real expenditure of government was for defence, the maintenance of law and order and the justice system and prisons, and the notion held that taxation should not exceed 15% of GDP. How different it all is today, with taxation in excess of 45%, three times greater! What is government doing getting involved with private industries, in which I include healthcare and education, and indeed there are still many private schools and hospitals? Why is government taxing the people's earnings only to pay for their health and education, a process costing about one-third at least of the wealth involved being wasted? Government cannot run these industries efficiently. Government should promote education by financing the buildings and the running costs as it did in my school in Kirkcaldy, but should never pay the teachers or tell them what to teach. A nation that enslaves its teachers in this way will itself end up being enslaved! Government has no business being involved to this extent, as if it knows best, none.

I noticed that Thatcher realized this as regard state industries and in the 1980s began to reverse the trend, and just in time and with positive effects on the overall wealth of the nation, but there is still a massive way to go. But may I ask you a question, as I have been dormant all these years now: why and when did government get involved in all these other areas in the first place, and why did the people let them?

Q: I think that after The Great War, the war to end all wars, with its great loss of treasure and blood spilt on the battlefield, meant the soldiers returning home to a damaged economy with much unemployment thought about what the King and Country, that they had served and died for, now owed them, and so their minds turned to security, which was soon reinforced by the experience of the Great Depression. Then along came the Second World War, and when it was over the people had had enough of war and depression. They loved Churchill as a war leader, but he was the first to go, and in came the Socialists who were going to give the battle-weary nation what the ordinary soldiers and their families wanted, which was Social Security. ABCA, the Army Bureau of Current Affairs, you see, was taken over by the Socialists while the fighting was still in progress and they indoctrinated the fighting men as to their post-war demands. And the first thing the Socialists did when they won power in 1946 was to give the people the National Health Service, and it went on from there.

A.S: I see. After a war many exceptional measures are necessary for a few years or even decades, but I think that it is time to revert to a more sustainable model. The "Invisible Hand of the Market" will make its presence felt in its own good time, probably in a crisis that challenges the bloated structures and forces urgent restructuring.

Q: We were talking about where the incidence of the taxation imbalance falls.

A.S: Where? On production, with increased taxes on labour! The Hands are over-taxed and the Lands are under-taxed, and the over-taxing of the Hands causes the cost of manufactures and other products to rise in price and the result of that is to lessen the Lands value available for taxation. So, the secondary imbalance is to reduce the tax harvest, which causes the politicians to seek yet newer taxes. Instead of the virtues of a judicial mix of tax between "Hands and Lands", today's society is left with the incidence of taxation in a bad state of imbalance, which as I have said was the hidden cause of the property boom and bust, in fact of all the post-WW2 property boom and busts. And the Chancellor has just announced that he is going to tackle his debt mountain by raising taxes on – production!

Q: You are referring to the $1/2$% increase in National Insurance, to raise £3.25 billion, another burden on industry's shoulders that will discourage new employment.

A.S: I should add that the French-inspired Value-Added-Tax is in its incidence an excellent tax and very much in line with my preference for a tax on luxuries, or commodities; the trick with this tax is to keep it away from necessities, which is understood, but not quite as well as it should be. The aim must be eventually to abolish enough taxes on production and shift them to luxuries and unimproved land values, as part of the switch of power to the counties and parishes and away from the central exchequer, thereby removing much of the value that is the security for excessive property lending by banks. The bankers would then have to lend more to industry.

Q: What will this imbalance of taxes result in?

A.S: A decline in productivity and therefore in wealth. The problem for the West now is that with the Orient rising again, with low-wage, low-taxed, energetic manufacturing, is that the loss of competitiveness will lead to a long and slow decline until the governments of America and Europe can no longer sustain the vital public sector services at anywhere near their current level, which wherever you look are already very near to non-sustainability in this Global Crunch. It seems to have been overlooked in 2009, that the public sectors of the US and UK, after adding in all the bank and other bailouts, now exceed over 50% of their country's GDP, which is not sustainable at all.

I bet old Marx is laughing in his grave! The sight of General Motors going bankrupt and re-emerging owned by two governments, Canada and America, the latter controlling over half its economy, and by the workers' UAW Union and their pension funds, and a gaggle of squawking bond-holders who have just been handed an ultra vires haircut by their own democratic government, is a communist solution par excellence. You look worried? Marx? Laughing? No, don't worry about him, he's buried in Highgate Cemetery. We wouldn't let him in to Canongate!

Q: How long has the West got?

A.S: Much less time than you think, but enough to make the fundamental changes. And the next decade to 2020 will be spent in trying to throw off the effects of Global Crunch, while the Orient will steal a march on you. What America and Britain need now is forward-looking radical governments that are not beholden to or blinkered by the past. It's the time for a new Whig Ascendancy in the intellectual realm, just as it was when we formed the club in 1762: where is today's Lansdowne when the world needs him, when today's political debate is just so much shadow-boxing and tinkering with petty ideas and percentages? How to take the right steps now must begin with the deconstruction of government itself: it has become far too centralized, far too expensive, and far too inefficient, and raising far too much in taxation. I read with great interest about Hyman Minsky, as the post-WW2 boom is over and real globalization is now forging ahead, with its implied ultra-competitiveness.

In Britain the central government has just got too big, and the people are tired of it. It is now vital to return the power to the people, by localizing power in the counties and parishes, so that they are self-financing, bringing education back to the *elected* County Education Officer and the same with *elected* managers to run hospitals, releasing the energies of the people through Jeffersonian democracy, restoring local pride and accountability. It's easy to do, it only needs the political will, as everything needed is already in place, especially the people. You will find if you look into it deeply that there are a manageable number of Bills to put before Parliament to transform the situation completely. That is why Britain must maintain sovereignty over its own affairs.

If the right steps are not taken in time, I can see a future of civil unrest in many countries, Greece, Ireland, Spain, Eastern Europe. It has also happened throughout British history: the Earls of Norfolk and Hereford won concessions from Edward I as far back as 1297, beyond what Simon de Montfort extracted from Henry III in 1265 and beyond the rights asserted by the armed barons at Runnymede from King John with the *Magna Carta* of 1215. Taxation issues were the trigger for revolutionary demand in the civil wars in 1258-1265, from 1642-1660 and from 1688-1690. When the fire takes hold in the British belly, there will be change.

I'm beginning to feel exhausted! It's been a long and glorious day, so just one more question, if you please.

Q: Well, Sir, what you have just advocated is the exact opposite of what our governments have been doing for the past twenty-three years, namely subscribing to unelected bureaucrats in this new and democratically unaccountable federal state of Europe, called the EU ...

A.S: Oh, No! Please, now I feel really tired! Britain's character, economy, currency and history are quite distinctly different to the Continent's, and that's all there is to it. Shakespeare said it all in John of Gaunt's dying speech. And the €uro's "One-Size-Fits-All" may be fine for Germany and France and their satellites, but never for Britain, surrounded by the good fate of having the open seas to earn our contribution to the wealth of nations. Thank you.

Q: Thank you, Sir! I am pleased to tell you that we have arranged an air ambulance to fly you home; you'll arrive at Edinburgh Airport shortly before dusk, and you'll be able to see the sun setting over the Pentland Hills and your native coastline as you come into land, and we'll have you safely re-interred in Canongate in the wee small hours, when no one else is around. Enjoy!

A.S: I am not given to excitements, but this my return is making me tremble in anticipation! I wish your work on Global Crunch well. The arguments must first be won, however, before the actions can be won. I remember Lansdowne writing: 'It requires no small labour to open the eyes of either the public or individuals, but when that is accomplished, you are not got a third of the way. Professor Adam Smith's principles have remained unanswered for above thirty years, but when it is attempted to act upon any of them, what a clamour!' [Exits laughing and waving].

A New World Financial Order?

Global Crunch, as we have seen, was forty years in the making. From Bretton Woods and through the 1950s and 1960s the capitalist system delivered the post-war recovery. No doubt the system needed to evolve, but not in the way wrought by Nixon unilaterally abandoning the Gold Standard in 1971, with no forethought of the consequences other than his own re-election. His decision unleashed inflation which morphed into stagflation and created the first post-war banking crisis of 1974. The second and greater error was the wholesale deregulation of money on both sides of the Atlantic, and the abolition of restraining legislation in the Anglo-sphere world over the last thirty years of the twentieth century, in the misplaced belief that regulation was the answer. This failed combination directly caused more banking crises, led by the S&Ls in the US in 1985, which was a warning that went unheeded, and specifically in the UK's deregulation of banks and building societies, which became a component of Global Crunch in 2007/8.

What Global Crunch really showed up, however, is that the regulators in a deregulated economy cannot replace the former well-conceived laws at the level above government. The fact is that the regulators are largely powerless to prevent anything at their level, if at the higher levels subtle laws are withdrawn and replaced by progressive laws drafted by dumb-downed legislators. If governments encourage the impossible in home-ownership for all and the US legislates that its own GSAs, or government-sponsored agencies like Fannie Mae and Freddie Mac, move in that direction, then it only needs the central bankers above them to lose control as well, and all is lost, and then there is nothing regulators can do that will make any difference. The way forward is the way back, in many respects, for as the wise man said: "The Old Ways are Best".

There is a school of thought which thinks that since Nixon abandoned Bretton Woods and really turned the Dollar into the naked reserve currency of the world, that there has developed what George Soros calls a "longer-term super-bubble" that stalks the world. In his book he writes: "There is not just one boom-bust process or bubble to consider but two: the housing bubble and what I call a longer-term super-bubble. The housing bubble is quite straightforward; the super-bubble is much more complicated". Well, after interviewing Adam Smith, I would say, along with Ben Bernanke, the exact opposite: "The housing bubble is very complicated, what Adam Smith referred to as "the potential fault-line in capitalism", involving the overall balance in the economy, the balance between "Hands and Lands", between the public and private sectors and between taxation and the quantum of credit allocation, whereas Soros's super-bubble doesn't exist, unless he's talking about the bubble in land values that arises if you get the critical balance wrong, which by and large the western democracies, with their free markets operating in regimes of total land enclosure, have indeed got very wrong.

The dollar-driven super-bubble theorists go on to conjure up a new world reserve currency and cast their eyes around and alight with glee upon the IMF. 'It has the power to issue Special Drawing Rights, so let SDRs be the new currency so that this dollar-driven boom-and-bust cycle is ended', as they overlook the cycles of Mother Nature and Petty's famous dictum. These theorists continue that the IMF could help the third world with their new SDRs, a proposal on which Soros himself remarked: "That's as close to a free lunch as you can get, as long as you don't eat it!" Well, he got that one completely right. The very idea of a super-IMF issuing SDRs or Globos or whatever is a dream beyond even the idea that the ECB can set interest rates across 27 disparate economies, but at least the ECB has an actual territory with a real GDP and is vaguely responsible to a Parliament of democratically-questionable origination that has a legislative, albeit bureaucratised, function.

This debate is also driven by the Chinese who have accumulated some $1.34 trillion in US/dollar assets and fear American devaluation, so they peg the Renminbi to the Dollar, a policy known as Bretton Woods II, and go look for a different reserve currency. The Chinese, however, already have a newly emerging reserve currency: they're sitting on it, in the form of gold which they are mining and hoarding, and within a generation the de-pegged Renminbi will challenge of its own accord the Dollar more than the €uro: in 2009 the Dollar accounted for 65% of the world's reserves, but the €uro only 25%. And the Chinese are in preliminary discussions about creating a Far Eastern bloc with a currency union, which makes sense to China's neighbours as the dollar-pegged Renminbi is swamping their economies with cheaply-priced Chinese exports, but China would be well advised to observe the fate of the EU €uro-zone first, and Japan too, for a decade or so at least.

Global Crunch partially eclipsed the emerging new world order.

The pendulum is now swinging from West to East with a vengeance; the US is still by far the largest economy with the greatest GDP in history, but soon it won't be, sooner than it realises, as it toils through the next decade laden with $52.8 trillion total debt and rising, which already equals over 3.73 times US GDP, while the BRICs and emerging markets quicken their unencumbered pace, and the growth of sovereign wealth funds has already reached $2.5 trillion and is growing exponentially. The Chinese-US currency peg is akin to a runner catching up Uncle Sam on his shoulder and holding him round the waste as they run together on the bend, holding him there until he's half a pace ahead and then has to let go of Uncle Sam as at last he strides away. Uncle Sam of course doesn't like this at all and has already said so, as he tries to devalue his Dollar and debts by discretely weakening his currency and boosting his exports, but the Chinese runner will only abandon the dollar-peg when it suits him, when he gets ahead.

The authors of the BRICs Report in 2001 reckoned their combined GDP would overtake the US's in 2050. Then in their follow-up 2007 report it was reckoned that India's GDP alone would exceed the US's in 2050; and in 2009 their revised predictions are that China's GDP, which will hit $5.4 trillion in 2010 as it overtakes Japan as the second biggest economy, will go on to overhaul the US's GDP by 2027. Already China is the world's biggest car market, where the post-Chapter 11 GM is making most of its resurgent profits. The new world order is not an idea in the mind of some more mature "Egghead with Attitude" or some daft notion of a "Global Regulator", it is a fact, a fact that evolves every day, as the Pendulum of Time swings with the Principle of Change.

Countdown to Catastrophe

So, what's the conclusion? We are back to that question of 'Have the Central Bankers Lost Control?' As the next Short Cycle begins in 2010, they think – hope would be a better word – that the banking crisis has at least been stabilised, that deflation has been defeated, that there is no sign of inflation, that unemployment is slowing, that growth has resumed, as the pull of the BRICs, especially China and

India, lead the recovery, and that interest rates will remain low for the foreseeable future, and that in 2011 they can begin to unwind all the bail-out loans, ease off on the QE and stimulus packages, and gently raise interest rates at the first sign of inflation returning, at which point they will all clap each other on the back for having saved the world economy. Such an outcome is devoutly to be wished, but all that would happen is that the casino banks would be off and running and ready to do it all over again, racking up more bonuses and indebtedness. Unless ...

Well, every aspect of this positive scenario is even questionable, beginning with the first assumption: banking crises last for 4.3 years on a historic average and this crisis is only half-way through and far from over. In November 2009, Dominic Strauss-Kahn of the IMF reckoned that the global banking losses were $3.5 trillion, more in Europe than America, of which only a half had been admitted to, let alone provided for. And that is after many G20 governments have unburdened these banks in the private sector and have transferred a great level of their indebtedness into the public sector, to the point where Moody's estimates total sovereign debt at $15.3 trillion, and rising to well over $22.5 trillion over the next five years, or even double this. Never has the world seen anything like these total debt levels, epitomised by Graph 3 for the US economy. The G7 are still experiencing reduction of the money supply as bank credit continues to contract and as banks continue to deleverage their balance sheets and this process will necessarily continue for the next two years at least. Interest rates are low and will probably stay that way for a time, but the cost of actual borrowing will remain high.

Next, deflation is still stalking the world, led by Japan, and asset values are still in decline, apart from stock markets that have gotten ahead of themselves as QE has seeped into the stock exchanges, but another rumble from the ongoing banking crisis will surely see them tumble once again. In the US, the Fed, the FDIC and the Office of the Controller of the Currency have communicated to auditors that implementation of FASB 157 (mark-to-market) has been suspended and that interest payments on NPLs, or Non-performing Loans, can be extrapolated into the future with no resultant provisioning of capital, a policy now known as "Pretend to Extend". And real unemployment is rising everywhere except in the BRICs, but the arithmetic behind the idea that the Chinese and Indian consumer will haul the West out of the mire doesn't even begin to add up.

Since the formation of the Bank of England in 1697, the Pound Sterling, along with the mighty Dollar, are the only two major world currencies that have never collapsed and been replaced. In 2010/11, however, there is realistically no spare monetary capacity for any further bank bail-outs for the UK, which is looking anyway at a ratings downgrade and possibly the attentions of the IMF, as the UK's fiscal deficit projection for 2010 at 13.3% is the highest in the OECD Group. The US and EU are of a size to go further with QE, and size in this crisis counts as we have seen, but the ramifications will be there for them down the cul-de-sac. If the embers of the banking crisis flare up again, further substantial bail-outs will effectively trigger the devaluation of fiat currencies and the debts expressed in them.

A currency or sovereign debt crisis would force higher interest rates and pitch the Anglo-sphere economy towards a double-dip W-recession, or even depression. When the indebtedness of the UK, as global interest rates rise, and the increasing interest payments are perceived to be creating a compound debt spiral, where the level of rising debt is eating its own head off with compounding interest charges, then Irving Fisher's debt-deflation model will take over, as capital flees and the currency effectively collapses, destroying savings, pensions and asset values, including house values, in real terms, while that which glisters soars like a Golden Eagle, clutching onto the Swiss Franc and Norwegian Kronor, as the only fiat currencies with resilient inherent value, as their *total* budgets are in *positive* surplus.

The next currency facing something of a similar plight would be the €uro, but it would have a very different effect than in the US or UK: it is more likely that Greece, whose debt rating was cut in December 2009 by Fitch from A- to BBB+ with negative watch, while Athens rioted, will be forced out of the €uro-zone as it is past the tipping point of wage-cuts or of a compounding debt-deflation spiral, and back onto the Drachma, probably to be followed by Ireland back onto the Punt after a riot or two in Dublin, and possibly followed by Spain onto the Peseta while they march again through Zaragoza, while Southern Italy languishes as usual as it anguishes about a return to the Lira, all of which positive probabilities were prefigured by the Pound's expulsion from the ERM on

"White Wednesday" in September 1992, courtesy of George Soros' Quantum Fund. The East European currency pegs to the €uro might snap as well, particularly in Latvia, Rumania and Hungary. The central core of the 'Original Six' will hold firm around the Franco-German axis, however, but this will make the €uro even stronger and the exits and de-couplings from the fringes of the €uro-zone ever more likely. Global Crunch will yet question the extent and speed with which the job-destroying deflationary €uro was rolled out across the plains of Europe, but the effect on worldwide confidence could exponentially feed the possibility of a global sovereign debt crisis. The flaw at the heart of the €uro-zone is already being mercilessly exposed: Germany's instinctive fear of inflation is pitted against Club Med's fear of minus-growth unemployment. The Germans are not about to lose that one, so it will inevitably be "Bye, bye €uro-zone" as Club Med once again becomes an affordable holiday-zone for the rest of us and Europe Continental rediscovers that it can build the whole of an Airbus. Hallelujah!

Alternatively, if public and private sector debt expands on the back of the next Short Cycle's tenuous recovery, basically in a repeat of the Noughties Decade, with US total debt moving relentlessly towards 450%+ of GDP or more, and Moody's forecasting a 50% increase in all government debt to well over $22.5 trillion over the next five years, if the usual remedies of lower interest rates and creating more liquidity do indeed seed a reflationary QE-driven recovery from 2010, then there may be a corrugated-shaped stagflationary Short Cycle series of wobbles, as the shock waves from bad debts cause more bank and state failures and batter the banking system again and again, as inflationary pressures and higher interest rates on this ever-mounting debt also begin to set up and eventually trigger the Irving Fisher Debt-deflation spiral across a broad front, with the G7, and especially Japan, all badly affected. That really would be the confirmatory moment that the so-called bankers of the shadow banking system had truly bankrupted the world economy in the greed and bonus-driven Noughties Decade.

In whichever scenario comes to pass, we are facing the possibility of the Debt-deflation model taking hold on a broad front when rising interest costs exceed 12.5% of public revenues, as they already do in Japan, and the US will be there shortly too, but that's on much lower interest rates than will pertain from 2011 on. At any time between January 2010 and 2019, in the new Short Cycle, the total indebtedness of the G7 world could implode and re-ignite the banking crisis. And lying underneath this unlit bonfire of unimaginable indebtedness lies the $600.0 trillion heap of unregulated derivatives, of which no one has any definitive assessment of the potential for systemic or counter-party risk, or even where the concentration of these new risks might lie.

If just one "Too-Big-To-Fail" bank becomes illiquid, just as RBS and HBOS and many others became in Global Crunch, the central bankers are already in the Macbeth Predicament where they would have little choice in this derivative-correlated world but to continue to support the system further, racking up even more and more debt until the unknown tipping point would render any further creation of fiat money self-defeating, and paper money and the economy would crash into hyper-inflation and Great Depression 2, where GDP would collapse by a material amount, if The Great Depression is any guide to today's economy, leaving the new Board for Financial Stability powerless and shaking like a useless and nutrition-less jelly, while the hard reality of "fire, sword and famine crouch for employment" in some very nasty and stricken corners of the globe. "When problems come," advised the Bard, "they come not singly but in battalions". And I hear the sound of marching feet to be almost upon us.

And if and when the catastrophe does come in this new Short Cycle, and it's more when than if in the light of the failure to address the real macro-economic issues raised by Mr. Adam Smith, and as the "animal spirits" are already back at work doing their worst all over again, there will come the critical moment for right decisions by Creative Persons to turn the ensuing crisis to immediate advantage and rid the system of dysfunctional governmental and economic structures, worthless currencies, failed banks, doubtful debts, devalued assets and the trappings and practices of Degenerate Persons, those careless persons who know not the powers and laws of Nature nor the Platonic Limit. Catastrophe will surely come with our current macro-economic structures, based on Thatcherism with its implicit fault-line, which encourages the relentless greed and lesser instincts of Degenerate Persons, those businessmen and bankers who are so infected by the thought of their gains and bonuses that they run, followed in chase by the hapless regulators, like the Gadarene swine of old as they all hurtle over the cliff-tops and drown in the shallows below.

Unless, as advised by Mr. Adam Smith, Creative Persons change these macro-economic structures and the incidence of taxation as a matter of rational analysis and conscious choice, or even as a moral and right choice forced upon us by catastrophe, and so return to balanced prosperity for all in the new Long Cycle, as if in some strange re-enactment of the Day of Atonement, by striking the natural and sustainable balance between "Hands and Lands".

Unless ...

Notes on Bibliography

T HIS edition is the result of over 45 years' study of economics seen from many different perspectives – student, City professional, businessman, observer, avid reader, and from many seminars and discourses with fellow-researchers.

In terms of author's works that have influenced these studies, they range from the early classical economists, especially Sir William Petty and Adam Smith, and on to Condorcet's *Life of Turgot*, through to the modern thinkers from the 1930s onwards, J. M. Keynes, J. K. Galbraith, Milton Friedman, whose theories I heard him describe at a lecture in London in 1979, Irving Fisher and Hyman Minsky.

These and others that seem particularly important are mentioned in the text itself. There are several modern commentators whose works were useful in a descriptive sense and provided or confirmed a multitude of facts, such as Alan Greenspan's remarkable and frank autobiography *The Age of Turbulence*, but they did not add new principles to those creative original thinkers named above.

This bibliography includes many newspapers, beginning with *The Daily Telegraph*, where anything written by Ambrose Evans-Pritchard is compulsive reading, *The International Herald Tribune, The Times,*

Le Monde, USA Today, The FT, The Sunday Times and *The Observer*, and many other newspapers.

Articles in magazines have also provided many facts, views and ideas, but they were ones that rhymed with the tenets of the original thinkers named above: *TIME, The Economist* and *Business Week* head this category.

Information briefings from banks and institutions have been very useful, especially those issued by Morgan Stanley, Credit Suisse, JP Morgan, the Institute of Economic Affairs, Monument Securities and Lombard Street Research

Finally, certain government publications are vital, especially the US Budget Reports and the UK Pink (formerly Red) Books.

Bloomberg TV is compulsive viewing – how does Betty Liu stay cheerful all day long and keep smiling through the apocalypse of Global Crunch at the same time? And Charlie Rose's interviews, just marvellous – as is CBS's *60 Minutes* and Robert Preston of the BBC, the one with the timed and timely pause, all of whose coverage of Global Crunch was quite brilliant TV reporting, importing drama to what was ineffable drama until they gave it their voice.

Index